Robert Sabbag is the bestselling author of the cocaine classic *Snow-blind* and the definitive book on the U.S. marshals, *Too Tough to Die*. His journalism appears in numerous magazines, among them *Rolling Stone*, to which he is a regular contributor. *Witness Protection*, a film based on his *New York Times Magazine* cover story 'The Invisible Family', was nominated for two Golden Globe Awards, including Best Picture.

Also by Robert Sabbag

Snowblind
Too Tough to Die

SMOKESCREEN

a true adventure

ROBERT SABBAG

CANONGATE

First published in the United States of America
under the title *Loaded*
in 2002 by Little, Brown and Company

Published in Great Britain in 2002
by Canongate Books Ltd,
14 High Street, Edinburgh EH1 1TE

10 9 8 7 6 5 4 3 2 1

Copyright © Robert Sabbag, 2002
The moral right of the author has been asserted

British Library Cataloguing-in-Publication Data
A catalogue record for this book is available
on request from the British Library

ISBN 1 84195 261 3

Printed and bound in Great Britain
by Omnia Books Ltd, Bishopbriggs, Glasgow

www.canongate.net

To the memory of my father

CONTENTS

GLAMOUR PROFESSION

1. EMERALD COAST   3
2. EL NIÑO PERDIDO   19
3. AZTEC TWO-STEP   34
4. CADILLAC MOON   59
5. GIVE A MAN ENOUGH
    ROPE AND HE'LL SMOKE IT   73
6. SMOKE OF A DISTANT FIRE   92

EL DORADO

7. RED, WHITE AND BLOND   113
8. PICKUP AT PERICO   139

9. AUTOMATIC PILOT 160

10. SMOKE AND MIRRORS 179

11. FIRE IS THE TEST OF GOLD 197

THE LORDS AND
THE NEW CREATURES

12. DISPOSABLE BIRDS 211

13. SMOKE ON THE WATER 235

14. VIOLETS FOR YOUR FURS 253

15. CEILING ZERO 267

16. MUCH HAVE I TRAVELED
    IN THE REALMS OF GOLD 292

    EPILOGUE 317

    ACKNOWLEDGMENTS 329

    INDEX 333

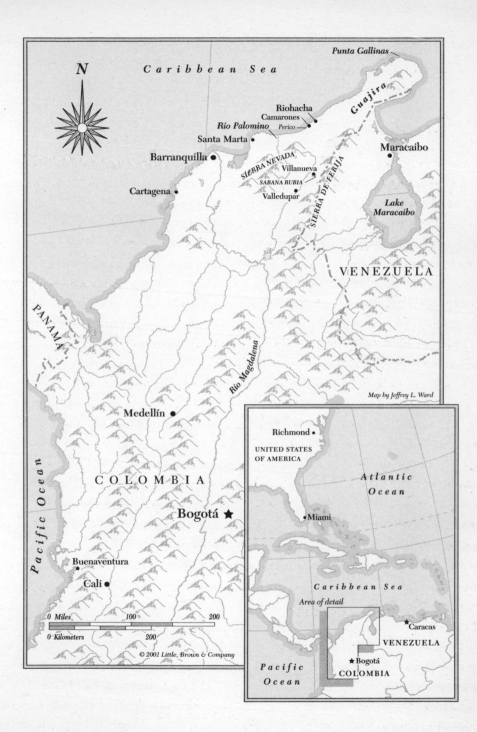

GLAMOUR
PROFESSION

1 EMERALD COAST

Allen Long descended from a short line of American aviators. He in effect was the first. One morning off the coast of South America, as his DC-3, with the break of dawn, violated Colombian airspace, there rose before him, as palpable as the peaks of the Sierra Nevada hovering on the horizon, the probability that he might be the last.

"Red to white, red to white, I have bad news for you, sir."

Bad news in Allen Long's business, of which aviation was only a part, was typically very bad news, and transmitted on an air-to-air frequency from a clandestine Colombian landing strip, the news had to be that much worse.

"Sir, I am sorry, but you cannot land," squawked the voice over the cockpit radio. "You must go back, you cannot land. Repeat, you must go back."

Long and his crew, who had been airborne for fifteen hours, stared stupefied at the source of this advisory, the three of them gazing at the instrument panel as if the radio itself were crazy.

3

Long's transmission was blunt. He keyed the microphone, and said: "We can't go back."

Nor could they put the aircraft down in nearby Barranquilla or over the border in Venezuela. To say that the plane was not "cleared" for that was an understatement at best, but Long said it anyway, and short of announcing the choices they faced, that was about all he said.

"We have to land and take on fuel, or we're going to crash this airplane."

As it happened, they did both.

The Sierra Nevada de Santa Marta rise out of the Caribbean in a sheer, almost vertical ascent to an altitude of 20,000 feet, the highest coastal range in the world, its perennial snowcaps dominating the tropical beaches of Colombia's oldest city. From the fertile forests of Santa Marta the mountains run parallel to the shoreline and reach one hundred miles to the east. Here their north face terminates on a hot, semi-arid peninsula, a flatland of hardscrabble and stunted vegetation that stretches to the northernmost point of the continent.

This inhospitable region into which the mountains decline, settled by Indians who survived the Spanish conquest and home to their descendants today, subsists outside the mainstream of Colombian life, sparsely populated, underdeveloped, historically bereaved of economic opportunity, and largely neglected by the federal government. Here in the northeastern desert is a Colombia untouched by the magical realism evoked by its finest literature, unenriched by the supernatural, a Colombia drained of its mystery, where the metaphysical happens only at night.

These are the Colombian badlands. This is the land beyond the Río Palomino. Independent, if not autonomous, unregulated, virtually lawless . . .

This is the Guajira.

This is where Allen Long conducted business in Colombia, trading on what the region's inhabitants extol as its principal natural resource: that "the Guajira is ruled by the gun."

In the fall of 1976, that morning as his cargo plane came within view of the mountains, Allen Long's business was booming. Up there, high in the foothills, waiting, lay the treasure of the Sierra Nevada. Up there, unburied, proliferating, was the Santa Marta Gold of legend. The finest marijuana in the world. And from there to the docks and the Mayday strips that were strung out along the Guajira, mule trains moved, by day, by night, in seemingly endless procession, under the weight of the find.

The gold rush was underway. Back home, 30 million American heads luxuriated in notions of getting twisted on nothing less than prime Colombian, and for almost a year now Long and his partners had been delivering it to them by the ton.

Among those partners were the pilots of the DC-3, Frank Hatfield and Will McBride. Allen Long American Flyer was really just a state of mind, his rating as an aviator being — well, call it unofficial. As architect of the criminal conspiracy and operational leader of the enterprise, Long was more than just along for the ride, but even in a mind as rich with fantasy as his, there abided no doubt that his taking control of the aircraft unsupervised was the functional equivalent of suicide.

McBride, an erstwhile musician, had known Long for about five years, and like Long, whose own pursuit of a career in the record industry was presently being ignored, he had been operating on the fringes of the marijuana business for much of that time. It was not in support of his musical ambitions that McBride had decided to take flying lessons. McBride was co-pilot of the DC-3. It was Hatfield who ran the air show, and it was Hatfield, the professional, to whom the other two smugglers looked when the radio message came in.

They were flying with the surf, following the shore break, having descended to about 2,000 feet on making landfall at Punta Gallinas. Banking southwest from there and running along the coast at a speed of 110 knots, they had begun picking up omens one by one as day was breaking behind them. Everything was different this time. The air was not crisp, but humid and heavy, the sunlight murky not bright. The underbrush below them was green, not brown. Clouds obscured the mountains. And just northeast of Riohacha, as the aircraft descended to a thousand feet, raindrops hit the windshield.

The precipitation merely suggested itself, a grace note, nothing more. Still, it was something new.

Breaking clear of it almost instantly, the smugglers started searching for smoke. A billowing column of thick, black smoke would bring them in to the runway. Spiraling from the flames of a burning tire, the plume could be seen on a normal flight to rise 200 feet in the air. Long, this time, was the first to spot it, and this time it hit the ceiling at fifty. At Camarones, they made radio contact. Only then did the omens add up.

"Sir, it has been raining here."

It had rained half the night. Torrentially. The downpour had ended only an hour before. Effectively, there *was* no runway.

The low drone of the radial engines, resonating through the cockpit, was the only sound for an instant. The ever-present hypnotic hum, the theme song of the operation, rising now on their collective silence, gave weight to the realization that they had seriously pushed the season.

The color drained from Long's face. He turned to Hatfield, the man in whose hands their fortunes rested — their lives and their fortunes literally, their sacred honor only if you stretched it — for something in the way of instructions. Hatfield, five years older than his partners, at thirty-three the oldest of three would-be millionaires whose lives were now up for grabs, differed from them most significantly in that he was not a smuggler by vocation. Marijuana, as far as he was concerned, was just a really good reason to fly. A professional pilot, Hatfield had been recruited the year before, and in a matter of months he had demonstrated an aptitude for crime that most pilots could only aspire to. But Hatfield remained true to his roots. His instructions were in keeping with conventions established by aviators throughout history, and characteristically brief.

He said: "Buckle up and hang on."

A flyover of the airstrip, under favorable landing conditions, revealed what could be called a runway only in the most optimistic interpretation of the term. Unidentifiable as such from the air, it was clearly discernible as a landing strip from only one point of reference. To see it you had to walk it, and trace for yourself the unmistakable tread marks of the various landing gear that had touched down there. The airstrip was invisible by design. Its engineering, or lack thereof, owed less to limitations of the local technology than to the threat of observation by government aircraft, which flew the coast routinely on drug-interdiction runs.

The strip began a couple of yards from the beach, which sloped up from the Caribbean to a rise of three or four feet. It extended eighteen hundred feet into the bush, a stretch of uneven ground, partially overgrown, the grass knee-deep in places. And today it was more than invisible. Today it was nonexistent, a third of a mile of fine, red clay that overnight had turned to mud. The field stood abandoned now, and crossing the strip, coursing the hardpan like rushing creeks, rivulets of rainwater ran so deep you could fish them.

Long's experience was limited, but what lay below him did not even approximate conditions as he had tried to imagine them when he had first heard a veteran flyer use the expression "soft-field landing." Just below the radar of his awareness, there was a sudden sense of his being in serious danger. The terror was stark and immediate. Catching sight of the airfield, he was overcome by a surge of adrenaline. His heart raced, his pulse quickened, his breathing grew rapid, and his palms began to sweat. It was a total and absolute physiological immersion in fear. And it was plain that he was not alone. The cockpit was filled with the smell of it.

Hatfield banked the airplane to starboard, circling north to make his final approach. He came in off the sea. With a wingspan of more than ninety-five feet, and standing almost two stories high, the airplane was more than sixty feet long and weighed 26,000 pounds. Buffeted by drafts and thermals, the wings of the aircraft seesawed as Hatfield nursed it down. He ordered McBride to lower the gear, and everything started to shudder.

The plane hit the runway at 80 knots, the gear throwing up mud, the trees visible through the cockpit glass speeding by in a blur. The instrument panel shook as the airplane thundered down the strip, the landing gear rumbling irresistibly through the depressions of the washed-out airfield. Struts thudding, fuselage rattling, the plane felt as if it were coming apart. Then the tail wheel hit. Momentum diminished dramatically. Shoulder belts and cargo nets strained under the shifting equilibrium of everything on board.

Hatfield's effort to slow the plane down was balanced now by an equally urgent need to keep it rolling. He had to circle the aircraft. He had to position it for takeoff, or no amount of fuel would get them home again. When the plane hit the end of the runway, the mud inevitably took hold, pinning it down as effectively as the arresting gear on a carrier deck.

Hatfield throttled up. He took all the power he could get out of the props. Engines roaring, tail wheel dragging, he slowly brought it about, inching the plane through the quagmire until the deep blue of the Caribbean filled the frame of the windshield. Moving just as sluggishly then, he taxied back up the strip, bouncing in the direction of the beach. Finally achieving the water's edge, he circled the plane again, pushing the revs to the redline to bring the tail wheel around. When he cut the power, the airplane sank, settling hub-deep in the mud, the cargo doors flew open, and the airstrip came alive.

Two trucks and twenty-five men broke cover. They bolted out of the brush from twenty yards off the runway, and they all converged on the airplane. The Colombians were in action now. Now there would be very few variables.

And there would be no testimonials. This was the Guajira. It was round-the-clock combat ops. Out-at-the-extreme, balls-to-the-wall flying was what it took to get business done here. It was the minimum required of aviators. The stunts typically associated with close air support on the battlefield were very cheap theatrics. Hatfield's would go unnoticed.

It was a routine pickup on the Guajira. A thousand gallons of flight fuel would be hand-pumped into the airplane's tanks from 55-gallon drums mounted on one of the farm trucks, as more than two tons of high-grade marijuana, nothing but gold and the finest Colombian red, were unloaded from the other. A well-ordered, methodical cargo operation, it would differ from the standard commercial procedure only insofar as it was conducted with unusual dispatch and almost exclusively by people wearing guns. Revolvers, semiautomatic pistols, shotguns, submachine guns, automatic rifles . . . It was a real festival of lethal hardware, a classic Latin American get-together, one in which the three gringos always took part unarmed.

Long threw back the cargo doors and stepped down into the mud He embraced the two men he did business with, the younger of whom, named Miguel, the one who had manned the radio, inevitably addressed him as "sir." Long took care of business with them, shook hands with a rugged character named Ernesto, the operational chief of the airstrip, and while Hatfield and McBride busied themselves shutting the airplane down, he set about inspecting the pot. Once approved for loading, each forty-pound bale would be hoisted aboard.

The first few bales had no sooner passed through the doors of the plane than they started flying back out. Long, bewildered, looked up to see Frank Hatfield standing on the cargo deck. Hatfield, at five-feet-ten, was about three inches shorter than Long, his military-cut, straight brown hair maybe that many inches shorter than Long's thick mane of blond. The lean but heavily muscled Hatfield was the beneficiary of quiet good looks, an easygoing manner, and an almost tangible good humor, the last of which appeared to have gone missing-in-action as he glared down at Long from the cargo doorway of the plane.

"What the fuck are you doing?" he said.

Granted, this was not the first use of the word "fuck," not by any of the three smugglers, and certainly not since the initial shock of the radio announcement had hit. But Hatfield's use of it here was like the overture now to an entirely new symphony of invective. In the next two minutes, replicated, mutated, compounded, and prodigiously exchanged by Hatfield and Long, the word would be traded so fast that its movement would be utterly impossible to clock. It would run through their altercation like gonorrhea through the crew of a merchant vessel on liberty in the Philippines.

"If you load this airplane," Hatfield said, schooling Long in the dynamics of flight, "we're not going to make it out of here."

Lifting off the runway in its current condition, even lifting off empty, was going to be a crapshoot at best, as any fool could see. Long, of course, was not any fool. Long was a fool of such sterling distinction that he was immediately willing to ignore the fact, even as he stood in ankle-deep mud, that having survived the landing just minutes before, he had already beaten the odds.

"I didn't come down here to go back empty," he said.

"We're not going back loaded," said Hatfield, and that should have been the end of it.

Long owned the franchise, it was he who ran the trip, but when it came to flying the airplane, and, yes, Long owned that, too, the chain of command started with Hatfield. The safety and ultimate success of the flight were Hatfield's responsibility. In the air Long always deferred to him. But right now Long was unable to think beyond a quarter-of-a-million-dollar payday, and for the first time in the months they had been flying together he challenged his pilot's authority. He started by taking a reckless position and elevating it to the arrantly ridiculous.

"Nobody said this was going to be easy," he said, challenging Hatfield's manhood.

Neither Hatfield's ability nor his courage, of course, was open to any question, but Long was not going to get very far by criticizing him for sound judgment. Hatfield, for his part, understood that in a beef as demented as this the last place to look for mileage was in an appeal to common sense. And so he fell back on simple intransigence. He just kept saying no, hoping that if the two of them screamed at each other loud enough, Long's delirium would burn itself out.

Long tried pulling rank.

"If we go back empty," he warned Hatfield, "you're not coming back on the next trip."

Not an entirely idle threat, but one Long was unlikely to act on, the remark was Long's way of telling Hatfield that he was nothing more than hired help.

To the Colombians watching, the shouting match was strictly a gringo thing, the fair hair, the flashing eyes — the very blue of the irises, so out of place in a place like this. There were six of them now, eyes as limpid as the surface of the ocean, as Will McBride was inevitably drawn into the argument.

As tall as Long, as blond, his impression upon the Colombians manifestly Nordic, McBride was clearly averse to jumping into the dispute. In what might be construed as the operation's table of organization, his authority outweighed Hatfield's, but he knew better than to think he knew better than Hatfield when it came to flying an airplane. When dragged into the fighting by Long, McBride, a man impatient with incompetence, ill-inclined to suffer clowns, shrugged his shoulders, threw up his hands, and voiced an opinion as brief as it was unequivocal: "Frank says no."

"If he doesn't want to go, that's fine," said Long. "I'll fly it out of here." He pointed a finger at Hatfield. "And I'll put a bale in your seat."

Maybe Hatfield really believed that Long was crazy enough to try it. If so, it was the pilot in him, his sense of responsibility for the lives of his partners, that made his continuing the argument with any conviction impossible. Maybe Hatfield was just exhausted. In any event, he finally gave up. In the end, the sheer force of Long's personality prevailed. The same insubmissive strength of will that had brought them all this far, that had enriched them each and fattened the bank of so many others, predominated once again in the face of conventional wisdom. In the end, every smuggler's story comes down to the triumph of greed over good judgment, and it would be no different here.

"You'll probably get us all killed," said Hatfield.

Long said, "I'd rather die rich."

It took every man on hand, and more, summoned from the local village, to push the airplane out of the ruts into which it had settled. The field was soft but firming up. The earth had begun to dry. Heaving on the undercarriage, muscling the struts, rolling the wheels up out of the eighteen inches of mud into which they had sunk, the Colombians inched the airplane forward, stepping away as Hatfield built up the speed of the engines. Props roaring, brakes on full, Hatfield pushed the revs, giving the airplane, standing still, more power than Long had seen him do in the months that he had been flying it. The airplane began to vibrate. The headphones crackled with static. Hatfield signaled the other two men to tighten up the straps on their seat belts.

"If we don't get airborne before we hit the end of the runway," he shouted, "we're gonna take the trees head-on. Just hope the cargo nets hold."

"It's not too late to unload," yelled McBride.

"No," said Long. "Let's go. Let's do it now."

He flashed the Colombians a thumbs-up through the cockpit window, and Hatfield released the brakes. Slowly the plane started to roll.

As the plane lumbered down the runway, the Colombians fired their guns, urging the gringos on. The Colombians applauded machismo in all its manifestations, no matter how ill advised. The expression of manhood exhibited here was all the more highly prized for being so poorly considered. Not lost on the Colombians, either, was the fact that if the Americans went home empty, nobody was going to get paid.

When the plane hit 35 knots, the tail came off the ground. The plane leveled off and picked up speed. At 65 knots it would fly. When Hatfield ran out of runway, the plane was doing no better than 60.

"Raise the gear!" he shouted.

To Will McBride, flying right-seat, this particular order was miles off the intuitive grid. Raising the landing gear of an airplane, he knew, while the airplane was on the ground would lead to rudimentary, aerodynamic instability of a kind covered in every textbook. A classic loss of equilibrium known to every pilot, it was one that was subject to quite specific, technical interpretation in the science of flight. It was called crashing.

"Raise the gear!"

They were skimming the brush now, and suddenly McBride saw the danger; he understood the urgency behind Hatfield's command. The mesquite, if it entangled the undercarriage, was going to flip the airplane. With visions of a massive fireball cartwheeling down the field, he raised the landing gear. The smugglers could feel the fuselage drop as the undercarriage came up. Long was sure he was going to die, and McBride gave voice to the certainty.

"Shit, we're going down," he said.

With that the plane caught air. Gear up, it achieved rotation speed, and lifted ten feet off the deck.

And stayed there.

They hit the high brush, and started churning it up, the beveled edges of the propeller blades slicing shallow troughs in the undergrowth. The rpm's dropped abruptly, the high-pitched whine of the engines backing off to a roar. Two perfectly manicured parallel tracks sculpted in the high mesquite, interrupted only intermittently as the plane, struggling, managed to catch air, would follow their passage for several miles. They gained a couple of feet, and then a few more. They disappeared from view of the airstrip. The Caribbean was just off to their left, but the salvation it promised was way out of reach. With the mesquite growing more than twelve feet high, Hatfield was unable to drop the port wing to bank in the direction of the sea. He was forced to maintain a straight flight path.

They were fourteen feet off the deck, moving at 75 knots, unable to get higher or go any faster. Periodically a tall patch of brush would drop them back down a foot. And then, in all its majesty, the Caribbean circled their way. As the coastline curved to the south, the ocean rose up to meet them. Once over the water, they were safe, they knew, and all three were now sure they would make it. The panorama, in stunning color, opened up gradually before them. Ahead of them, they could see the breakers. And then they could see the shoals. And then, finally, they saw the beach. And lining the beach, a row of coconut palms. An unbroken row of tall coconut palms.

"Shit!"

"Hold on! . . . Hold on!" said Hatfield.

"Ahh . . ."

They hit the palm trees.

". . . SHIT."

They actually uprooted one of the palm trees. They caught it full in the starboard engine. It remained hanging there as they flew. Smaller palms drove holes in both wings. Flight fuel poured from the starboard tank. Miraculously they were still flying.

They were about twenty-five feet off the water, gaining altitude now as they dumped fuel. Hatfield, studying the instruments, performed some rapid calculations.

"What do you think?" said Long.

"We can make it maybe four hundred miles. Which will put us maybe a hundred off the southern coast of Haiti."

Proceeding, therefore, was not an option.

One of the distinguishing features of the marijuana business, as pursued by Americans like Allen Long — one of the attributes that distinguished the marijuana business from other fields of criminal endeavor — was a conspicuous and, to those who thought about it, rather consoling absence of gunplay. This can be explained by the fact that, for many of the industry's pioneers, the marijuana came first, in both time as well as importance. The industry was created by pot smokers, a casual brotherhood of aficionados, loosely associated, relatively young, usually stoned, united around little more than a near-religious passion for the noble weed. A characteristically (and understandably) merry band of outlaws, who pledged at least passing allegiance to the values of the counterculture to which they and their customers belonged — "Peace and Love" being prominent among them — these people were accomplished pot smokers long before they were professional criminals. Prohibition would have gone down pretty much the same way if alcohol had been new in the Roaring Twenties and Al Capone had been one of a loose affiliation of drunks who had discovered bootleg whiskey in college.

Guns were a big fixture of the business south of the border and in American cities like Miami, where the money had begun to attract gangsters for whom dope was just one more commodity. Like a large majority of Colombians, whose disinclination was cultural, these were people who never smoked pot. But raise the issue of guns with smugglers like Allen Long, and it was axiomatic that you better bring lunch.

It brought forth dissertations. It invited an immersion in metaphysics, in a kind of mojo eschatology, with discourse on things like destiny and the implications of karma. In the end, what you came away with was . . . Well, there just seemed to be no place for guns.

Unless you were Frank Hatfield.

Frank Hatfield never embarked for the Guajira without a .45 caliber pistol within his immediate reach in the cockpit. The Colombians, who paid attention to such things, would recognize the handgun as a Model 1911 Government Colt. This single-action semiautomatic with the seven-shot magazine was at the time the official service pistol of the United States armed forces. And had been for sixty-five years. American pilots had been carrying the weapon into combat for generations. But it was not out of any sense of kinship with, or aspiration to the heroic stature of, the nation's military aces that Frank Hatfield always flew armed. He carried the sidearm not to use on the enemy. He carried it to use on himself.

Frank Hatfield sported an idiosyncrasy, a quirk that had become as definitive of his character as his brevity of speech, his winning smile, and his proficiency with airplanes and women. Frank Hatfield had a pathological fear of being eaten alive by sharks. It was the terror that alone haunted him. As brave as he was, as bold in the eye of danger, as brassbound as his aviator's balls had proved to be, it was the one manifestation of death's many faces into which Hatfield was unable to spit.

Haiti lay upon the island of Hispaniola, which, as islands will do, lay surrounded by a lot of water. And one hundred miles off the coast thereof, sharing a kitchen with the local marine life, was not where Frank Hatfield wanted to be.

Hatfield circled the airplane and headed back to the strip. The starboard engine was laboring, ill-equipped as it was to function with a tree choking the air intake of the cooling system. The temperature was rising, the oil pressure was dropping, and the engine was calling it quits. Then it went up.

"Fire in the starboard engine!" McBride yelled.

Flames licked along the cowling as the red-hot engine ignited. In fascination and horror, the smugglers watched the flames creep closer to the leaking fuel. If Hatfield shut the engine down, the airplane would explode. He had to keep her moving, had to keep the propeller turning, he had to hope the prop wash would blow the fire out.

The tongues of flame receded, and finally the fire died. Hatfield feathered the engine, and made for the airstrip on a single prop. As the starboard propeller went dead, he could see that the blades were warped — bent back at severe angles and twisted, violently and instantly made junk upon impact with the trees — and he had to assume the same to be true of the port-side prop as well. They never would have seen Haiti. They would be lucky now to make it back to the beach.

It was no place for endorsements, but not lost on any of the three smugglers aboard was the miracle of engineering being exhibited for their aeronautic enjoyment: The wings of the airplane were perforated by trees. The landing lights had been ripped entirely out of them, further deforming the airfoil. There was a palm tree hanging from the starboard engine. That engine was dead, and the propeller blades of the other, the one operational engine, were presumably warped to resemble the tines of a garden rake. The plane was dumping fuel. Soon the oil would be history . . .

And still the airplane was flying. And flying with a heavy load.

It flew that way for six miles.

Closing in on the beach, coming in dangerously low, the plane did not project any undercarriage. Deploying the landing gear was a luxury Hatfield could not afford. He could not risk adding a degree of resistance to the drag he was already up against. He had to make the runway. And he had to hope that what remained of the mud that had so effectively fouled his takeoff would now give him the skid he needed to land the plane in one piece.

With a smoking engine on the starboard side, with flight fuel pouring from the tanks, with hot steel glowing everywhere — with the likelihood of an explosion now came the added thrill of the bales. Some two and a half tons of lethal cargo would come crashing through the cockpit bulkhead if Hatfield came up short on the landing.

Hatfield skimmed the sloping beach, and put the plane belly-down on the runway. Sheet metal screaming, fuselage buckling on collision with the ground, the disabled craft crashed down the strip, slamming in with all the excitement of a freight train leaving the rails. The cargo nets held, the mud did its job, the plane slewed at an angle of about 30 degrees, nosed to a stop, and the smugglers bailed out.

Long obliged the starboard engine with a blast from the cockpit fire extinguisher, and backed away to wait for the explosion. The engine smoldered but failed to ignite. A column of smoke rose from the starboard wing, and would do so for better than an hour. The airplane refused to surrender.

Long offered a silent prayer for the well-being of the good people of the old Douglas Aircraft Company who forty years before had engineered the plane — this, the DC-3, the venerable commercial airliner in service since 1936, which as the C-47 Skytrain had become the most widely used military troop-and-cargo transport in history.

And now, more than just a part of history, the airplane literally *was* history. It was finished. It was the latest in a line of similar losses that stood as the hallmark of a new industry. In the multibillion-dollar enterprise that drug smuggling had become, such expenditures were a routine write-off, a line item in the operating budget under the heading "disposable birds." One preferred to write them off empty, however, on landing strips back home.

The Colombians had departed the airstrip. They had left after the airplane vanished from sight, assuming the takeoff had been successful. The smugglers were now on their own. Soon, a small group of Indians who had witnessed the crash assembled. No, they told Long, there was no phone in the village, they had no car, there was no way to reach Ernesto.

"Do you know what we need to do?" Long said. "We need to get rid of that airplane. We need to get the marijuana out of that airplane."

The villagers knew what to do. This was not the first plane that had crashed here, they said. A simple, familiar gesture of the hand served as the DC-3's epitaph.

"Fine, chop it up now," Long said.

"We can't just leave it like this," said Hatfield.

And he and McBride began removing from the airplane anything that might identify it, anything bearing its registration number, anything that might lead back to them. They destroyed all the documentation, then went to work on the hardware. The transponder, the radio transceivers — all the plane's avionics had to go. While the pilots, using screwdrivers, worked on the instrument panel, the villagers unloaded the pot. And once the starboard wing stopped smoking, the Indians started butchering the plane.

It was noon, and Long was sitting on the beach, the sun directly overhead. The air temperature was pushing 110, the humidity skyrocketing in the wake of the rain. With the local Indians to his back, cannibalizing the smoking aircraft, he stared out over the Caribbean like a man who had not only lost his dog, but had just seen its name on a witness list in a divorce proceeding against him.

"Look, man," McBride said, walking up behind him, "you told me and you told Frank, if anything like this ever happened down here, these guys would take care of it. You said the Colombians would get us out of it."

"I know."

"Well . . ."

"What?" said Long.

"Get us out of it."

"I'm working on it."

"Okay."

There were no arguments now about who was in charge. Their lives and freedom were in jeopardy. The responsibility for their escape rested with Long.

And Long was working on it.

Okay.

2 EL NIÑO PERDIDO

Allen Long was born the year Harry S. Truman was elected to the American presidency, and was first arrested for marijuana possession the year Bob Dylan released *Blonde on Blonde*. The year before, the year he took his first hit, Long dropped out of school. Dylan went electric. Not necessarily for that reason, nor even in that order. By 1966, when Long was arrested, certain cultural patterns were well established. By the end of the year more Americans would own the Dylan album than would even be aware of Leslie Bassett's *Variations for Orchestra,* winner of the Pulitzer Prize for Music. By the end of the decade more Americans would be in possession of marijuana than had voted for Truman.

When he was dragged off to jail by sheriff's deputies, Allen Long, seventeen, was living on Queen Street in Arlington, Virginia, a minute over the Potomac from the nation's capital, sharing an apartment with two other teenagers. The three misfits were students at the nearby Hawthorne School, a very exclusive, very expensive school for the deranged — or so Long liked to describe it. More accurately characterized, it was a school for those whose aspirations deranged the orderly function of others, an experimental, free-form academy for bright kids who marched to the beat of a different educational drum.

Several months earlier, Long, a senior, had dropped out of the private school he had been attending in Richmond. Not merely a Catholic school, it was a Catholic military school, and more than merely military, it was run by Benedictines. Long's father, who had enrolled him, was leaving nothing to chance in addressing the discipline problem his son had become. Long jumped scholastic ship to travel with a rock and roll band. Its members, older than Long, all of them in their twenties, had needed a singer with looks to front their new act. Tall, blond, and blue-eyed, passable as a teenage heartthrob in a kind of second-lead B-movie way, Long had the looks, but he had no musical talent. That, of course, deterred no one. He could jump and shout — a virtuoso at both, he had been proving it since infancy — and like others of his species with opposable thumbs, he could bang a mean tambourine. That was enough. With that and a record contract, the group, the Counts Four, picked up regular gigs in Georgetown, and just months before graduation, Long dropped out of high school to go on the road.

The tour ended in Los Angeles at the Whisky A Go-Go, where the band opened for the Byrds, an act whose cover of Dylan's "Mr. Tambourine Man" had recently hit the top of the charts. And there the band immediately dissolved, when the musicians, the real ones, were exposed to the chops of Byrds lead guitarist Jim McGuinn, and realized to their utter dismay that they would never be that good, nor equal to the achievement of even middling success in the music business.

Long persevered. To join the band, after all, he had dropped out of school, which carried with it significant consequences. And these he had risked for reasons that transcended the music. They were reasons anyone could appreciate, but none more readily than his classmates. As Long explained to them, being in a band was "the best way to get pussy," which to a seventeen-year-old was a quest that compared favorably with that of Percival for the Grail.

At that age, in those days, the only thing as cool, or seemingly so, as being affiliated with a band was being associated in some way with marijuana. Pot was forbidden fruit, the flesh of which was naturally suffused with the juice of romance and glamour. Shot through with totemic significance, it grew from the tree of knowledge around which Long's generation gathered, the talisman of a new age, the drug that would power the following year's Summer of Love and Woodstock two years after that. Marijuana, emblematic of the outlaw, was the badge of the burgeoning counterculture. As Long saw it, smoking dope — more importantly, having it, and thus being able to provide it — made you attractive to girls.

Having smoked his first joint as a member of the band, Long in 1966 returned to the D.C. area a man with experience to spare. He enrolled in the Hawthorne School, joined a new band, and moved with two of its members into the apartment on Queen Street. There, in that earthly paradise, nourished by the food-giving trees of the new Eden — sex, drugs, and rock and roll — he luxuriated. And in that idyllic garden he lasted about as long as Adam.

The music, the dope, they both played a part, but as Adam might have told him, had the two men shared a cell, you really had to hand it to the girls.

One of the young women who frequented the Queen Street apartment left there one night with a couple of joints she had been given by the members of the band. Busted by her father, who called the police, she made a subsequent visit to the apartment accompanied by a "friend." That he, the friend, was maybe twice her age and sported what was known at the time as "a Beatles haircut" provoked in Long and his roommates no second thoughts. These were the days of "harmony and understanding, sympathy and trust abounding." Everyone trusted everyone. To be mistrustful was just not cool.

"Do you know where I can get some grass?" asked the long-haired friend.

Police undercover work is a cycle of constants. Only the barbers change.

In exchange for a ride to their gig that night, the musicians scored a dime bag of weed, which they split with the undercover cop. Four days later, following a raid on their apartment, Long and his roommates were taken to jail. The parents of the other two boys intervened on behalf of their sons, whose cases were eventually adjudicated the way such cases usually are, much the way Long's was adjudicated four months later: the suspects released on probation to their parents' custody, the criminal record to be expunged after a year of good behavior. Long's parents, however, whose understanding of such things led them to suppose that their son was injecting marijuana into a brachial vein, thought jail was just what he needed. Rather than put up bail, they let the state lock him up until the case came up for a hearing.

To escape the predation of older, more dangerous inmates, Long, on the advice of a second-rate lawyer, applied to the court for a psychiatric evaluation, that he might end his pretrial detention in the safety of a hospital. The judge ruled in his favor — having smoked marijuana, the judicial thinking went, Long had to be nuts — and ordered him shipped off to Southwestern State Hospital, a mental health facility, where he was incarcerated in the wing set aside for the criminally insane. Not a bad approximation of his idea of hell, the curative bedlam served as his sanctuary for a full ten weeks. Long celebrated his eighteenth birthday in the custody of the state, and by the time of his release he had developed a grudge, a contempt for the legal system that would last his entire life.

Allen Long, born in Richmond, was six years old when his parents divorced, and he moved with his mother, a schoolteacher, and his infant brother to the small town of South Hill on Virginia's southern border. As a boy, he spent many days in the local auction barns there, lying atop bales of tobacco, lulled by the drone of the auctioneers, moving to Charlottesville at the age of eleven, when his mother married a psychology professor at the University of Virginia. Seeking the approval of his father, a prominent Richmond businessman, Long exhibited the values of the Virginia gentleman through his sophomore year in high school. At fifteen he spearheaded Virginia Youth for Goldwater, intending one day himself to be elected President of the United States. It was not his father but his grandfather from whom Long took his guidance, the elder man from whom he inherited his sense of risk and spirit of adventure, the very spirit in which, as a high school junior, he eventually twisted off.

Long's paternal grandfather, after whom he was named, arrived in the United States at the age of six. He had been sent from Ireland by his family to work for a distant relative in Tennessee. At eleven, he escaped what amounted to indentured servitude, stealing a mule and riding it a hundred miles to Louisville, Kentucky, where for the next three years he worked as a slop boy, cleaning the vats in a brewery. At fourteen he apprenticed as a factory tool-and-die maker, eventually moving to New Jersey to work for a lock-making company. Securing a patent on a suitcase lock he developed, he moved to Petersburg, Virginia, where in 1919 he founded the Long Manufacturing Company, which would become the world's largest manufacturer of trunk locks. Among the company's customers for the Long T46 — the trunk lock whose classic design would continue to be widely copied long after the patent expired and the company lost its dominance — was the United States Army.

It was into the fountain of money generated by this company, and eventually into the proprietorship of the company itself, that Long's father, John, fell by accident of birth. Long felt that his father fell into everything he did, navigating life with no purpose, a failing Long came to blame on the grandfather he so admired, who, holding out the promise of independence, tethered his son to a family enterprise whose control he never intended to cede. Long's low opinion of his father was not an opinion shared by everyone. John Long, in his own student years, had dropped out of Notre Dame to fight the Second World War. Achieving the rank of captain, he fought Rommel in the desert of North Africa and was part of the Allied beachhead at Anzio. He was awarded the Silver Star not for aimlessness but for gallantry in action. The Junior Chamber of Commerce named him Virginia's Man of the Year before, not after, his eldest son was arrested for pot possession.

It was into his father's custody that Long was released on probation in 1966. He moved to Richmond and earned his high school equivalency diploma while working at a lumber mill, a silk screen shop, and at a succession of other, low-paying jobs. Eighteen months later he returned to Charlottesville and entered the University of Virginia as a psychology major. While a student, he landed a job at a television network affiliate in Richmond. Rising to the position of night news cameraman, he was eventually promoted to head the news-film department. Convinced by then that his only competition for work was Federico Fellini, he put together a reel of film, quit the job, dropped out of college, and in the summer of 1970 departed for New York in a '57 pickup, determined to make waves in the film industry.

Choosing not to direct *Satyricon* — Fellini took that gig — Long accepted a job as a production assistant at a commercial production house, Motion Associates, on Madison Avenue. There he worked as a gofer on commercials for, among other clients, Eastman Kodak, Esso, Chanel, and Rival dog food. Capitalizing on the experience he gained, and exploiting the contacts he developed, he went on to secure backing for a documentary movie he wanted to shoot. A cutting-edge exposé, it was a project he sincerely believed would lead to an enduring and lucrative career in the entertainment business.

He was right. It was a movie about marijuana smuggling.

The trouble started with a guy named El Coyote.

A Mexican-American, born on the Texas border, the self-styled El Coyote was a thirty-year-old pot smuggler who lived in a penthouse apartment on the Upper West Side of Manhattan. He was the first of various characters Long would come to know whom he would remember as larger than life. Six feet tall, built less like a coyote than a greyhound (he weighed 140 pounds), El Coyote projected the image of a man of the world, a man as wily as the fabled creature from which he took his name: the legendary trickster of Southwest myth. Like that of almost any man whose Christian name is a definite article, El Coyote's image was simply that — nobody really bought it. But he projected it with magnificent enthusiasm, and the exhibition was always worth the price of overlooking the obvious.

A textbook of antic behavior, as high-strung as is stereotypical of a man proportioned in such a way that his photograph could be confused with his X ray, El Coyote transcended the manic in aspiring to the maniacal. A random urine sample from the excitable Chicano would screen positive for every recreational drug ever written about in the 1960s. They would show up all at once, all of them in the same test.

Long was living in the Village at the corner of Bleecker Street and Seventh Avenue, supporting himself on his production assistant's salary, when he met El Coyote. A West Village shop owner who distributed pot, knowing that Long owned a pickup truck, had offered him a chance to earn some extra money making deliveries. Long was driving his half-ton GMC around town delivering pot to the shop owner's customers or picking it up from his supplier, ten to twenty pounds of Mexican or Jamaican at a time.

The supplier was El Coyote. One of the customers was a guy named Crosby, who would gain notoriety several years later when he opened one of the more famous drug bars in New York. A downtown establishment with a video camera at the elevator and a bouncer at the door, it featured, where the back bar would ordinarily be, a blackboard on which were listed the various strains of dope available for purchase that day. Police eventually shut the place down, but failed to eliminate the concept, which later would be raised to an art form by the Dutch when such places became legal in the Netherlands.

One evening Long and Crosby — by now the Village shop owner had been bypassed as a middleman by all concerned — sat smoking in El Coyote's apartment, playing audience to the demented smuggler, while the latter regaled them with fascinating and largely hilarious tales of misadventure along the Mexican border.

El Coyote was all over the place, slipping in and out of coherence. There was something Long wanted to say, but before he could really get a handle on things the subject had shifted from dope to another equally urgent topic of the day: the vexing political reality that ten of the nation's larger corporations controlled the world. No attempt was made to identify them, but it was agreed that the fix was in.

"And they did it without controlling magnetism, that's the amazing thing," said Long.

This particular observation brought the colloquy to a stop. The other two men looked at him not with fear and pity at the terrible pharmacological mess he was in, but with anticipation of some germ of wisdom.

"Dick Tracy," Long explained. "'He who controls magnetism will control the universe.' Sundays. It was a recurring theme in the Crimestoppers Textbook."

Crosby ventured that if he remembered correctly it was also an essential element in the Revelation of Saint John.

Long made use of the hiatus to lead El Coyote back to the original subject of his oratory. He was eager to hear more smuggling yarns. El Coyote was happy to oblige, and as his performance began picking up steam, Long remembered what had been on his mind.

"You know . . ."

Politely brooking the interruption, El Coyote paused. Observing what a rhetorician would identify as the aposiopesis, he and Crosby once more turned their attention to Long and patiently waited for him to continue.

"You know, this would make a great movie," he said.

Stoned.

He was thinking of a documentary movie. And he was confident that its financing would prove to be no problem. Among Long's many friends in New York was the owner of an uptown saloon, a fellow by the name of Ives. Ives was El Coyote's age, and standing five-feet-six, weighing some 260 pounds, he was El Coyote's morphologic reciprocal — not simply obese, but morbidly so, he was as overfed as El

Coyote was undernourished. The two men looked, in each other's company, like some horrible livestock experiment. Bringing them together for the purposes of a movie, as Long was about to do, was certain to succeed if the movie were a cartoon and the two of them were cast in the leads. In default of that proposition, Long's project ran a very strong second.

With a contemporary soundtrack, a strong narrative line, and an audience base of some 25 million pot smokers to build from, Long's documentary was well positioned to make money, he believed, and that was how he presented it to Ives, a man whose ample waistline was dwarfed by the girth of his wallet. Ives's saloon was a mere indulgence. Ives was heir to one of the nation's older and larger industrial fortunes, one of the real ones, one of those corporations whose combined performance accounted for the Dow. Excited by Long's idea for the film, he readily agreed to be its producer.

Long, by way of research, planned to accompany El Coyote on his next trip to Mexico to pick up a load. Their friend Crosby would make the trip with them.

"He's going to finance the move."

"I thought I was financing the movie," said Ives.

"You *are* financing the movie," Long said. "Crosby's financing the move."

"The move."

"The move," said Long. "He's the guy who's paying for the pot."

"Oh," said Ives. "The 'move.'"

"The move."

They left New York for Guadalajara in August 1971 on an AeroMexico flight from JFK. Before they left, El Coyote, the professional, had given Long instructions on how he was to act: appear conservative in the extreme, cool in every respect, draw no attention to himself. El Coyote would dispatch a limousine to pick him up for the flight. The limo arrived at six A.M., and at six-thirty the car, with Long in back, was idling quietly curbside below El Coyote's apartment. Long was dressed as staidly as a stockbroker, everything on the up-and-up from the haircut to the briefcase to the jacket and tie. When El Coyote finally appeared the production values shifted. The tone of the masquerade went from Dun & Bradstreet to Barnum & Bailey.

El Coyote's suit, which had just come back from the cleaners, had been washed rather than dry-cleaned. The explanation for this travesty was rendered so incoherently by its victim that it was to be lost to history forever. As time went by, Long would learn not to seek answers to certain questions, his experience teaching him that with guys like El Coyote these things were just God's way. The suit was about eight inches short in the inseam, about five inches short in the sleeves. From his footwear to his fedora — yes, he was wearing a hat — El Coyote was as inconspicuous as a school bus. He wore black Carnaby Street boots, zipped up to his lower shin. And then his pants began. As if it redeemed respectability in the midst of this terrible fall from sartorial grace, El Coyote was wearing a necktie. And if the fashion statement itself were not sufficiently frantic, he had been up all night on cocaine.

His panic, however, arose from an altogether different disaster. El Coyote, a federal fugitive, had been unable to memorize the information on the false identification he was about to use to purchase his airline ticket. According to the birth certificate he had recently bought, his name was Kyle something, and he was desperate to get it right.

"Ask me my name," he said to Long. "Go ahead, ask me my name."

"What?"

"Go ahead. Just ask me my name."

"What's your name?"

"What?"

"What's your *name*?"

"I can't remember."

It was like that all the way to the airport.

Once inside the terminal, Long found a place to hide as El Coyote made his assault on the AeroMexico ticket counter. In calculating the odds on serious trouble, Long read the setup this way: El Coyote was wanted for smuggling. He was about to present fraudulent identification for the purpose of leaving the country. And as Long had just discovered minutes before in the limousine, these were only two of three conspicuous felonies for which the madman might be arrested. Around his waist, beneath his miserably shrunken suit, El Coyote was strapped with a money belt. In it he carried the cocaine, mescaline, opium, and hashish that, in addition to the variety of other drugs available there, he would need in Mexico for personal use. A maintenance stash, carried against the risk of any severe, psychochemical imbalance that his body might find itself running — against the possibility of his waking up straight — the bindle was necessarily hefty. There was no room in the belt for money.

El Coyote, issued a ticket, swaggered through the gate, and Long, nursing misgivings, joined him on board the plane. Crosby sat by himself. The flight was uneventful until they were about two hours out of Guadalajara, at which point El Coyote turned to Long and said, "Okay, now you have to put on the money belt."

"What?"

The possibility of a search was remote, virtually nonexistent. Customs officials were not thoroughly stupid. Nobody brought drugs *into* Mexico. Nobody who was in his right mind.

"Okay, I'll do it," said Long, realizing that El Coyote was not somebody who fit that description.

Upon arrival in Guadalajara, El Coyote rented a car, a Volkswagen painted a bilious, general-issue green. The three Americans climbed aboard, El Coyote behind the wheel, and stopping only long enough to sign into a hotel and deposit their luggage, drove directly to the Plazuela de los Mariachis and started drinking.

Guadalajara, located 300 miles northwest of Mexico City, is the country's second-largest city and considered one of its more beautiful. Situated a mile high in the Sierra Madre, the capital of Jalisco state, it is a city of narrow streets and intimate plazas, a city awash in bougainvillea, poinciana, orange blossoms, orchids, palms, lemon trees, and water, spilling everywhere, the water of 146 public fountains. Allen Long saw fountains everywhere he looked. The Plazuela de los Mariachis, just off the city's central square, was surrounded by cantinas and open-air cafés and resplendent with several groups of the street musicians for which the plaza was named, no fewer than five mariachi bands, all strolling the cobblestones, simultaneously playing requests.

Allen Long, moviemaker, sitting there in a cantina in the company of smugglers, was just where he wanted to be, alive to the magic and the promise of adventure, breathing the fragrant air of the Torrid Zone just below the Tropic of Cancer. Drinking tequila, chasing it with beer and chasing both with the stash of inebriants concealed in the recesses of the money belt, he and Crosby, after a couple of hours, were very severely bent, but not nearly so severely as their chauffeur. El Coyote's necktie was gone, his shirt was open — his pants were still way too short — his eyeglasses were off, and he had commandeered the entire cantina. The tables were pushed together, the patrons seated as if all of them were members of the same party, and urged on by El Coyote, all were toasting one another, drinking to America, drinking to Mexico . . . "*Viva la*" this . . . ! "*Viva la*" that . . . !

The sun fell, and the stars rose. It was a clear, balmy, late-summer night on the Plazuela de los Mariachis, and for a moment Long was overcome with what he would remember as a heavenly glow. Shortly thereafter he woke up lying face-down on the floor of the men's room in two or three inches of wet sawdust. That was when he remembered it, the heavenly glow. How long he had been passed out was a mystery. Why the sawdust was wet was not, but it made no impression on him, or on anybody else for that matter. He woke up, brushed himself off, and returned to the table, where his disappearance was remarked by no one.

In Long's absence El Coyote had organized a battle of the bands. There was $100 in prize money for the mariachis who impressed him most. There were three bands surrounding the table, musicians in full regalia — silver-studded *charro* suits, trimmed with piping, tricked out in braid, sombreros rimmed with pom-poms. One band was outfitted in pale baby blue, one lime green, the other yellow . . . There were guitars, violins, *vihuelas*, trumpets, and maybe a hundred spectators crowded around the table. The Americans had plenty of friends now.

El Coyote, living large, was laying out the cake. The cash was moving fast. He was buying drinks for everybody.

A hush came over the cantina when one of the bands played "El Niño Perdido," the lost child, a mariachi standard. It climaxed in a mournful trumpet solo, calling out into the night. When the music, echoing in the darkness, stopped, and the song drifted off into silence, the trumpet called out again, its music more forlorn. And once again it was met by silence. Then in the stillness, playing somewhere in the distance, a second trumpet could be heard. The first trumpet player responded. Again came the sound of the second horn. And now it was moving closer. A sigh went up from the crowd. The music of the trumpets, seeking each other, steadily converged, and by the time father and son were reunited, everyone in the cantina was crying, the sobbing mixed with cheers as the approaching horn found its way into the plaza, the second trumpeter suddenly visible, standing across the square. The two musicians, playing counterpoint solos, advanced across the cobblestones, and the trumpeters, standing side by side, rejoicing, began playing as one. The drunks in the cantina went crazy. And then the band kicked in.

And it just did not get any better than this, especially if you were wasted.

These mariachis took the grand prize.

Within minutes of proclaiming their victory, El Coyote, the toast of all Guadalajara, managed to work his way into a verbal pissing match with one of the locals seated at the table. A dispute over some asinine point of pride, it was one of those beefs that tend to make sense only when two people are equally drunk, one of those altercations that tend to resolve themselves in the throes of equally asinine, slobbering expressions of love. And more drinks. This particular quarrel, however, escalated beyond hope of resolution when El Coyote, enraged, jumped up onto the table, dropped his pants, and mooned his new drinking companion.

Long and Crosby instantly grabbed him and hustled him out of the joint, half carrying him to the Volkswagen.

Which El Coyote insisted upon driving.

El Coyote was thoroughly drunk — his pants were still down around his ankles — but he was El Coyote, and nobody but he was driving that car. Long and Crosby were drunk themselves, and the argument they put up, taking no probative value from the fact that they at least were wearing their trousers, was aimless, nonsensical, and ultimately of no effect. Long climbed into the back of the car, Crosby climbed onto the front passenger seat, and with El Coyote behind the wheel, the three witless pilgrims sped off. With predictable results. Turning down a one-way street, heading in the wrong direction, El Coyote ran the Volkswagen into the front bumper of a double-parked sedan idling just off the corner in front of an ice cream shop. The collision, which brought the Volkswagen thudding to a sudden stop, lit the other car up like the scoreboard on a pinball machine.

They had actually hit a police car.

The flashing red of the squad car's roof light instantly drew a crowd, and Long's thoughts instantly shifted from vehicular misdemeanors to the felonies stashed in the money belt. Prison came to mind. The police alighted, called the Americans out of the Volkswagen, and ushered them into the rear of the squad car. There, the prisoners were presently joined by a pair of Good Samaritans, a couple of civilian bystanders who managed to squeeze in with them. These self-appointed interpreters took seats on the prisoners' laps.

"Don't worry gringo, no problem . . ."

As the squad car followed the Volkswagen, driven by a third policeman, through the streets of Guadalajara, making its way to the station, Long tried to reason with the arresting officers. He took his cash out of his pocket and waved it in their direction. The interpreter sitting on Long's lap, making clear that he was there to assist — specifically to assist the Mexican police in relieving the Americans of their money — snatched the bills as they passed in front of him.

"One for you, one for you, and one for me," he said, sharing the cash with the cops. "Don't worry, gringo, no problem . . ."

This was Mexico, and because it was Mexico, events had a way of escalating beyond the narrative threshold at which they merely taxed credulity. Because it was Mexico, it was necessary that events, in their inevitable recounting, proved not merely hard to believe, but atmospheric of the supernatural. What happened next would have to be sufficiently strange, something implausibly operatic, something like a flat tire on the squad car. Yes. And it was while the policemen were changing the tire that El Coyote started working on them.

"We're brothers . . ." And that kind of stuff.

About fifteen hundred dollars later, the police decided that they and El Coyote were brothers, and that if Long drove the Volkswagen, and drove straight to the hotel, the gringos were free to go. With Crosby on his right, and El Coyote in the back, Long aimed the Volkswagen in the direction of the hotel, La Posada Guadalajara. "That way," the police had told them. And "that way" was the way Long drove. But El Coyote had descended so far into the affliction of drugs and alcohol that he saw chicanery and treachery in everything — El Coyote had really lost it now — and he was certain they were being directed to jail.

"It's a trick," he insisted. "A trick. Go the other way."

Long, dismissing him with a wave of his hand, told him he was imagining things. El Coyote lunged forward, and snarling with a ferocity worthy of his namesake, snapped Long's ear between his teeth.

"Grrr . . ."

"Arrrghh . . . !"

He bit down until Long obeyed.

Throwing the car into a quick U-turn, Long sped in the opposite direction.

Until he sped past the police.

When the police caught up to the Volkswagen, one of the officers stepped into the car, and *he* drove the Americans to the hotel. El Coyote by then had passed out in the back.

"What . . . ? What happened?" he grumbled, patting himself down for a joint while Long was hauling him into the building.

"Man, you shouldn't smoke," said Long, snatching the drugs. "It stunts your clothes."

3 AZTEC TWO-STEP

It was six A.M. and Long had been in town maybe three days when he was rousted from sleep by a knock on the door of his Guadalajara hotel room. Sunlight streamed through the window. He groaned when it hit his eyes. Half awake, he crawled out of bed and crossed the room, and standing in the frame when he pulled open the door was a tall, dark-haired gringo. He wore faded blue jeans, leather sandals, a white T-shirt and Ray-Bans, and carried a leather jacket slung over his shoulder. He removed the sunglasses when he saw Long.

He said, "Goddamn it, you're not them."

His eyes were dark, his complexion was fair, and when he opened his mouth to express his dismay he exposed teeth as bright and perfect as an octave on a Steinway.

"I guess I'm not," said Long.

"I'm sorry, buddy," the stranger continued, in a deep but pleasant baritone. "I asked the lady at the front desk where the Americans with long hair were staying. I guess my friends have checked out."

"I guess they have," said Long, whose hair, while in conformance with nonconformist counterculture standards, was positively short when measured against his intruder's dark halo of curls.

"Sorry," said the stranger again.

Long shut the door and went back to sleep.

The trip had become a complete downer. Two days earlier, El Coyote had made his connection. The meet had been set for two P.M. at the site of pre-Columbian ruins outside the city. The machinery of the marijuana-trafficking conspiracy had slipped smoothly into gear. At the appointed time Long and Crosby were standing with El Coyote at the top of a small pyramid at the site, when a truck arrived, and out stepped a Mexican in a cowboy hat. He climbed the steps, shook hands all around, and shared with El Coyote the obligatory *abrazo* — very masculine, very forceful, the signature embrace of the dope industry's brothers-in-arms.

"*Mi amigo.*"

"My friend."

"My good friend."

"*Amigo.*"

Crooks are always hugging each other. In the dope business such hugs are typically vigorous and the greetings accompanying them cheerful. They lack the ecclesiastical reserve of those hugs one associates with the mob, and they serve their purpose without the kissing, or other solemn affectations of piety. They are especially outlandish in those cases where the parties involved understand that in the course of business they will be trying to steal money from each other.

"I need two hundred pounds of your *best* merchandise," El Coyote declared. He needed it across the border, in Texas or Arizona.

The Mexican said, "Consider it done."

El Coyote, pleased, and playing it large for the benefit of his cinema-biographer, asked when he could take delivery — El Coyote, the consummate professional.

"I will be happy," the Mexican answered, "to do that for you in six months."

El Coyote was struck momentarily dumb. What kind of response was that? In El Coyote's facial expression you could actually read his accent. It was an expression that seemed to ask the question: "What you doing, *cholo,* you sticking some hot poker up my skinny Chicano ass?" El Coyote shook off his disbelief the way a dog shakes off water, and said, "What do you mean?"

"This is not the time of the harvest, my friend, you know that," answered the Mexican.

There was never pot in August. Not in North America. Of course not. El Coyote had forgotten that.

"What do you mean, you forgot?" Long gasped. "Are you absolutely out of your mind?"

Crosby, who had financed the trip, was that much more incredulous. He ordered the expedition back to the hotel, and started packing his suitcase. He and a chastened El Coyote left Guadalajara the next day.

Exeunt. They were gone, stepping not simply into the wings, but completely out of the theater of operations into which Long was now making an entrance.

Long, hoping to salvage the trip, had decided to stay in town. He had a movie to make, and would try, in the sudden absence of sources, to develop some contacts, scare up some leads. He knew no one in Guadalajara, but it was as good a place as any to start. That evening he drank alone in the Plazuela de los Mariachis.

On the morning he was awakened by the knock on his door, Long was heading back to the plaza when about halfway there he instructed his cab driver to pull over and stop the car.

"Hey," he called out the window, "remember me?"

Walking in the dust on the side of the road was the American who had interrupted his sleep.

"Yeah."

"You want a ride downtown?"

"Well, yeah, okay, I guess, sure," he said.

Stepping into the cab, the American introduced himself as Lee.

"Let me buy you a drink," said Long.

They made their way to La Copa de Leche, "the best bar on the Plazuela de los Mariachis," Long told him, sharing the weight of an opinion that had been in the family for, hell, almost fifty-six hours, and there he and his new acquaintance sat down and ordered lunch.

"What brings you to Mexico," asked Lee.

Long explained that he was a filmmaker, that he was researching a documentary. "It's about pot smuggling," he said. "I'm down here from New York."

He asked Lee where he was from.

"California," said Lee.

"What brings you to Guadalajara?"

"I'm a pot smuggler," he said.

Lee Carlyle, twenty-four, was a man of classically American enthusiasms, and characteristically Carlyle allowed those enthusiasms to run away with him. As a teenager in Escondido, California, indulging a youthful passion for hot rods, he had succeeded in building a low-rider so low that he could not get it out of his driveway. Adulthood did not temper his spirit. Later, when he was moving tons of marijuana out of Miami, Carlyle would purchase for his personal consumption the entire South Florida allotment of Château Lafite-Rothschild's 1972 Carruades de Lafite. It would take him — and his friends, and their various girlfriends, and all the hookers and coke dealers in Miami — a year and a half to drink it.

Carlyle got into the dope business the way most otherwise law-abiding Americans got into it: as a consumer, a pothead who bought weight and sold off the surplus to cover the cost of the pot he smoked. Carlyle began dealing as a teenager, selling nickels out of ounces, then ounces out of pounds. Soon, he and a couple of friends were smuggling pot out of Mexico and selling it by the brick.

Pot coming out of Mexico at the time was molded and packaged in rectangular blocks that mimicked the shape of the standard building or paving brick. A brick of Mexican marijuana tipped the scale at about two pounds, as its weight was expressed in standard English. Scientifically, it weighed a kilogram, or two-point-two pounds, which is how a kilo of anything is technically expressed in the U.S. Customary System of measurement.

In the 1970s, before that and ever thereafter, dope, worldwide, licit and illicit, was sold by metric weight. Cocaine, heroin, hashish, Bordeaux, aspirin, Valium, reds, Quaaludes, prescription speed . . . They were sold by the kilogram or liter, or fraction thereof, in keeping with the International System of Units, as the metric system is formally known. Mexican weed was no exception. Only after it crossed the border to be sold by Americans was commercial Mexican sold by avoirdupois weight.

And while that piece of cultural trivia might prove useless to a contestant on all but the hippest of television game shows, it serves as an illustration of the contraband-marketing skills of Allen Long's Colombian friends, whose merchandising genius would later change the world. For when Colombia entered the dope-dealing sweepstakes, traffickers there, right from the start, made marijuana available to smugglers priced by the pound.

When Lee Carlyle was twenty-one, he and his partners were running loads of pot out of Culiacán, moving maybe one hundred pounds of Mexican per trip to a group of buyers in Chicago. Carlyle was married to an aspiring actress, driving a new Camaro, and living in an apartment in Los Angeles. He was living the American dream, or the Lee Carlyle version of it anyway. As Allen Long would come to view it, Carlyle's was not a complicated horizon. On the last run he made before meeting Long, Carlyle was headed for the border with the dope in the trunk of a convertible, when he crashed the car, the trunk popped open, he was arrested for smuggling, and thrown into a Mexican jail. By the time he was released his wife had run out on him, taking with her everything he owned — the Camaro, the furniture — and all the cosmetic surgery he had paid for, the complete, marijuana-subsidized makeover, which had been instrumental in nailing her a gig on *As the World Turns*.

When Long and Carlyle met in Mexico, Carlyle was just getting back into the game. And to an observer unfamiliar with the rules under which it was played, chances appeared remote that Carlyle would ever cover the spread. His buyers in Chicago, running up against the seasonal drought suffered by pot smokers every year, would have done better than to take his call when Carlyle was released from jail.

"No pot," they told him.

"No problem," said Carlyle. "I have a friend in Guadalajara."

The friend and putative savior of all the pot-smoking faithful of Chicago's Near North Side was a Mexican named Jesús, with whom Carlyle had served time in jail, a connection who could load Carlyle up, he said, with all the weight he could handle. The Chicago distributors chartered a plane and flew down to Guadalajara. They had a forty-foot boat in Mazatlán, 300 miles away, which had been sailed down from San Francisco, ready to pick up half a ton of weed. They had sent a lot of people, moved a lot of equipment thousands of miles, and they had spent a lot of money — on a boat captain, a crew, on pilots, on marine and aviation fuel, not to mention the hotel rooms and other, exorbitant incidental expenses necessary to fund the move out of Mexico. Additional cash had been eaten up by logistics and personnel at the site of the scheduled off-load in Southern California. They had done all that only to discover that, yes, Jesús could load them up, but not that time of year.

They had cleared out overnight, leaving Carlyle behind.

That an operator as experienced as Carlyle could have miscalculated so seriously, or more to the point in his case, thrown the dice so recklessly, opened a line of questioning into the workings of the marijuana business that Long would have been smart to pursue. How the ambitious Carlyle had made the same mistake as the majestically confused El Coyote, a smuggler who had actually brought into Mexico more drugs than he had taken out, was worthy of investigation. But Long knew nothing about Carlyle yet. All he knew was that Carlyle was a marijuana smuggler, another American scammer coming off a deal gone bad in Mexico.

"What are you going to do now?" he asked him over drinks at the Copa de Leche.

Carlyle reached into his pocket. "You see this?" he said, and pulled out a dime. "This is what I have left. I'm going to take this dime," he said, holding it up, "and I'm going to turn it into a million bucks."

Sitting at the Copa de Leche, Long made two decisions. He decided, first, that this guy Lee was "off his rocker." And he decided that Carlyle's attempt to turn the dime into a million dollars was just the dramatic element that his documentary needed, the narrative thread that would pull the movie together. After listening to Carlyle's story, and hearing his plan, he said: "I want to use you as the subject of my film."

Carlyle said fine, undoubtedly thinking that if nothing else he would get room and board out of the deal. Long gave him $500, which was enough to rent a villa in Guadalajara for a month (Carlyle was now one two-thousandth of the way to his goal), and returned to New York to pick up money to finance the continuing research.

It would be two months before pot was available, and Long spent that time at the villa. Carlyle introduced him to Jesús and his partners, and a variety of other troublemakers in or on the periphery of the marijuana business in Guadalajara. While in residence at the villa, Long gathered a wealth of valuable material. And he had a lot of fun. Pot, unavailable commercially, was readily obtainable for personal use, as were cocaine and a variety of women. The region was abundant in visiting American art students, and a flock of young gringas, attracted by the drugs and the endless amenities of the villa, fell prey, not entirely unwillingly, to the ne'er-do-wells in residence. The swimming pool was always full.

Jesús came through with the pot on schedule, but the deal instantly went south when Carlyle's airplane failed to make the pickup. The pot had been waiting on a dry lakebed outside Guadalajara, and Carlyle's partner, Elwood, flying in from Arizona, had landed at the wrong location. When Carlyle dashed to Tucson to straighten things out, Long followed. The trip was memorable on two scores. Well, only one was actually a score: the amiable desk clerk who checked Long into his motel.

"Say, where'd you get those boots?" she asked.

"New York."

"Are they snakeskin, or what?"

"I don't know, I forget," said Long. "Gila monster or something. Some kind of poisonous lizard."

"Not too many poisonous lizards," she said. "Gila monster's about it."

"You a biology major?"

"Name's Rita."

With hair a shade darker than workingman's whiskey and eyes a shade darker than that, she sported the innocent, feverish gaze of the libidinous and congenitally nearsighted, and her wise-ass manner was punctuated by prominent lips that had supposed a perpetual pout. She was loose and in her twenties, she had nothing to hide, and which of them, she or Long, charmed the other into bed was unclear.

The trip was memorable on a second count for the speed at which the marijuana waiting in Guadalajara was sold. Long and Rita's romance was just one more one-night stand. Carlyle and his buddy Elwood, getting their act together fast, got the airplane down to Mexico before another night had passed. But by then the dope was gone.

A classic pot-smuggling clusterfuck, the deal represented Long's first foray into what Hollywood calls creative financing. With money earmarked for research, obtained from Ives in New York, Long had backed a part of Carlyle's load. He had invested the money in logistical support, intending to take a cut of Carlyle's profit and use the cash to subsidize the movie. The pot had been sold out from under the partnership in what amounted to two installments. The first half of the load was already gone by the time Elwood was set to make the follow-up flight. Carlyle's suggestion that the half in question was Long's half of the load raised an understandable dispute. Failing to move Carlyle with logic, Long threatened to call the police. Carlyle's response was the only response that was reasonable under the circumstances. Carlyle just hauled off and hit him.

"You can't go to the police!" he screamed. "Are you crazy? You *never* go to the police. No matter *what,* you don't go to the police."

Of course not. The first thing an outlaw, by definition, gives up is recourse to the law. In desperado school, it is a lesson you learn in kindergarten.

Rubbing blood from his lower lip, which had opened up with the fanfare of a circus coming to town, Long said, "I guess you're right," realizing the eminent sense of it. And then he hit Carlyle back.

What was notable about the altercation — the two men traded punches, put the fight behind them, and both got screwed on the deal — was that Long at this point did not think of himself as anything more or less than an honest filmmaker.

Optimistic in spite of the deal's failure, Long returned to New York ready to move the project forward. He figured that sooner or later Carlyle would get a load through, and until then there was plenty to work with. He would rendezvous in Mexico with a smuggler named Alejandro, a contact he had made at the villa, who had offered to introduce him to farmers in the mountains above Mazatlán. In the flowering marijuana fields Long would shoot footage of the harvesting and processing of the crop in preparation for its shipment north.

He leased $20,000 in equipment from General Camera in New York, choosing a state-of-the-art Eclair, the 16mm handheld camera that recently had made a name for itself as employed by director Michael Wadleigh in shooting the feature-length documentary against which all others were being measured: *Woodstock.* Hiring a soundman and an assistant cameraman, Long headed back to Mexico, traveling by way of Tucson. In Tucson he and his crew rented a station wagon — from Hertz, brand-new, a couple of miles on the clock — and planning to head for the border the next day, they checked into the motel at which Long had stayed on his previous trip to town, where Long checked in on Rita.

"Lee's at my place," she said.

This was the first sign of action in a developing pattern of behavior whereby Long and Carlyle, under the flag of the doobie brotherhood, would troll the waters of each other's casual romances, catch and release the castaways, and continue to steam onward, leaving women to drift like jetsam in the wake of the ongoing campaign.

Lee was at Rita's place, sitting in front of the kitchen stove, drying out brick by brick some 200 pounds of marijuana he had succeeded in moving across the border. The pot had been delivered to Arizona in the middle of the night, a night on which it had snowed in Tucson for the first time in any heavy smoker's admittedly questionable memory. The Mexican smugglers had stashed the marijuana in an arroyo that did what arroyos do — it filled with water — after a snowmelt. The dope was soaking wet.

Sitting there on the kitchen floor, speaking into the lens of a camera, Carlyle, drunk on 7-and-7s, expounded on his circumstances, the how and why of his becoming a smuggler. He was part of a revolution, part of a movement, he said, a cause. This was nothing less than a crusade. He was contributing, he declared, to the "positive change the earth needs to go through." And, he said, besides that, he wanted to make a lot of money. And he wanted a Playboy Bunny for a girlfriend.

The cannabis leaf: the Cross of the new Evangel. And here, enunciated by Lee Carlyle, were the essential tenets of the smuggler's Gospel. Motor whirring, machinery fluttering with the sound of film snaking through the camera aperture, Long's assistant cameraman, cross-legged on the floor, held the lens of the Eclair on Carlyle while Long conducted the interview.

"See this two hundred pounds of marijuana," Carlyle said. "I'm going to turn this into a million dollars."

An echo of his remark at the Copa de Leche, it was a dramatic expression of the smuggler's dream, just the kind of bullshit that Long as a filmmaker was looking for. And like the first time Carlyle had expressed it, its realization struck Long as being just about as remote as Alpha Centauri.

"How," asked Long, "are you planning to get it to Chicago?"

"Greyhound."

"Come again?"

Carlyle directed the camera's attention to the ten-dollar foot-locker — red-white-and-blue, still sporting its Sears Roebuck price tag — on the edge of which Long was sitting.

"I'm going to put the marijuana in it, get on a bus, and take it to Chicago," he said.

The guy *was* off his rocker. Long wished him luck, and the next day departed for Mexico.

Crossing into Mexico with $20,000 in camera equipment raised a predictable sea of bureaucracy on both sides of the international border. But invariably, Long discovered, when one ran into officialdom, however entrenched, and one happened to be in the movie business, the waters tended to part. The holy aura of Hollywood put the power of Moses in the shade.

Everybody, everywhere, wanted to help you make a movie.

High in the mountains above Mazatlán, with the help of his contact Alejandro, Long and his crew shot film of marijuana being harvested, gathered, dried, and processed. From Mazatlán, he and the crew drove to Guadalajara, where Alejandro promised them access to footage at a second location.

The day things came together, Long paid Alejandro $500, agreeing to meet him the following morning to make the run up into the mountains. Alejandro, spending the money in a whorehouse, which kept him up all night, showed up drunk at Long's hotel on a local rum and vanilla cream concoction commercially known as Ronpope. He and an associate, equally drunk, arrived in a rented Volkswagen, the same one the company rented to all the drunks in Mexico, as far as Long could tell — there it was again, that same bilious green. And naturally, being drunk, Alejandro insisted upon driving.

Long's assistant cameraman was a Puerto Rican named Joey Martínez. Long had hired him for his talent, for the fact that he spoke Spanish, and for his willingness to take the risk that the assignment in Mexico entailed. Long and Martínez were in the back of the

Volkswagen, Alejandro and his partner up front. Space being severely limited, Long's soundman had stayed behind.

Careering — and then, as he continued to drink, careening — down the highway, Alejandro blustered incessantly, talking over his shoulder as he drove. The straightaway over which they were flying ended in a high face of rock, visible in the distance, a cliff on which the local highway department had painted a bright yellow arrow, and Long took it upon himself to alert the bragging Mexican to its approach.

"Alejandro, better slow down, there's a turn coming up ahead."

"You want to see me make a turn? Motherfucker, I'll show you how to make a turn!"

Long would look back upon moments like this to explain why it took another twenty-five years, a full quarter century — and that spent under the day-to-day tutelage of criminals in Colombia, the most sophisticated criminals in the world — before Mexico became a really significant player in the international dope trade.

Taking the turn at seventy, Alejandro put the Volkswagen into a 180 degree spin. Long was looking out the rear window as the car went backward through the guardrail and pitched over the cliff. It tumbled downhill, rolling several times before coming to a stop, and when it did, it looked like a hard-boiled egg after you beat it with a spoon. All the windows were busted out, and through one of them Long escaped, miraculously unhurt. He pulled Joey Martínez out of the wreck. The big, handsome Puerto Rican, whose ribs were broken, had suffered a head injury that was to put him in the hospital. Alejandro's inebriated partner was uninjured, but his sunglasses were broken and he was really pissed off.

"*Mis lentes! Cabrón!*" my glasses, he screamed.

That was all he could say. And, drunkenly, he was saying it to Alejandro, who was dead. Well, he was nearly dead. "He'll be dead in a minute," Long remembered thinking at the time. When Long pulled him out of the car, and placed him on the ground, flies started buzzing around Alejandro's head. He was not breathing, not obviously, but he was still alive. He was *trying* to breathe. Blood overflowed his face, and Long placed a bandanna over it to keep the flies away. His partner did not get the picture, and was standing over Alejandro, yelling at him, bemoaning the condition of his sunglasses. *"Chinga tu madre! Mis lentes . . . !"*

Which cracked Joey Martínez up. Joey, his body flirting with the inevitable onset of shock, busted out laughing, and not even the pain of his broken ribs was enough to make him stop.

Alejandro's body had begun shuddering, and his partner, shouting down at him, was still casting aspersions upon Alejandro's parentage, when a police cruiser rolled up. An officer stepped out and approached down the hill with a notebook in his hand. With all the composure and dispassion of the typical U.S. highway patrolman, he asked who the driver of the car was. Long pointed to the body on the ground. The cop, dismissing Alejandro's partner, took over the conversation the latter was having with Alejandro, who by then had silently departed the cool sequester'd vale of life. While the partner rooted around the wreck for his bottle of Ronpope, grumbling because the sunlight was bothering his eyes, and while Joey Martínez continued uncontrollably to laugh, the cop questioned the late Alejandro, whose face beneath the blood-soaked bandanna was invisible to him.

And each time the cop asked a question, Alejandro said nothing.

"Your name, sir?"

Alejandro said nothing.

"How fast were you traveling?"

Alejandro said nothing.

"May I see your license, please?"

Tar-baby ain't sayin' nuthin', en Brer Fox, he lay low.

Joey Martínez was about to crack another rib, and Long, fighting the contagion of Joey's laughter, struggled to stifle his own.

"Muerto," Long finally said.

The cop looked up from his notebook.

"Muerto?"

Alejandro's body had gone still. Long studied it for a second or two, then nodded in affirmation.

"Muerto," he told the cop.

"Oh," the cop said. *"Muerto!"*

He flipped his notebook closed, walked back up the hill, and radioed for an ambulance.

The medics arrived, removed Joey and the body, and the cop drove Long and the other man to the hotel.

Long's soundman packed it in, and with Joey Martínez recovering in a Guadalajara hospital, Long returned alone to Mazatlán.

The first and most reliable pot connection Allen Long made south of the border he had made through a fifteen-year-old Mexican kid on the street outside a Mazatlán restaurant who offered to wash his car. The kid's name was Tomás, and Long, after paying him for a job well done, asked if Tomás could score him some pot.

To smoke. Long had run out of personal stash.

Tomás earned his money hustling tourists, and like every hustler Long would run into everywhere in Latin America, he operated on the fringes of the dope trade. Long was looking for an ounce of pot, and Tomás could handle that with no problem; in fact, he came up with a brick. It was his way of showing off. Like most hustlers on the periphery of the market, Tomás saw himself as a player. But Tomás was young yet. It would be a while before he moved up to the big show. The brick was supplied by his uncle, and was grown about 200 miles southeast of Mazatlán in the vicinity of Tepic, the capital of Nayarit state, where the first Mexican sinsemilla, the seedless cannabis prized for the potency of its flowering tops, would later be cultivated.

Long had first run across Tomás on a trip he had made to Mazatlán while living at the villa in Guadalajara waiting for Carlyle's deal to go down. Returning now to Mazatlán, upon Alejandro's rather theatrical drop from the payroll, Long sought out Tomás, the only lead he had, looking to score the additional footage he needed of marijuana cultivation in the mountains. Tomás reached out to his uncle, who eventually consented to a meeting with Long, an uncharacteristic move for an established criminal, attributable perhaps to the thrill of the movies, that and $500 in cash.

The meeting took place in a tiny cantina in the mountains surrounding Tepic. Long arrived with his camera, and no sooner had he stepped through the door than he suddenly stepped back in time. Within minutes of his taking a seat, gunshots rang out nearby. He swiveled his head in the direction of the noise. A figure raced past the open window. Long made ready to move.

"Just two men shooting at each other . . ."

The sepulchral voice from across the table, droning words of assurance, drew Long's attention its way. There was a near-imaginary, frontier quality to this stretch of Mexico's coastal mountains, and its essence was expressed in high relief in the visage of the man sitting opposite him. Tomás's Uncle Francisco embodied all the visual attributes, as gringos tended to interpret them, of the classic Mexican *bandido*. About forty-five years old, he had the broad face and prominent mustache that jumped forth from familiar, archival photographs of the legendary Pancho Villa, the revolutionary leader with whose countenance that of the stereotypical Mexican outlaw was commonly identified. Of medium height and heavyset, heavy in more ways than one, Francisco was outfitted to play the part. The tooled-leather boots were not for show, serving a preference for travel by horseback for which he was very well known, just as the twin revolvers in tooled-leather holsters served his local self-employment as the Man: the *traficante* who controlled the flow of marijuana out of Tepic. Many of the other outlaws Long would meet in the mountains that day would look as if they had stepped unblushing out of the same photo archive.

From Tepic, situated about 3,000 feet above sea level, it was a steady climb to Long's destination. Francisco and his men, staging from a ranch not far from the cantina, progressed from there on horseback, leading the earnest American up through the dry chaparral into the high reaches of the desert. Hidden there in the mountains, on the cleared slopes of shallow ravines that cleaved the rugged landscape, flared the rich green of cultivated marijuana planted row upon row. Hundreds of ravines were being worked, three or four to a farmer, and every ravine was productive. Long was struck by the industry that enabled the crop to prosper, by the primitive yet effective technique by which irrigation was engineered. A large stone placed at the head of a ravine diverted spring water to the uppermost row of plants. The crop rows traversed the canyon at a slight angle downhill, left to right, then right to left, and as the water ran down the hillside every plant received its share. Both sides of the canyon, alternately, were irrigated in this fashion.

Long got the footage he needed, and returned to Tepic with the promise of a second trip, sometime later, higher into the mountains — there, Francisco would show him the airstrip from which the pot was dispatched. Meanwhile, Long checked on Joey Martínez, recovering in Guadalajara.

"No way," said Joey, from his hospital bed.

"Forget it, Joey," said Long.

"I'm not letting you go without me."

"Joey, you can't go."

There was no need to point out the obvious. Joey, in his condition, would have a hard time making it to the door of his room, let alone making the difficult climb, much of it on foot, to the airstrip.

"You could get killed up there," Joey said. "You're a stupid American."

Joey, being Puerto Rican, reasoned that he himself in this situation was somehow not an American — well, not to the Mexicans, anyway — that his speaking Spanish would in some way mitigate any perception of stupidity in Long that the outlaws happened to harbor.

"They'll kill you," he maintained.

"You can't go with me on this one, Joey."

"I'm going."

"You can't go," Long insisted. "When I'm finished, I'll come back and get you."

The airstrip was located on a barely accessible escarpment high above the marijuana fields, at the upper reaches of the mountains' deciduous growth. When the trail became too steep for the horses and burros, Long and the smugglers walked, occasionally forced to secure handholds on the rock face overhanging the footpath. When delivering pot to the runway, Long was astonished to find, the smugglers, from the point at which the pack animals were abandoned, would have to carry the cargo on their backs.

Making the arduous climb, Long had good reason to be thankful for having selected the smaller, lighter, more expensive Eclair over the industry-standard Arriflex when he had rented his equipment in New York. Unaccustomed to the altitude, he had difficulty keeping up with the Mexicans. He fell behind. Then hurried forward. Then fell behind again. He fell behind rather rhythmically, in fact — he was running on a manual fuel pump.

Allen Long's romance with cocaine was like the worst of marriages. It was passionate and eager, but stormy. It was an arena for the indulgence of every tendency toward self-destruction, and it went on for years, infinitely lingering, doomed to everything but failure. It was a veritable circus for the expression of twisted behavior, and the big top never left town. From the moment he first encountered cocaine, Long was seldom without it. Buying it was like filling a prescription. He would carry it with him the way diabetics carry insulin. In the early years of his infatuation, the drug in debilitating amounts remained an affliction chiefly of the wealthy, and so the worst of it came later, the level of his engagement a kind of barometer of his rising fortunes. Time and the ravages of addiction would soon bleed the performance of its charm, but in the beginning, before things got way out of hand, there was an almost comic quality to his appetite. In the beginning, at a time when dope use in general was new — when dope was first insinuating itself into the collective identity of a generation — getting stoned, as a spectator sport, was not entirely unrewarding.

In scaling the mountains that day, as Long fell behind, he would pause to inhale a couple of thumbnails of flake from a stash he had purchased the night before. It had worked for the Incas for 2,000 years, and it worked just as well for him. It helped him overcome the effects of altitude and fatigue, and eventually to overcome the lead of the Mexicans rearmost in the line of ascent. Long would speed up the trail until the influence of the drug waned, the Mexicans overtook him, and he fell behind again. And did cocaine again. Acting out the fable of the tortoise and the hare, he found himself testing its hypothesis, and the result, he was dismayed to discover, was just as Aesop had reported it.

Ascending through stands of oak and maple, passing beneath the same foliage that flourished in his backyard in Charlottesville, Long followed Francisco and his men to the site of a high, cloud-free mesa, a narrow elevation with drop-offs of up to 2,000 feet on a side. The setting was surreal, of a kind that had existed up to then only in his imagination. Running out over the face of the cliff, like an optical illusion, stretched the landing strip, a phantom of a runway no longer than 1,200 feet.

"No margin for error," one pilot later told Long. "You're perfect or you're dead."

It was like hitting the deck of a carrier. Overshooting the landing meant instantly picking up sufficient speed to achieve lift before falling off the front of the mesa. It was the only correctable miscalculation, and correctable only within a window of seconds. Any other miscalculation and there was no coming around for a second pass.

Entering a small hut in which a fire was going and coffee was brewing, Long settled in with the Mexicans and waited for operations to begin. Activity picked up the next day with the delivery of pot to the runway, and the appearance overhead soon after that of a single-engine Beech. Scaling the peaks, the plane circled the airstrip, nosed in at an acute, almost acrobatic angle and dropped onto the runway. Out of the plane stepped a smuggler from Tucson named Bobby, who generously consented to Long's shooting footage of the load-up and takeoff.

"But don't shoot the tail numbers," he said.

The Mexicans threw 600 pounds of reefer aboard, and Bobby — no time to chat — jumped back in the cockpit, threw up a thumb, and took off. The Beech, before catching air, dropped precipitously off the edge of the cliff, tail dipping, just like a Navy F4. It picked up altitude, banked to the left, leveled off and disappeared, heading for the border.

Another load, off to market. There would be joy in Tucson tonight.

When he returned to Guadalajara to pick up Joey Martínez, Long received a call from the States. It was Ives, his producer, phoning from

New York. Long, since leaving town with the camera equipment, had spent a couple of months in Mexico, and Ives was calling now to remind him that all the money was spent.

"I hope you've finished the movie," he said.

Long had footage of Carlyle, he had all the footage from the fields, and now he had the footage he had shot on the escarpment above Tepic. But he still lacked the narrative element, the simple story value, that would raise the movie above the level of those documentaries typically found on public television. What he had right now, at best, might secure his movie a slot there, but he wanted more than that. If he went back to New York, it was over, he would have to start raising money again. Figuring he could stretch things for a couple of days, he decided to hold on to the equipment. Joey Martínez, a stand-up guy, told Long he would stick it out with him.

Long called Rita's number in Tucson to see what Carlyle was up to. It had been a while since the crazy Californian had voiced his determination to take the pot-filled footlocker and turn it into a million dollars.

Rita said, "Lee doesn't live here."

Of course not, Long concluded. That ship would have sailed a long time ago. Captain Carlyle, circling the party boat, passing the SS *Rita* in the night.

"But he left a phone number," Rita continued, "and said to give it to you if you called."

Long reached him at an apartment in Chicago.

"Come on up, buddy," Carlyle said. "Get up here, man, I did it."

"Did what?"

"Just come," he said, "you'll see."

Long dumped the station wagon at the airport in Guadalajara, and he and a heavily bandaged Joey Martínez headed for Chicago. Carlyle met them at O'Hare. He arrived in a blue Maserati convertible. Long hopped in, and with Joey and the equipment following in a limousine, the three men sped into town. They dropped off the gear at Carlyle's place, and Carlyle took the filmmakers to lunch. Carlyle, whom they had last seen squatting on the kitchen linoleum of a half-duplex in Tucson, was now renting an Oak Street penthouse with a panoramic view of Lake Michigan and a good stretch of Chicago skyline. Over lunch at a three-star restaurant, Carlyle, last seen draining a bottle of Seagram's, squatted now behind three longnecks of Dom Pérignon and told the two filmmakers his story.

Taking the money he had made selling the 200 pounds, he had returned to Mexico and paid his suppliers, who then fronted him another 400. When he sold that, the Mexicans sent him a thousand pounds. He bought a truck, hired a driver, and doubled up again, after which his Chicago buyers offered to put a fleet of trucks on the road. All this time the Mexicans had supplied the pot on-the-arm, and because the pot was fronted, Carlyle's margin was necessarily thin. He was making somewhere between $5 and $10 a pound. He had been operating only a couple months, but, now, with enough of his own money, he was in a position to pay for the pot in advance, to buy it from the Mexicans himself. He was in the process of moving serious weight, somewhere in the vicinity of a ton, and on it he stood to make as much as $100 a pound. He was investing everything he had in this truckload, and Long and Joey Martínez were just in time to see him celebrate his success.

Joey Martínez turned to Long and said, "Now you've got a story."

Carlyle was about to turn his original dime into a cool quarter million. And he had done it in a matter of six months. In two months he had gone from traveling by Greyhound to driving a new Maserati. At his penthouse later that afternoon, he introduced Long to his new girlfriend. Valerie, who had been featured in *Playboy*, was employed in customer service at the magazine's flagship Chicago club — yes, Carlyle had landed a Bunny. In the apartment, Long and Joey set up their gear and committed the smuggler's story to film.

It was magic hour in the movie business. The sun was setting on the black anodized aluminum and tinted bronze glass of the Hancock Tower, which rose like a whale spout on a windless ocean just beyond the window. Its lights and all the lights in Chicago were just beginning to show. With Long conducting the interview, Carlyle paced the penthouse, moving between the window glass and a black leather executive chair that appeared to have been upholstered by the same guy who had fitted out the interior of the Maserati. Expansive, uninhibited, no longer the picture of failure and resignation that had become familiar to Long, Carlyle shared his wisdom with the people, the big-time smuggler high on cocaine, Quaaludes, and champagne.

Staring into the camera, falling into silhouette, Lee Carlyle enlightened the world. He explained how things were done. He told how he had pulled off the move, talked about his plans for the future. He edified his fellow Americans. He revealed the true meaning of life. As only a twenty-four-year-old could do it. Lee Carlyle was in possession of the secret. He held the key to the Kingdom of Heaven. And Allen Long had the story he needed. With a little fleshing out in the middle — footage of the smugglers loading trucks in Mexico, transporting the dope to Chicago — Long had his documentary.

The telephone rang, and Carlyle uncradled the receiver, taking the call, being the executive that he was, even as he spoke into the camera. His side of the phone conversation went something like this: "Hey, man . . . Oh . . . What? . . . Yeah . . ." He turned away from his audience. "Oh, shit, they did? . . . Oh, God . . . Oh . . ." And then he said, ". . . No."

Carlyle sat down, hung up the phone, held his head, and started to cry.

"They caught him."

The guy driving Carlyle's truckload of pot. A six-foot-three-inch bar bouncer posing as a minister, right down to the clerical collar and the phony driver's license. They caught him in Arizona. They busted the load. It was gone. Carlyle was broke.

"It's a rags-to-riches story."

"No."

"It's the American dream personified. Rags to riches, back to rags, and back to riches, as far as I know."

"You've spent a hundred and forty thousand dollars, and you have nothing to show for it. If you want to finish the movie," said Ives, "you'll have to raise the money yourself."

According to the professionals for whom Long had run the footage, he needed an additional hundred thousand to finish the film. His mentor, a cinematographer at Motion Associates, the production house at which he had worked, told him the story was there, but that he would have to go back and rebuild it. And to do that he needed more footage. Included in the overall estimate was $60,000 for processing and editing.

"And," said Ives, still hemorrhaging money, "I want you to go get the car."

The car?

The station wagon, rented brand-new from Hertz, which had been driven into Mexico from Tucson, and was still sitting there after two and a half months. The car parked at the airport in Guadalajara with several thousand miles on the clock. *That* car.

Long, retrieving the station wagon, turned it in at El Paso, about 200 miles closer than Tucson to where the car was parked. He made the trip in a hurry, traveling virtually nonstop, fueled on pharmaceutical speed, high on a handful of Black Beauties he bought from a Guadalajara filling station attendant. He traveled as well with an ounce of very good pot, every leaf of which he was determined to smoke rather than give up before he arrived at the border. About fifteen miles short of the Rio Grande, where the landscape was desolate and the mountains were as black as the pills he was popping, he pulled off the highway to smoke a joint that was big enough to stop a door and emptied the car of all the drugs he could find. A half-hour later, with his body racing on amphetamines and reefer, he made the bridge at Juárez.

He pulled up at U.S. Customs, and with the car having been out of the country so long, was ordered as a matter of form into the inspection lane.

Run up and down the mountains for a couple of months, carrying people who just maybe smoked a joint once in a while, the car looked like it had been through some protracted and possibly psychedelic guerrilla insurgency. A careful examination was almost certain to show its interior to be littered with shake. When Customs inspectors approached the car with a German shepherd on a leash, Long knew he had some fast talking to do. In his condition, under the influence of a blood chemistry that could honestly be called festive, the talking was going to be fast whether he liked it or not.

"Look," he told the woman heeling the dog, as the other agent lowered the tailgate, "I smoked pot in that car . . ."

Just around the edge of her aviator shades, the inspector's eyes shifted his way. There he stood, yellow-eyed, sallow-skinned, and reeking of the skunk weed he had smoked moments before, going on as if the same aroma, currently choking the vehicle, might prove to be the source of some mystery to officers of the United States Customs Service working the Mexican border. Just around the edge of her aviator shades, her eyes seemed to say: No shit?

"There's no marijuana in it," Long continued, "but . . ."

"Then why worry?" she said, and released the dog into the car. She glanced back at Long and confided, "That dog's never caught anybody."

The dog sniffed around, executed a quick pirouette, sat down on its haunches, and stared out over the tailgate, panting, as if waiting for a ride into town.

"Go," the agent told Long.

The Hertz agent in El Paso was not similarly unruffled. Freaked out but faced with no other choice — after pathetically failing to intimidate Long with a fifty-dollar drop-off charge — he took possession of the marijuanamobile. The damage, billed to Ives's credit card, amounted to more than $6,000.

Long, in Mexico, had struck up a friendship with an American he ran into in Mazatlán, a troublemaker by the name of Pomeroy. A California biker, Pomeroy was a member in good standing of the Oakland chapter of an organization he reverently called the Angels and official law enforcement documents called the Hell's Angels Motorcycle Club. Having recently wiped out on his bike, he had ridden into Mazatlán with his girlfriend on the back of his Harley and plaster casts on both of his feet. Long met them at the same tourist trap out-side of which he had encountered Tomás. Maybe fifteen years older than Long, with dark brown hair that was going gray and the body lan-guage of a rodeo cowboy, Pomeroy, a lovable rascal to Long's way of thinking, had been smuggling marijuana for years, and the two took to each other immediately.

Intrigued by Long's idea for a movie, Pomeroy had given him the name of a friend, a concert promoter in New York who had just been given a record label, suggesting that Long might be interested in talk-ing to the man at some point. Pomeroy, convinced like most smugglers that his life story was worthy of immortalizing, offered to help the would-be filmmaker any way he could, and invited Long to look him up at a Marin County address if he ever got out to the Bay Area.

Returning to New York from El Paso, Long put in a call to Pomeroy, figuring that maybe Pomeroy's promoter friend could help him get the movie going again. The project was hopelessly stalled now, and Long was running out of options.

"My friend wants to meet you," Pomeroy said, before Long got around to asking.

There are character traits, both personal and collective, for which the Hell's Angels are notorious. Inefficiency is not among them.

Pomeroy's friend had an office in New York's Gulf & Western Building, and Long, when he stepped through the door, knew that he had come to the right place. The promoter sat at his desk gripping a bone-handled knife, and centered on the desk pad below the blade was a rock of cocaine the size of a lab rat. Long, to be gracious, helped Pomeroy's friend snort it. Their conversation opened where conversa-tions in such circumstances invariably do, with casual but predictably earnest expressions of their appreciation for the agriculture of Peru. It was agreed — for etiquette in such circumstances always demanded it — that this particular sample was excellent, as pure as either had ever seen his life, and by inference significantly better than that which somebody else might be willing to share. With that rap meandering to a conclusion, the meeting turned to a more pointed and professional discussion of their common interest in documentary filmmaking.

Pomeroy's friend saw in Long's movie an excellent vehicle for a sound-track album. Long concurred with the view. Both men knew that the right album would generate more revenue than the film itself. Pomeroy's friend said he would very much like to work with Long.

"How much do you need to finish the movie?" he asked.

Long, elated, answered that he could get the job done for a hundred thousand dollars.

"All right," the friend said, wiping his nose. "Call me when you get the money."

And that was the end of the meeting.

Long had a good mind to grab the guy by the shirt and tell him his cocaine sucked.

Failing to raise financing for the film in New York, Long refused to give up. Determined to keep the project alive, he did what any film-maker in similar circumstances would do. "Hell, I can do this," he said, and did what all the great filmmakers before him had done . . . Ford, Truffaut, Fellini, the giants of the art, Orson Welles . . . He did what all of them had done in establishing their careers in the cinema.

"I can go back and do a load."

Sure.

He became a marijuana smuggler.

4 CADILLAC MOON

Marin County, California, lay at the confluence of every cultural stream of any importance to a man of Allen Long's ambitions in 1972. In Marin the values of the youth movement that had flowered down the road in the sociological greenhouse of San Francisco's Haight-Ashbury district were being expressed in the backwash of their inevitable commercialization. In Marin, on the Sausalito side of the Golden Gate Bridge, free love, dope, and music, five years after the Summer of Love, were being celebrated in the hearts and hormones of the steadily employed.

Having tapped every source of potential financing for his documentary and come up dry, Long had called Pomeroy again.

"How'd the meeting go?"

"I need to raise some money," said Long.

"Come out here," said Pomeroy. "I got a job for you."

And Long, if not on the next, was on the next best flight.

He spent his first evening in California with Pomeroy and his girl-friend, Justine, hanging out with Quicksilver Messenger Service between the band's sets at Winterland. After the gig they all went to the Trident in Sausalito, one of the more popular joints in a town where hospitality demanded that smoking dope be something you do without leaving your table. Sitting with Pomeroy and the easy-going Justine, the blonde who had ridden into Mazatlán on the back of his Harley-Davidson, Long, stoned to the point of embracing religion, was made to feel instantly at home. Little was there at home, however, to compare with the waitress who was serving him drinks. A redhead named Fleurette, she so exceeded Long's aspirations for a waitress that to order his first shot of tequila he was forced to adjust his breathing. The first time she asked if he wanted another he had to adjust his clothes.

In Marin that night and those that followed, under the dutiful ministration of Pomeroy, Long was received like a visiting dignitary. Call it a sales pitch. Long was sold. The breathtaking Fleurette would seal the deal, Fleurette, an authentic redhead, whose pubic hair, he would later discover, was trimmed in the shape of a heart. Long fell in love — with both — and in the fragrant blush of her topiary he languished for the next six months. He moved into Pomeroy's Mill Valley house and swiftly got down to business. He had a movie to make. There was a cinematic muse to satisfy. It was time to try some professional smuggling.

Pomeroy had been moving marijuana in loads of between fifty and one hundred pounds, and was getting ready to step things up when he brought Long on board. He had just taken on a partner, a small-time hustler by the name of Big Jim, a San Francisco bus driver who had been augmenting his income dealing herb. Big Jim was eager to move weight. He had a growing clientele and money to invest, and needed a dependable source of dope at a decent price. Pomeroy, who had been supplying him, had the personnel and equipment and the organizational skills necessary to get marijuana into the country. What Pomeroy did not have was a connection in Mexico sufficiently reliable to supply the necessary weight on a regular basis. That was where

Long came in. Long impressed Pomeroy as a guy quick enough on his feet to be an asset to any operation. He was a guy who knew his way around Mexico, and Pomeroy believed him to be the guy who could help him establish the connection he needed.

Long, proving to be as quick with his hands as Pomeroy believed him to be on his feet, reached into his hat and pulled out a rabbit. A mustachioed bunny in tooled-leather boots wearing six shooters on both hips. Long had Francisco in Tepic.

"Olé!"

Long went to Mexico to set up the deal, and once it was made, was joined in Tepic by a fellow named Tex. Tex was there to check out the airstrip. Hangared in a barn on his ranch in El Paso, Tex had a surplus T-6 trainer unregistered with the FAA. Tex, a man of few words, as if honoring the stereotype of characters so named, was the more matter-of-fact of the aerial cowboys riding for the Pomeroy brand. There were two pilots on the payroll. The other was Pomeroy's hairdresser, Decidedly Effeminate Frederick, as he was known to the Mill Valley crew. Thanks to the flamboyant Frederick, Pomeroy was one of the more fashionably coiffed outlaws ever to wear Angels colors. Frederick owned a single-engine Cessna.

With all the players in place, and a 600-pound load sitting on the runway in Tepic, the team went operational with the approach of the first full moon.

Long awoke early that day, and he and Pomeroy descended to the garage. The house in Marin was a four-bedroom, two-story rental on a half-acre north of Mill Valley. A second-floor balcony overlooked an in-ground pool, which was one of two main attractions of the gray-clapboard hillside property. The other was the large, below-grade garage on which the house was built and in which one could park three cars end-to-end and close the door behind them. Parked there were two Cadillac limousines.

The rear panel as well as the passenger seats of each car had been removed. Everything behind the driver was cargo space, all the way through to the trunk. The rear suspension of each limousine was outfitted with air shocks. Pumping them up raised the tail of the car, which when loaded with cargo would then level out, and appear as if it were traveling empty.

The impact of what Long was about to do gave him a moment of pause. It was one thing to be in Mexico — *bandido* country to him, where no law applied, where you could buy your way out of trouble — and quite another to be here, he decided, here in the USA, getting ready to drive off and pick up a planeload of dope. Having set up the deal was nothing. This was inescapably hands-on. This was narcotics trafficking.

"Are you going to back out?" he asked himself. "Or are you going to grab your balls and get in the car?"

He got in the car. And they drove.

With the fog lifting off the redwoods, they drove up through Northern California, following Interstate 5. They wound through the Sacramento Valley, and swung northeast at Redding. They followed Highway 299 across the Cascade Range, skirting the Shasta National Forest, and a couple of hours after midday, at about 6,000 feet above sea level, they hit Cedar Pass and descended to the alkali lakes. Maybe eight hours out of San Francisco, Pomeroy pulled into a filling station, and drew Long's attention to a narrow dirt road.

"You see that bypass? That little track that goes past those houses up there and into the woods? That's the road we're going to take on the way back."

It would allow them, he said, to circumvent California agricultural inspection.

In Cedarville they ate, drank a couple of beers, smoked a joint, and waited till dark, then pumped up the air shocks and made for the border, heading south on Highway 447. As they ran down the hills on the eastern slope of the mountains, the scenery changed dramatically. They dropped from the lush, four-color world of the California foothills to the floor of the Nevada desert, which greeted them like a postcard from the surface of the moon. The highway undulated through a series of valleys in which huge irrigation systems gave rise to everything that was green. The road seemed to disappear into infinity, to run endlessly in places between one change of elevation and another. South of Lower Alkali Lake, for mile upon mile, as the two-lane blacktop entered the Smoke Creek Desert, the valleys were flat and the road was straight.

On that highway, that night, Pomeroy received a radio transmission telling him the flight was delayed. Smuggling was waiting. It was axiomatic. Nothing about the trip would prove more characteristic of the work Long had chosen than the fact that the load was late.

They would have to put up for the night. The nearest place to do that with two Cadillac limousines, without drawing too much attention, was Reno, some 160 miles south. They arrived there early in the morning, checked into a motel, and slept. When Long awoke, which was sometime after one P.M., Pomeroy was gone.

The next several hours, Long's first stretch alone as a federal offender, bordered on the existential. Before turning in, on the chance that Long might wake up before him, Pomeroy had given orders: "We leave at six. Until then, don't go out. Don't go anywhere. Stay here."

Now Pomeroy had disappeared. And Long labored for hours under a restriction he was too inexperienced to break. Pomeroy had made it clear that Long was a link in the chain of responsibility upon which the success of the operation hung. Others had placed their faith in him. And others were at risk. If Long slipped up in the slightest, others might go to jail.

Not far beyond the door flashed the neon lights of Reno. They flashed around the clock. The desert town was one large caravansary in which casinos were the water. And Long was exceedingly thirsty to be anywhere but by himself. "Stay here," Pomeroy had told him, and "here" was a cheap motel room somewhere on the outskirts of town, with two beds, a telephone, and a color TV. The telephone was bolted to a table. The television was bolted to a dresser. The dresser was bolted to the floor. The walls were painted white, and all were free of artwork. The only colors, and there were all of them — all those dazzling, artificial colors one imagines when one imagines Reno — jumped from the bedspread and the carpet, their design, which was enough to make any guest vomit, having been engineered intentionally to be unaffected when he or she did.

Long paced the room like a zoo animal, compulsively studying the checkout notice posted on the door. He wondered what he was supposed to do if Pomeroy did not come back. He had been gone for four or five hours. Right about now, Tex, the T-6 cowboy, would be refueling south of Nogales, and sometime after midnight he would be on the radio to Frederick the hairdresser, making contact 5,000 feet over the valley Long had driven through the night before. And Long had better be there.

At six P.M., Pomeroy returned.

"Okay," he said, "let's go."

"Jesus, where the hell were you?"

"Calm down," said Pomeroy. "Relax."

"Where'd you go?" Long wanted to know.

"Relax," repeated Pomeroy.

"I've been here, man, I've been ready."

"Just get in the car and follow me."

Where Pomeroy had gone is where Long would go, systematically, later in his career, doing to a hundred other people what Pomeroy had done to him.

"You gotta stay here, and you gotta stay straight," Long would tell the people who worked for him. "Don't go out and get wasted. Don't go anywhere. I don't want you to move."

And then, in the same way that Pomeroy had gone out to kill some time at the blackjack tables, Long would go out to play — in his case probably pick up a woman and all the drugs he could find — to return just before the load was due, and tell everybody, "Okay, let's go."

They revved up the limos and headed east, hitting a service station outside Sparks and pulling up to the air compressor, where they pumped up the Cadillacs' shocks before turning into the desert. They traveled north through the Nightingale Mountains with the cars riding high in the rear. Long's fear conspired with the moon and the night to throw the land's features into stark relief, altering his perception of everything. As the road rose to meet the mountain range, the peaks, like distant pyramids, ascended as if on elevators into his line of sight. Wheeled carriages, supporting the pipes of vast irrigation systems, dominated the flat terrain, the pipes themselves, traversing the landscape, stretching to opposite horizons.

Just southeast of the alkali lakes, the smugglers pulled to a stop and backed the limousines off the road, edging into the brush bordering the blacktop. Removing eight portable strobe light assemblies from the trunk of his limo, Long positioned but did not activate them, four on either side of the highway, delimiting a run of about 700 feet. He returned to the car. And they waited.

The cars were parked three feet apart. The broken white line of the highway dashed off into infinity. The night was still, and every second seemed like an hour to Long, scared to the point of shivering, sweating in the cool night air. Pomeroy fired up a joint. He laid out a few lines of cocaine. He handed Long a beer. The moon, suspended over the left-front quarter panel of Long's black limousine, full-blown, ostentatious, was doing what it could to wash the heavens clear of stars. Every now and then there was a sound. A mule deer on the move. Jackrabbits rustling. A coyote.

"What was that?"

"It's a jackrabbit, man, relax."

Long would get cool later.

High above the desert, Frederick circled. The valley floor stretched below him, revealed in the glow of the moon. From the cockpit he could read the highway, able to pick up oncoming headlights almost an hour away. In air-to-air contact with Tex, coming up from the south, and ground-to-air contact with Pomeroy, he could call off the rendezvous at the sign of any activity. Only then would Pomeroy hear his voice. In the absence of danger, Frederick would maintain radio silence. To signal a landing, he would simply key the microphone twice.

The windows of both Cadillacs were down. Pomeroy was smoking a cigarette. The desert was silent, the breeze was light. Long was staring over his sideview mirror, watching a jackrabbit change its mind. And then on the night, in the stillness of it, came the sound of radio static.

Click. Click.

Pomeroy fired his engine, Long did the same, and using only their running lights, they powered the Cadillacs up onto the highway. They pulled side by side, facing north. Long jumped out and set the strobes, then jumped back into his car.

Seconds passed. The strobe lights pulsed.

Silence again.

Click. Click.

The smugglers hit the headlamps. An explosion of incandescent light, as the eight sealed beams fired simultaneously, illuminated the highway for a mile. And then, in the silence, Long felt a shiver in his neck. As though a bat had just flown through his hair. There was no sound but the flutter of a feathered prop, and the airplane was there over the hood of the car, lurching down out of nowhere, flared out to catch ground effect with its forty-two-foot wingspan. Wheels down, accessing the highway at an angle of maybe 25 degrees, it glided in on the beam of the headlights to touch down on the asphalt in front of him. With a single squeak of the gear as the rubber hit the blacktop, it made a perfect three-point landing and rolled north at about 65 knots.

Throwing the Cadillacs into drive, the smugglers hit the accelerators, and chased the airplane down the highway, catching up as it braked to a stop and 300 bricks of Mexican weed in burlap hit the asphalt. They executed rapid three-point turns, backed the Cadillacs up to the plane, popped the trunks, and loaded the dope. Before Long could pick up the strobes, Tex and the T-6 were airborne. From the moment Frederick had first keyed the microphone, maybe 130 seconds had passed.

They drove through the night. And as Long followed Pomeroy through the wilderness, his body running with sweat, it occurred to him that he was a criminal now. In the eyes of a beer-swilling, pill-popping nation, Allen Long was a felon. He was driving a car in which 300 pounds of dope were stashed. And there was no way to pretend that he was somehow unaware of it. Pulled over by the police, for any reason, he was busted.

A few hours after sunrise, they pulled into a service station off Interstate 5, driving the limousines up to the pump on opposite sides of the same island. It was 1972, and America had yet to realize the vision of an Interstate highway system entirely free of the scourge of human assistance. The self-serve island, in glorious ubiquity, from sea to shining sea, was just a gleam in the nation's eye. It was a *service* station into which they had driven — always an exciting stop for a smuggler.

"Hey, what's that hangin' out the back of your car?"

It was the guy pumping gas, he was talking to Long, and he might just as well have been asking him, hey, what is that gushin' out your aorta? What was hangin' out the back of Long's car was reefer, an extrusion of weed, projected from a kilo onto which the trunk had been slammed in Long's haste to gather up the strobe lights. And it had been hangin' out the back all morning, all the way from Nevada.

"Oh," said Long, "that's lespedeza."

"What?"

"Yeah," said Long, retreating to the cover of monosyllables.

"What's that?"

"It's a special kind of clover," he said. "We're carrying it down to the horse farms in Marin."

"Huh," said the attendant, who nodded his head. "I'll tell my uncle about that."

His uncle had some horses, he said.

When the attendant stepped away from the pump, Long stood there paralyzed, certain that the California Highway Patrol, after taking the man's call, would soon be asking the same question. Pomeroy walked over and, gauging the weight of Long's apoplexy, engaged him in what seemed from a distance to be a conversation about the weather.

"After we leave here," he said quietly, "pull over, push the brick back in the trunk and close it."

Sure. That is what Long had intended to do.

"Lespedeza?" Pomeroy said. "What the fuck is that?"

"A kind of hay, you feed it to horses."

"You made it up?"

"No," said Long. "It's real. It's green and it comes in bales."

Pomeroy smiled. He nodded his head.

"You're going to do just fine," he said.

From the beginning, Pomeroy had been telling him that.

"You can do this," he had said, when Long signed on. "I know you're the guy for this. When I met you, I knew I could trust you."

Pomeroy had really laid it on, and as Long would discover later, using the same technique on others, when you lay it on them, they *have* to do it. It was a man thing. It was a characteristic, Long believed, that lived somewhere in the American spirit. A Frenchman, for example, would back out. Any good *parisien,* he theorized, would say, "What? You have to be kidding." But Pomeroy had told him that he was the guy, and as downright terrified as he was, he had to *be* that guy, because Pomeroy was counting on him.

Long would look back on this point in his life and see Pomeroy as something of a surrogate father. He would see Pomeroy as the man who had given him the chance to be great, the chance to be great in his own way. Pomeroy said, "You can do it," and he never went back on it, never reneged. Not once did he ever look at Long and say, "I'm not sure you can handle this."

When Long left Marin, he would leave having learned something about himself, and having discovered something at which he was good. If he had not discovered his destiny, he had discovered something that looked a lot like it. To his mind, he had taken something from start to finish, risked it all and won. It would be a defining moment in his life.

Once a month for the next five months, he and Pomeroy landed 600 pounds of Mexican pot in the desert southeast of Lower Alkalai Lake. And they did it with the efficiency and reliability of a very expensive Swiss watch. Long made $5,000 a load, which would not have been enough to finish his movie, even if he had saved the money. But the prospect of saving it reflected a flaw in his logic that had not been apparent to Long when he decided to finance the movie smuggling dope.

"If you have money and a Harley in Sausalito," he reported to Lee Carlyle at the height of it all, "it's amazing how much pussy you can get."

The silence on Carlyle's end of the phone line was a clue to how ridiculous that sounded. Not the revelation itself, but the fact that Long had felt the need to announce it. He was talking to Carlyle, after all, he was proselytizing before the converted. Hell, he was preaching to the mission's Apostle.

Long had the Harley. He had Fleurette. And numerous other young women. He was twenty-four and living in Marin. What more could any man ask for? On a typical day on top of the world, he would roll out of bed about three P.M., smoke his first joint, drift over to Sausalito for coffee, and kill time in no particular way before heading for the Trident at night. From the Trident, it was off to wherever the party happened to be: Winterland, some club, some musician's house in the hills. And he did it all with a buzz on, just one more pot-smoking outlaw in what seemed to be an entire generation of them.

"It's true, I have a lot of friends in politics, but they wouldn't be friendly very long if they knew my business was drugs instead of gambling . . ."

"You gonna Bogart that thing, or pass it on?"

"Shhh . . . !"

"Drugs is a dirty business . . ."

"Sorry, man."

"Don Corleone . . ."

Long was sitting through a movie about real gangsters, attending a late showing of *The Godfather,* and a joint was making its way down the aisle from his left.

"Here, man," whispered the guy behind him.

Another joint came over Long's shoulder.

"Very righteous shit," the guy told him.

"I think that's mine," said Long.

He took a hit, and passed it on, handing it to the woman in front of him.

"Delicious," she said, and thanked him.

Counterculture ritual, as he and his contemporaries celebrated it, was ripe with a feeling of ease, and Long himself took pride in his share of the responsibility for fueling it. Stoned on one drug or another, doing whatever they did — student-athletes at schools back east were playing intercollegiate hockey on acid — an entire generation was tripping to the same popular, four-color fantasia. It was hard to imagine that a time would come when America did not know what it was like for a good chunk of the population to be completely fucked up all the time.

"*. . . Ups, downs, acid, mescaline, cocaine, Salk vaccine, what do you need, aspirin, I got that, too . . .*"

Everybody was doing everything, all the time, with the possible exception of smack (at least among Long's acquaintances), the really effortless purchase of which probably meant a trip to the city. There was always someplace to hook up, plenty of places in the Bay Area, but if you lived outside New York, the best and by far the easiest places to score heroin were Vietnam and prison, the latter being the place where most marijuana smokers were exposed to it.

Estimates out of Washington that year were running as high as 25 million for the number of pot smokers nationwide, and Marin County, with a significant share of them, was ground zero for all that was cool. And all was going along splendidly for Long as well as his associates. Pomeroy and Big Jim, who owned the franchise, were each probably pulling in about $20,000 a load. On Pomeroy, the veteran scammer, the money had little discernible impact. With a lifestyle that cycled through alternating periods of wealth and relative poverty, Pomeroy was accustomed to being rich whenever he was not broke. For Big Jim things were a little bit different. It was not only his first taste of big money, but his first taste of the outlaw life. He fancied himself something of a drug kingpin now, and in a man of largely middle-class aspirations, the metamorphosis was amusing to watch. His living out the image of a crime lord expressed itself in such goofy ambitions as stealing other men's girlfriends.

Greed, megalomania, and paranoia were just around the corner for Jim. He and Pomeroy shared the combination to a large safe in the Mill Valley house, and in it they deposited the money generated by each shipment of marijuana. Once the balance of a shipment was sold, the two men divided the profit. For all the time they were smuggling pot, money never came between them. The operation from the outset was as gratifying as a Japanese tea ceremony and as predictable as a Catholic Mass. Until they started messing with karma. And in the good-old-boy-herb-smoking-and-smuggling brotherhood, karma, of the negative variety, when not brought to bear on the subject of guns, usually meant cocaine.

Not far down the fat-and-happy trail to success, with the plane bringing in loads every month, the partners decided to have the Mexicans throw some cocaine on board with the pot. They landed ten keys, put the cocaine in the safe, and three days later, Long walked into the house to find Jim holding Pomeroy by the throat, trying to throw him off the second-floor balcony.

"I'm going to kill this motherfucker!" he shouted, accusing Pomeroy of stealing cocaine.

"Motherfucker, you're the one stealing the shit!"

Long jumped in to separate them.

Both of them and neither of them were stealing the shit — they were not stealing it, they were simply doing it. Had Long known the safe's combination, he would have been doing it, too. All of them had a taste for it.

Up to that time, as Long viewed it, the safe had represented the honor and trust of the partnership. But they had put twenty-two pounds of cocaine in the safe, and three days later, by his count, they were trying to kill each other, literally.

Men must endure their going hence even as their coming hither, and in the immediate aftermath of the episode, seeing ripeness in the moment, Pomeroy took Long aside and told him: "This is probably a good time for you to get out."

The Marin County adventure was over. A mere six months had passed, and Long was on his way home.

New York. Where the deer and the antelope play.

With the documentary footage in hock to the film-processing lab — by now, Ives, his producer, had written off the investment — it was hard for Long to know what he was going to do next. Or maybe it was just hard for him to say. Maybe it came to him smoking a joint at 37,000 feet. He left Marin with what he told himself was no great sense of criminal purpose, but he had not been home more than a New York minute before it became pretty obvious to him that a movie camera was the last thing he needed.

5 GIVE A MAN ENOUGH ROPE AND HE'LL SMOKE IT

Aspen, Colorado, American folklore's answer to such exotic wonder-lands as Sodom and Gomorrah — in the contemporary mythology a kind of drugs-and-deep-powder, post-alphabet Babylon without the agriculture — was singularly appropriate to Allen Long's launch into the rarefied air of big-time smuggling. Situated just west of the Continental Divide in the valley of the Roaring Fork River, 8,000 feet above sea level and about 4.3 light-years removed from the nearest star with an apparent magnitude greater than that of any one of its resident celebrities, the big-ticket ski resort and upmarket-bohemian hideaway owed its reputation to a brand of renegade income that only the glamour professions could provide. Arriving in December 1975, Long walked through an airport in which even the innocent passengers fit the federal drug profile: the gold Rolex, the hand-stitched lizard skin boots — a DEA shakedown every minute at any other port of entry. Long, of course, was not among the innocent. Since leaving California some three years earlier he had been earning his money moving dope, and in doing so had been preparing for just such a meeting as the one he was in Aspen to attend.

Returning to New York from Marin in the fall of 1972, Long had rented an apartment downtown at the corner of Prince and Wooster Streets. Sporting his new California threads and displaying a newly acquired swagger — pursuant to his success as an outlaw, having pretty much redecorated his life — he made a big point of making the uptown scene, made a lot of new friends, and burned through what remained of the money he had made smuggling. In the course of going broke, he looked up a guy by the name of Little Eddie.

The world of the marijuana smuggler, in many ways, was a small one. While the traffic in cannabis stretched across three oceans, several continents, and numerous national borders, its flow was restricted by narrow channels of affiliation. The search for sources and outlets was conducted by word of mouth. Owing to the rigors of an illicit market, in which neither buyer nor sellers advertised, reliability and trust came at a higher premium than in the legitimate business world. Solid connections were seldom abandoned, and the same was true of one's customers. It was not unusual for numerous reasons for a pot wholesaler in Denver, say, to be buying his weight from a smuggler who lived in Boston. Just as Lee Carlyle had traveled from Los Angeles to market his product in Chicago, a New Jersey dealer like Little Eddie might quite naturally travel to Mill Valley to investigate the possibility of doing business with someone like Pomeroy. That is how Long and Little Eddie had met.

Despite the dope-smoking, the dark mustache, and the hair that fell to the middle of his back, Little Eddie, seemingly anchored in the counterculture, was the nearest thing Allen Long had ever run across to an early-talkies mobster. A short, tough, street-smart operator, who had been hustling since his teens, Eddie followed all the old rules. In a business where squealing came with the turf, where state's evidence was the lingua franca, Eddie was a stand-up guy, proudly observing the code of silence adhered to by the gangsters he and his New Jersey friends looked up to. In addition to being a man of his word, Eddie was meticulous. He seldom made mistakes. He and Long would remain friends for years, well beyond the point at which Eddie was eventually busted and, refusing to cooperate with the government, followed the old rules right into jail.

When Long looked him up, Little Eddie was doing a big hash trip, part of a crew that was moving some 5,000 pounds of hashish out of Morocco.

"If you know somebody who can buy this hash," he said — he had access to 1,000 pounds of it — "we can both make some money on it."

Long thought he did know somebody. Through a series of random associations that started with the various pot and cocaine dealers he patronized, Long had begun moving, if only socially, in pretty fast company in New York. Among the people with whom he was running were members of the Howie Fuchs organization.

Howie Fuchs, twenty-seven, a former city welfare investigator, soon to be dubbed "a Horatio Alger of crime" by a New York district attorney, would querulously claim a Bronx beer distributorship as the source of his wealth. That he would protest his innocence in a press conference was an indication of the level of celebrity the Yeshiva University graduate would eventually come to enjoy. In addition to whatever amount of beer Fuchs might have been distributing, he was, when Allen Long knew him, distributing cocaine by the key, along with a variety of other drugs. (Conspiracy to distribute sixty kilos of coke was the crime of which he would be convicted in federal court. Later he pleaded guilty in state court to smuggling some 270 kilos of cocaine and 4,000 pounds of hashish.)

Howie Fuchs was a guy who could move a lot of hash, and Long's approach to him, proposing that Fuchs take a share of Little Eddie's Moroccan load, led to an immediate change in Long's standing with him. In the spring of 1973 Long was invited to participate in a high-stakes poker game hosted by the flamboyant crime lord in a suite at Manhattan's Essex House hotel, a nonstop, no-sleep, three-day coke-and-hooker binge at which only the anointed were welcome.

Of such moments were memories made. Long felt warm all over.

The Moroccan arrived a couple of months later. There was, however, so little room in the deal that Fuchs declined to take it. "There's not enough room in this deal for your dime," was how such things were traditionally explained, the dime being a figurative reference to whatever "your" take on the transaction happened to be.

In short, the hash was priced a little high for Fuchs and his boys, one of whom, a friend of Long's by the name of Danny, volunteered the following: "That guy Jeff, he'll probably buy it."

"Jeff . . ." said Long, shaking his head.

"You played poker with him," said Danny.

Like all gatherings of its kind, in the corporate as well as the criminal world, the card-game-cum-bacchanalia had been underwritten by Howie Fuchs in support of business as well as pleasure. People came and went, and among those present was a severe, rather secretive, tight-lipped character with an oddly studious air and an accent straight out of the Bronx. Aloof, in his early thirties, introduced as Jeff, he and some guy named José from Detroit were among the few men who attended the gathering who remained unknown to Long. Jeff made it pretty clear that he was not interested in getting to know anyone, or more to the point, in anyone getting to know him. The name was almost certainly a phony. It was a good bet that "Jeff" was somebody significant in the dope business, as was everyone else at the party. José was definitely a player.

"What do you know about Jeff?" asked Long

Jeff, according to Danny, was the biggest marijuana dealer in the Midwest.

"How do I get to him?" Long asked.

Danny could not help him there. He knew Fuchs was selling hash to Jeff. The two had been dealing through another buyer whom they recently had managed to jump. (Not enough room in the deal for *his* dime anymore.) Danny said he would ask around.

He got back to Long a few days later.

"Physics?" said Long.

"Maybe engineering. Someone thinks he heard him say the guy once taught at Harvard."

The name Danny had come up with was no name at all, but a description he had pieced together from bits of conversation picked up by various players the night of the game. Long could get to Jeff through a certain college professor, Danny told him.

"He's here in New York?" asked Long.

"That's what I assume."

And with little more than that to go on, Long eventually tracked him down. He reached him by phone.

"Hi, I'm Allen Long. I met a fellow named Jeff . . ." he began, and kept it vague.

"Mm-hmm."

"I've got something he might be interested in."

"Give me your number."

Twenty minutes later the professor called back from a pay phone.

"Jeff," he said, "is very security-conscious. He doesn't want to talk to you. I, however, would be interested in hearing what you have to say."

A college professor? No kidding. Could this be for real? Long figured what the hell. He said he had a load of hash.

"The only way Jeff would be interested would be if he were to see some," the professor responded.

Howie Fuchs would have put it differently — Howie Fuchs *had* put it differently — but the sentiment was the same; notwithstanding the mobilization of a conditional clause that featured elegant employment of the subjunctive, the professor's response was the appropriate one. Wondering what academia was coming to, Long said fine.

He met the professor, whose name was Abe, a few days later at Teterboro Airport in New Jersey. Long had assumed that, flying out of Teterboro, Abe was traveling on a private flight rather than a commercial carrier. But when he spotted the professor standing beside a single-engine Cessna, he was surprised to find him unaccompanied by a pilot.

Hairdressers, science professors . . . all God's creatures had private tickets. Misery had nothing on dope when it came to acquainting a man with strange bedfellows.

Abe, who held a doctorate in physics, was very much the scholar, sporting the acquired slouch of the academician — he had the slouch down cold — and the affected, pseudo-tribal stammer that betrayed an undergraduate degree from Harvard. With the deliberative speech and deferential manner that when necessary could be deployed in a backhanded show of superiority, he gave the appearance of being unfocused, which stood him in stark contrast to the anything-but-absentminded, blunt-spoken Jeff. Tall and slim, his hair a laboratory study in arranged disarray, he was wearing a houndstooth jacket, a bow tie, and desert boots, and carrying $4,600 in cash, which he gave to Long for a four-pound brick of blond Moroccan hash. He said he would be back in touch.

The call came two days later.

"This is John."

"John?"

"We met in New Jersey . . ."

Of course.

". . . His name's Jeff, my name's John."

His name's cloak, your name's dagger.

"Okay, " said Long.

"You understand?"

Long understood.

"Call me from a pay phone."

Instructing Long, from then on, to call him only from pay phones, the professor gave him a number. Long hit the street.

"Here's what you do . . ." said Abe, when Long called him back.

Long and Little Eddie, in a rental car with 150 pounds of hash in the trunk, drove to Ann Arbor, Michigan, and checked into Weber's Inn, located on Jackson Road. There, the following morning, Long received a phone call and was instructed to proceed to the Paul Bunyan restaurant.

"You can't miss it," Long was told. "You'll see a big statue on the highway of Paul Bunyan and his ox."

"Babe."

"What?"

"Babe," said Long. "Paul Bunyan's ox. Babe the Blue Ox."

"Babe the Blue Ox. Yeah. Be there at eleven."

Long entered the restaurant alone, caught sight of Jeff sitting at a table with a view of the door, and pulled up a chair.

Tall and trim, no more physically imposing than the average long-distance runner, Jeff was dark-haired, fair-complexioned, well-groomed, and dressed for croquet. He wore loose khaki trousers over white canvas shoes, a plain sweep-face wristwatch with a simple leather strap, and his tortoiseshell sunglasses were tucked neatly into the collar of a blue, short-sleeved knit shirt free of ornamentation but for an embroidered trademark crocodile. He shook hands with the enthusiasm of a man surrendering his wallet.

If he remembered Long from the poker game, he gave no indication of it.

The pleasantries were kept to a minimum. Jeff passed Long a briefcase. Long found his way to the men's room, locked himself in a stall, and counted the $172,500 the briefcase contained. He returned to the table and passed Jeff the keys to the rental car. Jeff left the restaurant, returned an hour later, handed the car keys back to Long, and slipped him a piece of paper.

He said, "Here's a number you can reach me at if you can ever do this again."

And left.

Long and Little Eddie made $15,000 apiece on the hash (their collective "dime" being $200 a pound). About a week after they got back to New York, Howie Fuchs, already facing trial on drug-trafficking charges in state court, was arrested on a federal complaint. Long's name came up in the latter investigation, and rather than talk to an assistant U.S. attorney who asked him to drop in for a visit, Long packed up and left town.

Long moved back to Richmond, and for the next year or so he behaved himself. Or tried to. He went to work for a friend, a building contractor, but not before blowing six months on a failed Jamaican ganja trip — a Lee Carlyle extravaganza, horribly conceived — in the course of which he managed to burn through the $15,000 he made on the hash. Eventually, he and his builder friend went into the contracting business together. And did no better financially than he and Carlyle had done on the Jamaican deal.

It was while living the straight life in Richmond in the fall of 1973 that Long met a young woman who, in her ability to piss him off and play fast and loose with his ego, drove him slightly crazier than other women he had known, and with whom in consideration of which he necessarily fell in love.

Cherie Harris, all energy, longing, and imagination, aspired to a career in literature or "something in the arts," but at the age of twenty-one the only thing she knew how to be was a movie star. A student at Virginia Commonwealth University, where she majored in being cool, she found an outlet for her creativity in the invention of herself. Cherie was five-feet-seven, her dark brown hair was long, her eyes were brown, as big as doughnuts, and a good old boy would tell you she was pretty as a crocheted afghan. But when history was written, Cherie would be remembered for something other than her looks: Cherie, as the cultural record showed, and as she herself acknowledged, was "the first girl in Richmond with platform shoes."

In creating a place for herself in the world, Cherie, a thrifty shopper, paid special attention to her clothes. The look that she was going for, which she explained to her contemporaries as "a glam-hippie thing," was only half in evidence on the cool blustery day in November when Long first saw her on the street. She was bundled up in a long, black, imitation-fur coat that she had purchased from the Salvation Army, her feet were clad in construction boots, and she was carrying a big umbrella. A day later, when Long picked her up for a date — they were off to a club to hear music — he did not recognize her at first. Over an evening dress and platforms, she wore a big, white, loop-stranded wig, a contraption that played out somewhere between Afro and astrakhan, which she had sprayed with football grip and sprinkled with sparkle and glitter. It was a look Long associated with New York streetwalkers and entertainers like Mozart. Noting his disappointment, she changed in the club's ladies' room.

Upon first spotting Cherie on the street that day, Long unleashed what Cherie and her friends — and many of his friends — came to refer to as "that Allen thing." That Allen thing was charm. Affability and plenty of it. Observable in the stereotypical Southern gentleman and a certain variety of sociopath, it was a gift Allen Long possessed in abundance, and one he cultivated assiduously. His expression of it was state-of-the-art. It worked on everybody, not just women, and was notable for remaining seductive well after Long had demonstrated that there were risks attached in getting to know him. To say Allen Long had personality was like saying Secretariat had legs.

Cherie thought Long was cool — so, right from the beginning of the relationship the two had something in common — but played unimpressed, at the same time trying to figure out how she could take things further. Cherie did not possess a wealth of sexual experience, but knew enough to realize that Long was going slow, and she found herself having to push a little to get him to pay attention. Eventually Long would come around, and the sum of their years together would outnumber those of Long's earlier love affairs combined. But by the summer of 1974 Long had other things on his mind. Returning home from work one day — he was renting a room from a friend — Long received a message that a guy by the name of JD had called, leaving the phone number of a local motel. Long returned the call wondering who he might be.

"Lee gave me your number," said JD, over the phone.

Carlyle's friend JD. Long remembered meeting him in Florida, briefly, on that failed Jamaican trip.

"Can you come out here?" he wanted to know.

Long made his way to the motel.

"You remember me?" JD asked, when Long showed up at the door.

It was like asking him if he remembered Mount Rushmore.

JD Reed, twenty-three, stood six-feet-five-inches tall. The 220 pounds he weighed looked to consist entirely of muscle and cartilage.

The overall physical impression he made smacked of the landscape that gave rise to his clothes — the blue jeans, white T-shirt, and Tony Lama boots, the Stetson hanging on the door hook — the gene pool on which he drew seemingly financed in the closing of the American frontier. He had arms the size of railroad ties, long brown hair, combed like that of a renegade cavalryman, and eyes as resolute as Manifest Destiny. Meeting him was like crossing paths with Crazy Horse — lighting upon the venerable Sioux at the close of business that day in the valley of the Little Big Horn River.

Reed introduced Long to the other man in the room, a skinny guy by the name of Speed, who when not traveling with Reed held down a lucrative gig as a valet parking attendant at one of the larger Las Vegas hotels. The two had just driven in from Tucson in the Chevy Suburban parked outside loaded with 1,200 pounds of Mexican pot. Reed's buyer in Richmond had failed to come up with the money he owed for the load Reed had fronted him on his last trip to Virginia. Reed needed to unload the 1,200 pounds and get paid before he went home.

"Lee said maybe you could help me."

In the biographical scheme of things, it was like Mrs. Wright saying to her son Wilbur: "Maybe your brother Orville could help."

(And maybe someday, when things worked out, there would be room in the deal for her dime.)

JD Reed, born in West Virginia, raised in Las Vegas from the day he could walk, took his first toke on a joint in high school. After dropping out of college in Southern California, he started growing pot in the mountains of Ranchita, about fifty miles north of the Mexican border. Self-possessed and soft-spoken, in those instances where he spoke at all, Reed was imperturbable, cool in a way that he was happy to let strangers misunderstand as cold-blooded. He emanated what on first encounter seemed to be an air of menace. One got the feeling he could be very dangerous. It was his habit, even at his happiest, to tear in half the telephone directory of every American metropolis it was ever his pleasure to visit. He looked upon Manhattan the way Agamemnon looked upon Troy. His instinct was to cut fence. It was his nature to think of everything west of the Divide as his own.

Reed's appetite was huge. If he wanted a drink of water, he drank a gallon of water. When he wanted something to smoke, he rolled a joint that outweighed his hat and smoked it all by himself. He was neither rude nor stingy. "If you want to smoke some, help yourself, it's over there," he would say. "This one here's for me." And he was never without something to smoke. Upon checking into a hotel room, everyone who knew him would tell you, the first thing he did, before halving the phone book, was remove a drawer from the dresser and use it to clean his pot. Separating the buds, crumbling up enough of the weed to fill a decent smoke, he sifted out the seeds, shaking the drawer side to side like a miner screening gold. It was what he was doing that day in Richmond when, sizing up his new acquaintance, he said, "Lee said maybe you could help me."

And Long said, "I believe I can."

In moving Reed's 1,200 pounds, Long's first call was to a casual acquaintance, a local business owner and R&B bass player by the name of Will McBride, who had been dealing pot by the pound. McBride took half the load. Another friend put Long in touch with a dealer he knew in D.C., who "could probably move a lot of this." In fact, as Long discovered, he could have moved it all.

Easy Matthews, a Washington-area contractor, was one of the more coolheaded pot distributors Long would ever meet. A big-boned, bearded redhead with hands as broad as banjos, he was self-reliant, self-assured, endlessly unruffled, and had excellent instincts for the work. A dealer in significant weight, Matthews was a major player. As large as JD Reed, with a resounding laugh and expansive gestures — "I want it all," he would sing, when offered a piece of the latest load — he had a wife, four children, and a partner, a fellow motorcycle enthusiast named Myles, a soft-spoken, skinny character who played serious basketball, always wore coveralls, and never did drugs. Together Myles and Matthews managed an apartment building in which all the units were occupied by dealers, drivers, money handlers, and others employed as part of their distribution network.

Matthews paid half the cash up front for the balance of Reed's 1,200 pounds and the other half two days later, which was all the time it took him to sell it. Long put a nickel-a-pound on the pot. In three days, without leaving town, he made $6,000 on the load.

"When I was a little boy," said Long, reporting his success to Carlyle, "my grandfather told me it's better to make a fast nickel than a slow dime."

"Yeah, I remember your telling me," Carlyle said.

"Often enough that today it remains imprinted upon my consciousness."

"And mine."

"Volume is everything, man. The way to riches is to sell volume. Quick turnover, low overhead. Whether it's the drug business . . ."

"Or the car business," said Carlyle.

"Yeah."

"I remember," Carlyle said.

The drug business differs from the car business, however, in at least one way that jumps to mind, and a fast nickel selling weed conveys certain advantages not necessarily apparent to the typical Oldsmobile salesman. Selling dope, alas, is illegal. Getting the contraband out of your possession as fast as possible (removing the evidence) and dealing with as few people as possible (reducing your exposure) substantially minimizes your risk of arrest.

Within ten days, Long had rented a new apartment, opened a bank account, and made the down payment on a BMW sedan. And Reed was back with another load. Two hundred pounds went to McBride. Matthews was clearly the man now. Waiting in Richmond when the pot arrived, he took the bulk of the shipment, a thousand pounds, and turned it over in two days. From then on, no matter how much weight he was moving, Long would always manage to keep Matthews supplied with a piece of the load. He would never limit himself to one buyer: Sell to a single buyer, he knew, and soon *he* will be telling *you* what the price is.

JD Reed, by this time, working with a partner in Tucson, had moved thousands of pounds of "lime green," as he described the commercial Mexican he was selling, but had yet to progress beyond "ground smuggling," picking up his pot in the American Southwest and driving it cross-country to sell. Now, with Long moving 1,200 pounds of the product every couple of weeks, it was time for him to step things up. To do so, Reed partnered with a hillbilly in Tucson by the name of Cactus Jack. Toothless, Tennessee-born-and-reared — "He'd be the guy drivin' them mules," said Reed — Cactus Jack was sixty-five and just about as cool as they come. A flat-out American original, he was a married to a Mexican national who had family in Sonora, and working with him, Reed went on to establish an operation south of the border.

Using a Piper Navajo Chieftain, Reed did two trips a week out of Mexico. He brought the first load into the country using a whorehouse airstrip near Las Vegas. To off-load subsequent flights he used a series of dry lakebeds in the desert. Everything after the landing — unloading the pot, driving it east, and selling it — Reed handled by himself. On the first trip, he went to Mexico and loaded the airplane as well. He moved 3,600 pounds a week, most of it to Long. So busy did he become that often he would just drop off the pot and immediately turn around, leaving collection of the money to Cactus Jack and a peg-legged partner named Arlo. Long, when they first showed up to collect, had to ask neither of these guys for ID. When he turned over the cash the only problem he had was picturing the pair — the halting Arlo trailing behind the toothless Jack, who was carrying a knapsack with nothing but money in it — trying to board a plane at National Airport.

Long had been doing business with Reed for just about a year when Reed found a DC-3, and Long saw the opportunity to walk his own operation upstairs. His plan was to take an entire shipment, 4,000 pounds, and move it all at once. Knowing only one man who could move that much weight in a hurry — knowing that Easy Matthews, as good as he was, did not have the cash to handle it — he told Reed to get the pot to Ann Arbor.

"This guy up there has a lot of money, he'll pay right away," he said.

The pot had to be moved in a hurry, and it had to be moved at Reed's price. On the line was Reed's credibility with his suppliers.

Long, therefore, was taking a risk when he guaranteed the deal without ever talking to Jeff.

It was the first of many times that Long would take such a flyer, gambling everything on intuition. He knew if he tried to negotiate over the phone, the deal would probably never go down. But could Jeff say no to a load-in-hand? Long's gut told him no. And he had to take the chance. Nailing down quality and price was always contingent upon speed, upon rapid turnover of the product, and just as importantly, rapid turnover of the money. Few were the people who could buy drugs in volume, and they were not known to more than a few others. This was Long's opportunity to exploit his access to Jeff, and in a way that, if all went well, would allow him to continue to do so.

Assured of a *reasonably* rapid turnover, "right away" being a relative term, Reed loaded up in Las Vegas, and drove the pot to Ann Arbor. Only after meeting him and taking the truck did Long put in a call to Jeff, not even knowing whether Jeff was in town.

He was. And soon Long had him looking at a sample.

"You know," said Jeff, with a put-upon air, "I got a whole barn full of the same kind of weed." Here we go, thought Long. "And your price is not that much different."

This was to be Long's first taste of a new, hybrid style of negotiating, a tough but eminently polite brand of bargaining transplanted to the upper Midwest from the busy streets of the Bronx. In one way he was reassured. He had made the right decision in coming. But he had also put himself in a serious squeeze. He had told Reed the deal was done. He had to close the deal, he had to do it now, and he had to get Reed his price.

"I'll do it for you . . ." sighed Jeff.

Long knew what was coming next.

". . . but I can't pay right away."

Meaning Jeff would have to sell it first. That was not good.

"How soon?" Long asked.

He had promised Reed a rapid turnaround.

"I don't know," said Jeff. "Tomorrow? I can probably get it done by tomorrow."

Long looked like a dummy who had been hit by a quiz, like a kid in the last row who had been instructed by his teacher to, maybe, name the nine Muses in alphabetical order. His mouth was hanging open, but he had nothing to say. Looking at Jeff, he thought, here is a guy who can move two tons of pot overnight. And get paid for it. Overnight. Reduced to a complete nonplus, he gave Jeff the keys to the truck. The following day, when he and Reed left town, he was $20,000 richer, and Reed was paid in full.

The gamble paid off big.

"Bring me all the pot you can at this price," Jeff told him. "I'll take it all."

It was like Willy Loman landing the Macy's account.

Long, with money in his pocket, driving a BMW that was now paid for, moved out of his apartment, rented a house just south of Charlottesville, and flush with success in the marijuana business, reinvigorated his pursuit of simultaneous failure in the music business.

For all the years he smuggled pot, Long would maintain a presence in the legitimate world by way of a half-assed career in the record industry. He did not consciously intend it to be half-assed — though a fear of success was almost certainly embedded somewhere in his character — but his subordination of it to a criminal career presupposed an outcome that even he could not fail to predict. It was as an aspiring cameraman, while working at Motion Associates, that Long had first approached executives at CBS Records in New York to propose the idea of his filming rock concerts. His promoting the concerts himself was a natural follow-up to the idea. Never having done so before did not prevent him from trying, and while his efforts met with little success, they were courteously received, solidifying a relationship with one industry executive that would last for many years. Over the course of that time Long demonstrated an aptitude for the music business that might have been amply rewarded had he followed through on any of his projects beyond the point of initial enthusiasm. His indulgence in the charade served various purposes.

First, of course, it provided a cover for his criminal activities. It made questions about what he did for a living — how he earned his money — all that much easier to answer. But more than that it served a necessary self-delusion. Long, clearly proud of what he was able to achieve as a smuggler, and understandably so, given the enormous challenges it presented, was not secure in that pride of achievement. Notwithstanding all his justifications — the victimless nature of his crimes, his alleged membership in a brotherhood of pioneers and cultural evangelists — Allen Long, given his upbringing and education, was unable by virtue of both to ignore the reality that he was a criminal. If he was not ashamed of what he did for a living (and in some deep subconscious place he was loath to dredge he might have discovered that to be true), neither could he brag about it with impunity. The only people he could trust to show what he saw as appropriate respect and admiration for his accomplishments as a smuggler were other smugglers. The music business gave him something to brag about. And more than that, it allowed him the opportunity to tell himself that being a smuggler was merely a temporary diversion from his more laudable aspirations in life.

Had he actually pursued those aspirations wholeheartedly, chances are he would have been successful. The entrepreneurial aspects of the music business, the development and management of talent, came naturally to Allen Long. The necessary instincts were there. He proved to be very good at it. But that would come as no surprise. Anybody who could go up against the odds he was about to go up against, and not only survive but prevail, anybody who could succeed as a smuggler, doing business with the kinds of people he was about to do business with, was perfectly suited to an industry controlled by even bigger criminals.

The music business dovetailed rather naturally with the pot business. Rock and roll and marijuana, music and dope in general, if not actually born under the same sign, came together at so many crossroads as to insure that Long, so deeply involved in the latter industry, would make numerous friends in the former. He would develop those friendships and the sundry professional contacts that followed — CBS being a good example — very early in New York. By the time he had left for Richmond, he could easily claim as many friends in the music business as in the dope business. The industries fed each other. Each was home to operators who had segued from one to the next. Some were involved in both.

Long, who had first smoked dope as the member of a rock and roll band, had remained as enthusiastic about music as pot, and impressed by the talent of singer-songwriter Steve Bassett, whose performance he caught at a club in Richmond, signed him to a management contract. Over the next three years he would invest a substantial amount of money in the act. (Eventually signed by John Hammond to Columbia Records, Bassett recorded an album produced by Jerry Wexler. Yielding a single that hit the R&B charts, the LP suffered commercially when, as Long understood it, the soul stations discovered that Bassett was white.) Long later managed songwriter Robbin Thompson, whose first album in a three-record deal with Atlantic made the *Billboard* charts. (Thompson, who later collaborated with Bassett on the song "Sweet Virginia Breeze," was dropped by the label when he failed to follow the LP up with material its executives liked.)

For years Long would remain energetic in his support of these acts — he paid for the national tour to promote Thompson's album — but he was far more energetic in escalation of his own activities as a smuggler. The decision by now had been made. Smuggling pot was not some dubious adjunct to filmmaking, and it had risen well beyond the level of an experiment. He was in it. All the way. It was what he did for a living. More than what he did, it was a large part of who he was. And it was time to take control of it. He wanted to be the biggest scammer he could possibly be.

JD Reed and his partners had been bringing pot into the desert at Lake of Wells, Nevada. Nearby, supposedly unknown to the world, stretched the vast nuclear test site at Indian Springs. When the DC-3 pilots, low on fuel, had landed within the boundaries of the installation, bringing down not only government heat, but national security heat, Reed bowed out of the deal. (The airplane was busted on the next load.) With Reed in temporary retirement, it was time for Long to underwrite an operation of his own. And he was not the only one making a change.

Will McBride had learned to fly.

"I want to do something big," said Long.

It would be a while before McBride checked out in multiengine aircraft, but he knew a guy with a lot of hours who might be interested, he said.

"You set it up," said Long. "I'll talk to him."

Long called Reed in Las Vegas, and told him what he had in mind.

"What kind of airplane we gonna use?"

"Haven't decided," said Long.

"What does your pilot say?"

"I haven't talked to him yet."

"What about the money?"

"I figure maybe two hundred and fifty thousand to get it going."

"Where do you figure to get it?"

"We get it from my friend in Detroit."

"Talked to him yet?"

"No."

No plane. No pilot. No money.

No problem, not for Reed.

"If you're waitin' on me," he said, "you're backin' up."

And two weeks later, Long was stepping off an airplane in Aspen, Colorado.

Aspen, the playground of choice to a high-scale hobo collective of American celebrities and the lower echelon nobility that journalist Hillary Johnson in 1982 would be the first to describe as Eurotrash, was esteemed for already having a coke problem as early as 1975. A mile and a half high in the Rockies, a resort in the throes of giving birth to a solar-heated airport piped with music by Steely Dan, it was a town sanctified by the passage of every major dope smuggler of the day, and

Long, had he been aware of it, would have been proud to be joining their number.

Walking through the airport, he and JD Reed stepped directly into a taxi and headed for a house on Red Mountain. Night had fallen and it had been snowing for a couple of hours when they entered on the lower level of the modified, multilevel A-frame. Removing their boots, they were ushered into a wood-paneled den, the windows of which, with an unimpeded view of the ski trails snaking their way into the valley, overlooked the flickering lights of a town jumping at the height of the season.

Jeff had arrived in Aspen a week before with his family. Long had not discussed his purpose with Jeff when he called Ann Arbor to schedule a meeting, nor had he told him, when Jeff suggested they meet in Aspen, that he would be arriving in town with Reed. Jeff knew better than to think that this was a social visit, however, and showing his guests to red leather armchairs warmed by the heat of the fireplace, he was quite happy to get down to business, interested to hear what Long had to say. Long, after all, had proved he could deliver good Mexican pot at a price. Jeff had put $25 a pound on the 4,000 Long had sold him, and turned it over in twenty-four hours. He was that much more interested when Long told him: "We're not going to Mexico."

6   SMOKE OF A DISTANT FIRE

Ann Arbor, Michigan, in 1975 was not the cannabis capital of the world. On a given day there would be more dope on hand in, say, maybe, Morocco. But for per capita consumption of pot, the university town forty-one miles west of Detroit was pretty tough to beat. The annual Ann Arbor Hash Festival, the on-campus "hash bash" held every April, was known to attract thousands, and the city's "$5 herb law" was counterculture legend.

The youth vote in Ann Arbor in 1974 constituted a full one third of the city's population. That electoral bloc drew substantially from some 40,000 students at the University of Michigan. A charter amendment enacted that year (voted initially into law in 1972, voted down the next, and reinstated in the more recent election) made possession of marijuana, even in amounts exceeding a pound, a misdemeanor subject to no greater penalty than a $5 fine. The amendment carried the added force of restricting Ann Arbor police to enforcement of the local ordinance, the state law being more punitive. That summer the Michigan

Court of Appeals upheld a similar marijuana law in Ypsilanti, home to Eastern Michigan University, ten miles down the road. Pot was interwoven so naturally into the fabric of the two cities that when the *Ann Arbor Sun,* a nonprofit community newspaper, ran its "Win a Pound of Colombian" contest in January 1975, the winning entry was drawn by a county commissioner in a ceremony conducted at Ann Arbor City Hall.

Announcing the winner, the newspaper cited the "limited supply" of Colombian, and acknowledged paying "the hefty price of $350" for the weed. The best Mexican pot was worth maybe half that.

To pot smokers nationwide, Colombian marijuana was not the stuff of myth. It was certainly available, but came around infrequently and in relatively small amounts. And characteristically what came around was Colombian marijuana of the commercial variety. Only a few smugglers were bringing pot up from Colombia, and of those going down to get it, fewer still were connoisseurs. The pilots flying it up, one could readily assume, were pilots first and smokers second; the boat traffic was dominated by Cuban-Americans organized in South Florida who did not smoke marijuana. Insensitive to any subtleties, neither pilots nor boat captains knew what they were getting when they loaded on the Guajira. By the same measure, neither did Colombian traffickers, nonsmokers themselves, really know what they were selling. Between the Sierra Nevada Indian and the dedicated American smoker, who both identified differences among varying strains of Colombian, stood businessmen who did not.

Into this quality-control vacuum, Allen Long was about to step.

To connoisseurs like Long and legions of American heads, there were only three kinds of Colombian pot. There was gold, there was red, and there was everything else. *Punta roja,* the red, compared favorably with Thai weed, the gourmet grass of Southeast Asia. JD Reed said that it was when he tasted his "first little *punta roja* bud" that he knew he would one day go to Colombia. In the Western Hemisphere, it was generally agreed, there was only one thing better (with the possible exception of Hawaiian, which was cultivated so near the International Dateline as to be considered oriental, and was for the most part unavailable). That one thing better came from the pale leaf of the plant that the Indians of the Sierra Nevada identified as *mona,* or *rubia,* the blonde. The Americans called it gold. This was the legendary gold of Santa Marta.

Everything else, everything other than gold and red, was commercial Colombian, and everything else was what typically turned up in the United States. Commercial Colombian was what the *Ann Arbor Sun* gave away. And commercial Colombian was as good as anything on the everyday market.

The best Colombian, by contrast, was as good as anything in the world.

Allen Long knew this. Long had tasted connoisseur Colombian, but had never seen it in great supply, and he had never seen evidence that it existed in great supply. But Long had heard the stories. It was out there, he was told. Everyone spoke in awe of the bounty of Santa Marta. The tales of it lived on and had grown into legend. The Sierra Nevada held forth the promise of a mythical land of gold, and like the conquistadors who centuries earlier had gone deep into Colombia in epic search of El Dorado, Long, in dreams of smuggler's glory, had come to believe in this land of plenty. He imagined entire mountain valleys carpeted in leaves of gold, there for the taking in fabulous abundance. He nurtured a vision of Colombian treasure awaiting discovery, and for him, bringing it home presented an adventure that by the fall of 1975 had assumed the heroic character of a quest. When he raised the notion of an expedition, Reed had been quick to sign on, and the two explorers had set out for Aspen seeking an audience, paying a call on a Michigan businessman who, for the purposes at hand, looked to them very much like the King of Spain.

Jeff had company in Aspen. Visiting that week was Abe, who proved a source of entertainment when, wandering into the den, he sat in on the conversation. Excited perhaps by the intrigue to which he was suddenly a party, Abe made the innocent mistake of addressing Jeff as Jake. A spirited argument between them followed, conducted at the level of a whisper, in which "Jeff" rebuked "John," an argument that appeared, in one form or another, to have been in progress for years.

Jeff's name was not Jeff, and he was not, as Danny in New York had asserted, the biggest marijuana dealer in the Midwest. He was not even the biggest in Ann Arbor, which in 1975 was probably home to as many pot dealers as Guadalajara, Mazatlán, and Tijuana combined. In Ann Arbor you could always tell when a load was in town — that night, Whiffletree, a popular dining establishment on West Huron, would be overflowing with counterculture capitalists, their number divisible by the busful, ordering champagne.

The marijuana market in Ann Arbor, a town defined by its concentration of university students, mirrored the national market as a whole in 1975 in that the typical pot smoker was — or certainly saw himself as — part of an American counterculture that even then displayed the characteristics of a discernible movement. It has been argued that not until April of that year, with the fall of Saigon, did the 1960s as they are commonly appreciated really come to an end. But while the typical consumer might have reflected a certain, even if only vestigial, opposition to the establishment, the typical dealer did not. Dope dealers, like dealers of almost any commodity, while paying lip service to their customers' cultural values, were firmly anchored in the mainstream of American commerce.

Jake, aka Jeff, was no exception.

Jake Myerson had arrived in Michigan as a college student. As a young businessman in the late 1960s, several years after graduation, he started selling pot because he liked to smoke it — an ounce here, an ounce there, just to keep himself in personal stash. By 1970 he was getting loads from Mexico. By 1975 he was buying pot by the ton. More than ten years older than the oldest undergraduate, Myerson probably had more in common with the university's administrators than he had with its students. Serious-minded, highly organized, and almost avuncular in his dealings with the people who worked moving his pot, he was in many ways a generation behind the customers he served. By temperament, he differed not only from his clientele, but from many of his competitors as well. Easy Matthews, for instance, was an outlaw who acted like one, fun-loving, flamboyant, anything but uptight — he had the personality of a pirate. Jake Myerson was an outlaw with the disposition of a grocer.

Not so much disobedient as dyspeptic, Myerson was neither voluble nor particularly expansive. He spoke in a nasal, almost metrical monotone, and played a rich array of interpersonal cards close to a heaving chest. He seldom raised his voice, even in disagreement, choosing instead to meet antagonism with a show of injured dignity, retreating from confrontation to the cover of a conversational style that had its parallels in jujitsu and its antecedents in the ancient marketplace. Talking to him was like talking to a guy who was talking to a cop. But while the hangdog demeanor masked a forceful will, it was incapable of disguising the attributes that inevitably defined him: generosity, loyalty, and a hopelessly kind heart. Eminently responsible, reliable, and utterly efficient, Jake Myerson was a man whose measure could be taken from the value of his phone number. If you ever found yourself in a jam, he was the first guy you called.

All the time he was in the pot business, Myerson, a discriminating smoker, remained as devoted an epicure as he was a merchant. In Allen Long's opinion, Jake Myerson was "a true head." Paying for the two tons of Reed's Mexican weed that Long had delivered to Ann Arbor, he had told Long to bring more, saying he would take all he could get. "But if you can bring me this," he had said, furnishing Long with a fistful of Santa Marta Gold, "we can make a lot more money."

Long figured he said it to everyone who supplied him with product.

Where a pound of Mexican pot was worth about $100 wholesale, Colombian pot, at the same level in the market, was worth about $300. Where a "single" of commercial Colombian, like the pound given away by the *Ann Arbor Sun,* was worth $350, the same pound of Santa Marta Gold, sold individually, was worth in excess of $500. The gold was that much better, and it was what everyone wanted to smoke. Including Myerson himself.

What was immediately obvious to the businessman in Long would be obvious to almost anyone, but few were the businessmen who could truly appreciate what was so readily apparent to the pothead in him. Or so irresistible to his ego. If Long could get gold — as a true head like Myerson need not remind him — not simply could they make more money, they could lay claim to a small stake of counterculture stardom.

The meeting, then, in Aspen between Long and Jake Myerson bore witness to the wedding in each man's personality of the shop-keeper and the swashbuckler. Neither man, however, came to the mat-ter of marijuana smoking with more authority than JD Reed, one swashbuckler in whose nature the shopkeeper did not abide. At the meeting in Aspen, there was no truer head than he.

Reed was a head who, at length and unapologetically, could pro-vide poetic discourse on "the energy, the magic, the beauty of the herb." And mean it. He was a smoker who had started smuggling pot because he got tired of looking for it. Feeling quite emphatically that "it should be in hand when you need it," he was religious on the sub-ject. Literally. Marijuana was not an article of faith, it was the Faith itself, and Reed was its Defender. All the money he made smuggling herb he reinvested in smuggling more. The millions never caught up with him, he was always working. Reed, like other smugglers, lavished disposable income on cars and boats, but only on those in which he could haul marijuana. Where another scammer might seek joy in the extravagance of a platinum Rolex, an indigo blue Maserati, or a house with eight bathrooms on the rim of Red Mountain, Reed would be quite happy, he argued, "if I could keep enough smoke around me."

"Dope will get you through times of no money better
than money will get you through times of no dope."
Freewheelin' Franklin
Fabulous Furry Freak Brothers

It was smoke, no doubt, that had led JD Reed to his appreciation of the transmigration of souls. Reed believed that he had been a great warrior in a previous life. "Many lifetimes I had to be a warrior," he rea-soned — "I got the build for it, I got the instincts" — and he took pride in the fact that, after coming of age in his present life, he had never inflicted harm on anyone. "With my body strength and knowledge," he explained to Long, "I manipulate 'em, I don't hurt 'em. That's what marijuana did for me. It turned my warrior-ness into peace."

Reed was a warlord who had established his kingdom securely in the realm of the ethereal, and to achieve the celestial precincts thereof, he followed his very own *camino real*. The journey began with his laying hands on the highest grade ganja any man could possibly score, and rolling a joint the size of a prairie dog. He would soak the joint in Afghani hash oil, a bottle of which he always kept handy, and hang it in the sun to dry — he would clothespin the oiler to the laundry line outside the kitchen of his Las Vegas ranch. Picking it at just the right moment, Reed would fire it up and smoke it until nothing but ash remained. That was how he started his day.

For anyone smoking with him, it signaled the end of the day.

Hash oil is chemically extracted from the cannabis plant and purified through repetition, and good hash oil can be up to four times as potent as the resin itself. In 1975 it sold for about $20 a gram. A pound was worth a little over $5,000, and Reed was known to buy all he could get. A big deal on the dope market, it was a hot item in Las Vegas, especially among show folk. Carrying an ounce or so in a medicine bottle, and removing it with an eyedropper, the typical smoker — that is, a smoker other than Reed — would paint a line of oil on the side of a cigarette, take a couple of hits, and get instantly stupefied, as high as he or she could ever hope to get on a bowl of hash. A sidereal sort of high, the sort of "mental medication" that Reed enjoyed, it held no appeal for smokers like Allen Long, who preferred the "up" high of good grass.

The meeting in Aspen, if for nothing else, would be memorable for the union of opposites to which it ultimately gave rise, for the bonding in eternal brotherhood of the pothead and the egghead. For no more unlikely a friendship would come out of the meeting than that which developed between Reed, practicing noble savage and sagebrush philosopher, and the earthbound, empirical man of hard science, intellectual Abe, Ph.D., "Q.E.D.," theoretical physics. Within a few months of the meeting in Aspen, back on the East Coast, these two characters, in holy communion, would be scouting landing strips, stoned, in the cockpit fumatorium of a single-engine Cessna. Abe, manning the stick, would be smoking an oiler as plump as Schrödinger's cat, while metaphysician Reed, mystic of the Mojave, theorized on the way of the warrior:

"If I was a general, my army'd be cannibals, we wouldn't carry no food . . ."

"Interesting, I can dig that . . ."

Abe's effortless drift from the halls of the academy to the ranks of the American felonry, his full gainer from the ivory tower, prompted no questions in Allen Long. Long, because it was true of him, believed that the glory of big-time drugs was irresistible to everyone. Learjets, cocaine, reckless young women — it was like being a pop star, only better, to Long's way of thinking, because you were not on the road so much.

The academic life has its own rewards, and many of them in their own way are probably just as tawdry. But in the end the glory of intellectual endeavor would seem to feed at its hungriest on provender more rarefied than the gruel available to the average criminal. Or so one would assume. Well, forget it. Long was right. Notwithstanding the academic accomplishments both admirable and enviable from which Abe could proudly take sustenance, the intrigue and excitement of pot smuggling, the lure of the scammer's life, were just too much for him to resist. His hanging with Reed gave new meaning to the notion of extracurricular activity.

The meeting in Aspen was relatively brief. On the surface it was quite straightforward. Long was proposing a partnership, a merger of sorts. Admittedly ill-defined, it was met by Jake Myerson with understandable misgiving. But Myerson's well-tempered skepticism was rapidly displaced, superseded by his undisguised annoyance with Abe — presumably in Aspen to get some skiing done — and the latter's sudden intrusion into discussion of the deal.

"I've got two expert pilots," Long was saying. "And I have JD here, who has done more than twenty airplane trips this year."

"Would you say five thousand pounds, Allen?" interrupted Abe, who was running calculations on a yellow legal pad.

Myerson swiveled his head and hosed Abe down with a menacing glare of which the latter was joyously oblivious.

"Say forty-eight hundred," Long answered.

"How much do you need, Allen?" Myerson asked, refocusing his attention on Long.

"I figure one hundred and fifty thousand to buy the plane . . ."

Myerson, in the naked face of the number, looked like a man who had taken a bullet.

"Forty-eight hundred," mumbled Abe, calculating the return on a planeload of Colombian, "at three hundred a pound . . ."

Myerson said, "That's a lot of money."

"That's one point four four million," said Abe, impressed with his own figures.

Myerson, turning to face him, said, "Abe, you can put that thing away."

"Gross," said Abe, defensively.

"You're not being asked to put up anything now," said Long. "We're going to go to Colombia and firm up the connection before we spend any money on the plane."

"I thought you had the connection in Colombia . . ."

"Excuse me, gentlemen . . ." said Abe.

Myerson, like a prizefighter clearing blood clots, heaved a chestful of air through his nostrils, and fixed his eyes on Abe. "Forget the one point four four million," he muttered, pointing a finger at the legal pad. "You can put that aside."

"I'm sorry . . ." said Abe.

"That's okay," Myerson said.

". . . but I'm about to agree with you," said Abe. "Allen, you said one hundred and fifty thousand dollars. That might be enough to out-fit the airplane, but what about paying for the pot. You've forgotten the pot. Add forty-eight hundred pounds to the cost of the plane, and you're looking at a quarter of a million dollars."

"Let me see that," said Myerson, reaching for the pad.

"Actually," Long said, "I figure the down payment on the pot at maybe fifty to sixty thousand. The Colombians will front the rest. Say thirty-five to forty thousand dollars in expenses between now and the time we do the first load . . ."

"Wait a minute," said Myerson.

"I need two hundred and fifty thousand, cash, to do this," Long concluded.

"Allen," said Myerson, stopping him before the number went any higher, "you're asking me to invest in something brand-new — something brand-new even to you."

"JD has been doing airplanes for over a year now," said Long.

"From Mexico," said Myerson.

"Allen, I think Jake's main concern —"

"Please, Abe," said Myerson, raising a hand to silence him. The professor as crime lord. Just what he needed. He said, "A quarter of a million, Allen, is a hell of a lot of money to bet on an operation with no track —"

Reed got to his feet.

It was bad enough for Myerson that he had Abe to deal with. Bad enough that he had Long, who as trustworthy as he seemed to be, was essentially running a con: no connection, no plane, he probably had no pilots. That was bad enough. But now the beleaguered Myerson had JD Reed to deal with. Up to now, Reed had been silent. Up to now, he had been motionless, albeit having chosen somewhat disconcertingly to sit on the floor rather than take a chair. To people like Myerson an impassive JD Reed was the human equivalent of a hand grenade with the pin securely in place. It was not Reed's habit to explain to strangers that standing before them, blocking the sun, looming in their path like some heavy-equipment breakdown, was a 220-pound Man of Peace. It was not Reed's habit to say much of anything. One's immediate response to greeting him was reflexively to ask oneself whether there were women and children in the house.

Reed stood up and said, "Come on, let's go, Allen, it's time to get out of here. We'll get what we need somewhere else. I know five people in Vegas who'll give you the money to do this. Shit, I got that much cash at home. If this man don't see it, fine. We don't need his money. Let's go."

"Hold on," said Myerson.

Jake Myerson, misgivings aside, had every reason to welcome the partnership that Long and Reed were proposing. Here was the opportunity to set up his own line of supply, to get product at his own price, the opportunity to dig that much more deeply into the financial structure of the deal: his opportunity to control the load. Such a setup was worth a substantial amount of money to Myerson as a distributor. In the face of a solidified Mexican market, pricing had become a pivotal issue. And the Colombian market was wide open. No one knew the true value of cultivation in Colombia — four million pounds in a single valley, some said. It was known that in both quantity and quality the Colombian crop dwarfed that of Mexico. And the product sold at a higher margin.

But Long did not need to explain any of that to Myerson. It was Myerson who had explained it to him. The advantages of the proposition were self-evident, and would be so to any distributor. Myerson was not the only major distributor accessible to Long. There was Matthews in Washington. But Matthews did not have the necessary cash; he could not move and pay for two tons of pot overnight as Myerson had proved capable of doing. Long was therefore gratified, if not especially surprised, when Myerson very politely waved Reed back to his seat — or floor, as it were, in his case — and advanced the discussion.

"You said you have pilots."

Long said he had pilots, and assured Myerson that there were none better.

"So, who is this guy?"

"He's my flight instructor," McBride responded.

Long said, "You're kidding."

When a few days later, Long caught his first look at Frank Hatfield, he turned to McBride with a dubious look, and said: "You really *are* kidding."

Chest out, shoulders back, all squared away, the haircut apparently unchanged since the day he asked for his first "regular boy's," Hatfield impressed Long as very much the stereotype of the kid next door. You could put him on a cereal box. Well built and classically handsome, with the cool, unstudied confidence that eluded men like Long, he introduced himself with a smile, speaking in an unhurried drawl the geographical source of which was difficult to nail down. He was wearing khaki chinos and a navy blue nylon windbreaker, and in service of some functional utility beyond Long's understanding he wore below the jacket both a sweater and a short-sleeved shirt. His handshake met the specifications of good adjustable locking pliers. Long's instinctive reaction to seeing him was: This is not going to do it.

It was a brisk December day, and McBride, by way of setting Long up to lay out the proposition, had booked him a flying lesson. But Long's characteristic impatience, coupled with his gut response to Hatfield, prompted him to forgo the charade.

"Let's just get right to it," he said.

McBride explained to Hatfield that he, McBride, would be going up also, and the three men climbed aboard a Cessna 172.

Frank Hatfield had taken up flying upon his discharge from the Army, using the GI Bill to cover his advanced training after picking up a private license. In the early 1970s, after bouncing around the country, Hatfield moved to Virginia, divorced and out of a job, and went to work as an instructor and charter pilot for a general aviation outfit in Richmond. He had about 2,500 hours when he was introduced to Long.

"Frank, do you know what I do for a living?" Long asked, once the plane was airborne.

Long was wearing a jacket, no tie, a French-cotton shirt of the collarless sort, seventy-five-dollar blue jeans, and smooth lizard-skin boots. The jacket was silk and he had paid more for his wristwatch than Hatfield had paid for his car.

"I think I have a pretty good idea," Hatfield said.

"Well, before I tell you" — it was not in Long's character not to presume that Hatfield gave a damn whether he told him — "I want to ask you something. Do you think you have the balls it would take to risk your life for a million dollars?"

"What do you have in mind?"

Long told him.

Hatfield smiled, and said, "I thought you'd never ask."

Long cast a glance behind him, eyeing McBride.

"What kind of airplane are you planning to use?" asked Hatfield.

Long said he was not sure, that he hoped to discuss it with the pilot, but knew he wanted a large cargo plane. Hatfield told Long he was type-rated to fly a DC-3.

"Where would I get something like that?" asked Long.

"Well, Will and I were looking at *Trade-A-Plane* . . ."

Long glanced at McBride again. The latter simply threw him a smile.

"I've been waiting for you to ask me to do this," said Hatfield, "since Will first told me about it."

Long said, "You want in?"

"I have some questions I want to ask first."

He wanted to know what Long was offering in the way of guarantees. He wanted to know what would happen if he got arrested, who would get him out of jail. Long, conceding that the questions were reasonable, assured Hatfield that the proposition on the table was not.

"First," he said, "there are no guarantees."

And, he continued, going to jail was in fact a very real possibility. Smuggling, conspiracy to smuggle, possession with intent to sell — on a first offense they were looking at maybe five to ten years. Hatfield, he warned, had better understand that up front. That was the deal he was buying into.

Hatfield wanted money placed in escrow to cover his legal fees.

Long said, "That's not gonna happen. I don't know," he concluded, shaking his head, "I'm not sure you have the balls for this."

Hatfield nodded, shrugged his shoulders, put the Cessna into a dive, and cut the airplane's engine. Nose down, in free fall, the aircraft plummeted.

"How do you feel now?" he asked, folding his arms, turning to study Long's face, his evaluation quietly clinical. "How are your balls?"

"In my mouth," Long, who admired the tactic, admitted.

Hatfield fired the engine, pulled the plane out of its dive, and without looking at Long, said he was in.

Long still had his doubts. And in the car, leaving the airport, he shared them with McBride.

"I'm worried about that guy," he said.

"What are you worried about?"

"Will he be there? Will he do it when the time comes?"

"He'll do it."

And that was just about everything Will McBride needed to say. To know McBride was to know why.

Will McBride, a native Virginian, grew up amid the peanut farms just west of the Great Dismal Swamp. Attending college in Richmond, he dropped out to play bass guitar in a series of rhythm & blues bands. He met Long, then a college student, at a party at which he was performing. Setting off to travel the country in 1971 with the pit crew of a racing team, McBride returned to Richmond at about the same time Long returned from New York, and the two remained casual acquaintances until JD Reed showed up in town.

McBride, by then, was running his own company, a small service agency in Richmond to which he had turned his talent for selling ideas, and one of two ambitious endeavors to which he had turned his entrepreneurial skills, the other being a small but thriving marijuana distributorship in town. He and Long had been doing business for a little over a year, and Long had come to know McBride as a guy who got the job done. McBride did not tolerate improficiency or a willingness on the part of anybody to yield to failure without a fight. McBride's confidence in Hatfield sealed it for Long — if McBride believed in the pilot, that was enough. Long was being asked to believe in McBride, which made things pretty simple.

Had Long asked Cherie, things would have been simpler still. Her opinion of McBride was uncomplicated. She adored him. In judging

Long's friends, Cherie took a narrow focus. It was a point of view she had refined working high school summers as a lifeguard, a role she later resumed out of necessity as Long's girlfriend, evaluating a large cast of reckless characters. And McBride measured up to the standard that mattered: He was trustworthy. Beyond that she admired his attitude. In the no-bullshit department he ranked in her opinion right up there with JD Reed. He would tell you when he was not going to go a step further.

McBride and Hatfield were in.

Allen Long, like other scammers, evinced an abiding faith in human corruptibility, and he discerned in Frank Hatfield the workingman's approach to crime. He believed that any red-blooded American male, when offered the chance to make close to a million dollars for doing thirty hours of work four times a year — for flying an airplane, for doing anything thirty hours straight — was going to say yes. In Long's estimation, jail as a deterrent carried very little weight. A criminal who really believed he would end up in jail would never break the law in the first place. Sure, in his mind the possibility existed, but until the cuffs were biting his wrists, until that door slammed shut, jail was just not a reality. At the outset of any criminal enterprise jail was no more than a hypothesis. And once the gig paid off, once a man got a taste of the money? In Allen Long's view of the world, it was all over, pal.

Hatfield's saying yes was the first move in getting air operations underway, and the last encouraging move for quite a while when it came to the airplane. The airplane itself was the problem, as airplanes always were. Airplanes, boats — the vehicles were always the problem, as Long would discover time and again. They were what kept you from doing the deals. And the Drug Enforcement Administration knew it. The DEA knew where to look for people looking to register an airplane for no immediately evident, practical purpose. The agency knew where to find people looking to establish an airline, or to buy any craft that could conceivably be put to the purpose of carrying cargo. They were the ones who had the ads in *Trade-A-Plane* saying "DC-3 For Sale."

Trade-A-Plane magazine, "the aviation marketplace," is a color tabloid published three times a month out of Crossville, Tennessee. Promoting itself as the "world's largest general aviation resource," the magazine is distributed in a hundred countries, and has been bringing together buyers and sellers of airplanes since 1937. In its pages, through contemporary display ads and an enormous classified ad section, those in the general aviation market can find virtually any type of new or used aircraft. The first place an aviator would look if he wished to buy a used airplane — the place Hatfield and McBride would have gone under any other circumstances — the magazine was the first place the DEA would look for someone wishing to do so. And consequently the last place someone in Long's position would go. Long's best bet in escaping the scrutiny of the government was to buy an unregistered airplane. The best way to do that was to buy the airplane in parts. And the best way to buy an airplane in parts was to go to Tucson, Arizona — to go to Davis-Monthan Air Force Base — and buy the airplane from the government.

At Davis-Monthan sit some 5,000 decommissioned planes, "retired military inventory," 80 percent of which can be returned to flyable condition. Most of the mothballed aircraft are maintained to be sold for parts, chiefly to those overseas governments in whose military arsenals the models are still in service. In 1975 the C-47 Skytrain was still in military service in the United States and in more than ninety other countries. Twenty-five years later, its civilian equivalent, the DC-3, would still be in commercial service with small airlines throughout the world. Unlike the fighter jets and other serious combat hardware in the government graveyard at Davis-Monthan, the C-47s were available for civilian purchase through airplane brokers around the country. Hatfield and McBride managed to find a broker in Long Beach, California, who specialized in locating and reassembling surplus aircraft, and who was willing to accept a contract to do so without asking too many questions.

The DC-3 would cost $110,000. On the contract the buyer was listed as ALL Air, Inc. (A.L.L. for Allen L. Long). The incorporation of ALL Air, which was necessary to the advancement of the smuggling enterprise, broadened the criminal conspiracy in the customary way; expanded it in the time-honored manner predictable in such cases. For no drug-smuggling conspiracy of any significance was complete without the participation of a member of the bar.

By the standards of the legal profession Buddy Blanchard was pretty young. Long put him in his mid-thirties. By any standard, Blanchard was a pretty slick individual, and in Virginia vernacular that made him "a smart old scoofer." A connoisseur of fine wine, food, and antiques, Blanchard, with a home and practice in Richmond, held fast to a position in the upper echelon of Virginia society and was highly regarded as one of the better lawyers in the state. Blanchard was six-feet-five-inches tall, and had a face like a gargoyle on the Cathedral of Notre Dame. His ears were big, his nose was long, and his lips looked like they had been laid on lovingly with a trowel. He was one of the more ill-favored men it had ever been Allen Long's pleasure to meet, and Long could not have been more pleased to meet him. He had been recommended to Long by a satisfied client, whose referral carried with it all the unrestrained faith and outspoken assurance that women bring to the sharing of their gynecologists. "He'll do anything for money," is how such lawyers come advertised.

Long presented Blanchard with an entirely hypothetical question on a matter of law. Suppose, he said, someone wanted to buy an airplane for some undefined illegal purpose. How would one go about backstopping the purchase to protect himself, Long asked.

"Hypothetically?"

"In theory," said Long.

"Strictly hypothetically," Blanchard said, "not that I would ever advise someone to do this . . ."

The someone in question, Blanchard said, would ascertain a fictitious address, say a vacant lot, get a Post Office box attached to that address, and use it as a mail drop for a party who existed in name only. One would then write a letter to an attorney in the name of that party, enclosing a $5,000 money order and a guarantee of available funds for the purchase of the aircraft. One would retain the attorney to establish a corporation, to act as business agent for that corporation, and acting in that capacity to purchase the aircraft in the name of the corporation for said party.

". . . should anyone want to do that," Blanchard concluded.

Neither Long nor Blanchard, of course, knew anyone who might want to do something like that. Pursuant to their conversation, however, Frank Hatfield flew out west, and using the address of an empty lot, opened a Post Office box in the name of a fictitious leasing company. Long typed a letter to Blanchard from the fictitious owner of the company, retaining the lawyer to incorporate ALL Air for the purpose of flying cargo throughout the Western Hemisphere. He enclosed a $5,000 cashier's check, and stated that upon receiving correspondence from Blanchard in care of the PO box he would arrange delivery of $110,000 for the purchase of a DC-3.

A few days later Long was back in Blanchard's office.

"Funny thing," Blanchard said. "You know that question you asked me the other day? I got a letter right here . . ."

Jake Myerson gave Long $110,000 in cash, which was placed in an escrow account opened by Blanchard to be paid out to the airplane broker in Long Beach. ALL Air, Inc., seeking to hire ferry pilots to supervise reassembly of a DC-3 and fly it from Long Beach to Richmond, placed a help-wanted ad in the Richmond classifieds. Two local pilots, looking for work, responded to the ad and were quickly hired.

Dispatched to Southern California, the pilots — Frank Hatfield and Will McBride — would not return to Richmond for some time. Getting the airplane up and running would drag on seemingly forever. But that was yet unknown to Long.

With the pilots taking the sun out west, he and Reed headed south.

Booking passage on Avianca Airlines, Long and Reed, poster boys for pot smoking in the land of the free, for the first time since hearing its name, for the first time since having located it like some dreamscape on the map of the world — for the first time since learning to spell it correctly — flew to the Republic of Colombia.

EL
DORADO

7 RED, WHITE, AND BLOND

Barranquilla, Colombia, some 1,600 nautical miles due south of Richmond, sits about ten miles upstream of the Caribbean on the west bank of the Magdalena River. An industrial city, fifty-eight miles southwest of Santa Marta, it is Colombia's principal port of entry from the north. Long and Reed arrived on a nonstop Avianca flight from Miami, and when they stepped out onto the airport tarmac, the heat hit them like a shovel. When they stepped inside the terminal, they were hit by knowing smiles from customs and immigration inspectors, whose experience had taught them that few gringos like Long and Reed traveled to Colombia for any reason other than the reason for which Long and Reed were there.

Of those Americans who did visit Colombia, fewer still lingered in Barranquilla — they remained no longer than the time required to catch a connecting flight. Barranquilla was that kind of place. As described in the travel literature, it was "a lively, happy city," and tourists, for whom it held "little interest," were quite happy to take that for granted. As far as the typical traveler was concerned, the city's 700,000 inhabitants could have it.

The two smugglers took a cab downtown and checked into the Del Prado, the city's only hotel of consequence. Everything that happened in Barranquilla happened at the Del Prado, every deal that went down went down there. As every gringo knew, you simply did not go any farther. The two checked into a poolside room, Reed turned on the air conditioner, and said, "I need something to smoke."

Long had arrived in Barranquilla with the typical Colombian connection, which was no connection to speak of. His friend Little Eddie knew a guy in New York who knew a guy in Miami who worked for Avianca named Felipe who had a cousin in Barranquilla. Or something like that. As often as not, the cousin, a cab driver whose name was Benito, could be found parked outside the Del Prado. (At one time or another throughout the day every cab driver in Barranquilla could be found parked outside the Del Prado.) After a couple of drinks at the hotel bar, Long and Reed stepped outside. Slammed once more by the punishing heat of the day, they walked the curb in front of the hotel, and found Benito at the wheel of one of several cabs stationed there, snoozing in the shade of a tree.

Long, introducing himself as an acquaintance of Benito's cousin Felipe in Miami, came right out and told Benito, a small, fast-talking fellow in his thirties, "I'm here to buy marijuana." Had Long not been hooked into Benito, he would have said pretty much the same thing to the driver of the first taxi he hailed. It was the natural place to shop.

Benito smiled, and as expected, assured Long: "I am the man."

U.S. currency went a long way in Colombia, and a hell of a long way in the dope market. The difference between a five-dollar and a ten-dollar buy was the difference between an ounce and two ounces of street-level marijuana. When Benito asked Long how much he wanted, Long figured what the hell, might as well get down to it.

"Yo quiero cinco mil libras," he said.

Long had picked up some Spanish in Mexico, and like many Americans who had spent time there, unable as they might be to converse fluently, he did know how to buy dope. Benito understood what he said — in the matter at hand Long's limited vocabulary presented no problem, and his grammar, syntax, and pronunciation bordered on excellent.

He wanted to buy 5,000 pounds.

With an audible intake of breath, Benito exclaimed, "I am the *man!*"

Long said, "Benito, my friend, I don't think you're the man. But I think you can help me find the man."

Both Long and Reed, in operating south of the Rio Grande, had learned what to look for in "the man." If you needed a runway, the man was someone, no questions asked, who could see that you had a runway. If you needed fuel, he could pick up the phone and within minutes get you a truckload — any of three grades of gasoline, kerosene if you were landing jets. The man was not a taxi driver. Nor was he a bartender, or your local dealer in the city. The man was a guy with clout. The typical profile of a guy like this was a man in his early to mid-fifties, maybe as old as sixty. He lived in a compound surrounded by servants. He owned a Mercedes or two, he had been to Miami, or at least he had been around. He traveled with a retinue of yes-men, lieutenants, and bodyguards, a variety of people whose job description was to do nothing but his bidding, much like the assortment of citizens and slaves who traversed the Forum behind Roman senators in the years of the Republic.

Benito was not the man. But of course, he knew the man — in Latin America everybody on the hustle knew a guy who knew a guy who knew a guy who knew the man. Everybody knew where to score dope.

"I know where to get it," Benito said.

"Yes," said Long, "you know where to get it, but I need to talk to the man who's got it."

Benito said, "I'll take you."

And so began the predictable climb up the chain of associations leading to a marijuana connection, each Colombian along the way assuring Long that he was "the man."

Through Barranquilla's crowded streets, the yellow taxi made its way to the outskirts of town, pulling into a neighborhood that was home to little prosperity and the dope dealer with whom Benito did business. About ten years younger than Benito, more on the slick side, more in the style typical of the nightclub trade, a Latin American street hustler in the Hollywood mode, he leaned through the window of Benito's cab, and told Long he was the man. He could get him all the marijuana he needed.

"Okay," said Long. "Tomorrow, I need to go see a three-thousand-foot runway, a thousand gallons of flight fuel, and five thousands pounds of pot."

"Oh, I can't do that," he said.

"Well, you're not the guy I'm looking for, then. But if you have some marijuana, I'll buy some for my friend."

Ten dollars bought Long all he needed for now. He and Reed returned to the hotel, and fired up a couple of joints. Long agreed with Reed that the pot was not especially good.

Doing big business with gringos was every gangster's Golden Fleece, everywhere south of the border. Neither monsters nor magicians would deter the serious small-time dealer in quest of that particular prize, and never would a simple "No, thank you." So it came as no surprise when the next morning Long answered a knock on the door, and standing there when he unlatched it were Benito and his dope-dealing friend. They had someone waiting outside, they said, whom they wanted the Americans to meet. Long and Reed made their way to the street, where they were introduced to a man named Moisés. Moisés was slender, with sleek, brown hair and an earnest, honest, ovoid face that came to a point like the face of a flying squirrel. Moisés was a taxi dispatcher, and looked to be in his early thirties. He said, "I am the man you are looking for." He knew someone who could show Long the things he wanted to see, but meeting this person, Moisés confided, meant going to Santa Marta.

Well, thought Long, if only mildly encouraged, that would be the right direction.

Moisés had to work that day, but that night, as soon as he finished work, all five men — he, his friends, Long and Reed, the last two carrying their luggage — squeezed themselves into the dispatcher's cab, a tiny yellow Fiat, and sped up the coast to Santa Marta. They hit several government checkpoints on the way.

Highway 2 along the Caribbean coast was a bracelet of security checkpoints manned by soldiers and federal police. Part of an internal customs system designed to interdict traffic in contraband, including the time-honored domestic smuggling of merchandise like whiskey and cigarettes, such checkpoints were a fixture of Third World life, providing a federally sanctioned form of local extortion. In Colombia, a country in which violent civil insurgency was rooted as deeply as coffee and homicide enjoyed popular endorsement as a form of political expression, such installations served the government further as a means of gun control, keeping weapons from the interior. And they took on added significance when it came to the traffic in dope. East of Santa Marta armed guerrillas of Colombia's assorted leftist insurgencies improvised numerous checkpoints of their own, stepping out onto the highway to shake down people in transit. Between Santa Marta and Riohacha a motorist might hit as many as twenty.

At each government checkpoint the taxi was stopped, and once the gringos were spotted all five men were ordered out of the car and they and the taxi were searched. At nine P.M. the smugglers reached Santa Marta. Long and Reed checked into the Irotama, a first-class hotel just north of the airport. Moisés told the Americans to wait, and he and his friends disappeared. An hour later two strangers appeared.

The older of the two men was a few years older than Long and a good eight inches shorter. He was lean and balding, wore gold, wire-rimmed spectacles, and was dressed the way Americans of Long's generation had dressed in high school. He wore a white cotton shirt with a button-down collar, casual slacks, and dress shoes. He was introduced as Dr. Cepeda. A manifestly emotional, high-strung man, clearly working to suppress his intensity, Dr. Cepeda vibrated beneath the casual clothes with the undifferentiated energy of a Chihuahua, which worked to exaggerate the physical contrast between him and the man introduced as his associate. The latter's name was Miguel. He was all poise and self-possession. He was even-tempered, tall and plump, a credible human analog of the North American harbor seal, his body on a longitudinal plane perfectly elliptic. He had a broad, tranquil, good-humored face and skin the color of honey, unlike his friend the doctor, who had no Indian blood in his background. Miguel spoke English well. He explained that he was a medical student and was present to serve as a translator for Dr. Cepeda, who did not.

"My name is Pablo Cepeda," Miguel said, as the doctor spoke, "and I am the man you are looking for. I can do whatever you want. It is my business to sell what you want. This is my associate, he is helping me."

Long said he was expecting an older man.

Miguel, translating, said, "Dr. Cepeda wants you to know that he is the man for you to do business with. He says he has what you need."

What Long needed had been outlined for him by Reed, who had worked with DC-3s in the past, and Hatfield, who adding to what Reed knew, had schooled Long in the specifics of the particular aircraft they would be using. The standard DC-3, which carried 800 gallons of fuel, had a range of a little more than a thousand miles. The airplane being assembled in Long Beach had auxiliary tanks in the wings, each with a capacity of 400 gallons, effectively doubling its range. More than a thousand gallons of fuel would be needed to fill the tanks when the airplane reached Colombia. The flight fuel Long was looking for, Hatfield told him, was green. It was gasoline, not kerosene. The latter, with a lower octane rating, was used as jet fuel; it was colorless. The extra fuel carried in the wing tanks — amounting to some two and a half tons if the tanks were filled to capacity — reduced the plane's military-maximum payload to about 5,000 pounds on a decent runway. Hatfield would need a half a mile of hard-packed earth to take off. There were other things to look into — did the Colombians have ground-to-air radios, for example — but Long would look into them later.

"What I need," Long responded, "is to see five thousand pounds of the very best marijuana."

"*Mercancía.*"

"Merchandise. Yes. The best."

Miguel communicated this to the doctor, who answered in the affirmative.

"Dr. Cepeda says to you, if you want him to show you the merchandise, he can show you the merchandise," said Miguel.

"I need to see a runway."

"*La pista?*" Miguel said, consulting his associate.

"*Sí,*" replied Dr. Cepeda.

"Dr. Cepeda says you can see a runway."

"Flight fuel," Long continued. "I need to see eleven hundred gallons of high-octane gasoline."

"*Gasolina,*" replied Cepeda. "*Sí. También.*"

"That Dr. Cepeda can show you also."

"And I need to speak to the man."

When the latter remark was translated for him, the good doctor exploded. The accumulating energy with which he had been oscillating finally achieved critical mass. Clearly outraged that his credibility was in question, he sputtered unintelligibly, as if he were possessed by a demon, frantically waving his arms to punctuate his remarks.

Miguel just nodded in reply.

"Dr. Cepeda says he is the man. He tells you, do not ask that question anymore. Dr. Cepeda says that tonight he will bring you something. If you like that, he will show you much more tomorrow, when he takes you to see the runway."

Reed did not say a word.

Dr. Cepeda, Miguel explained, wanted to know if Long had brought money.

"No," said Long, "but once you show me that you have what you say, I will come back and bring you the money."

It's not a setup, they're not cops, it doesn't feel that way . . .

Yet, still, as he found himself thinking this, Long could not help wondering whether these two Colombians were for real. Were these the people he was looking for? Are these the guys? he asked himself. Could this demoniacal doctor really be the man?

An hour after the two men departed, Dr. Cepeda returned, handed the Americans a folded newspaper, and said he would see them in the morning. Wrapped in the folds of the newspaper was a half-pound of Santa Marta Gold.

Santa Marta Gold, a product that ranges in hue from a deep, varnished oak to a pale, buff manila, owes the lightness of its leaf color to the nitrate content of the soil in certain stretches of Colombia's coastal mountains. Described accurately as blond, *rubia,* or *mona,* and identified by some Colombians as *la rubia de la costa,* "the blond from the coast," it was known to connoisseurs like Long not only for its color but its unmistakable aroma: pungent, spicy, a single note. There was nothing that smelled quite like it.

It was doubtful that Dr. Cepeda and his associate, nonsmokers as were most middle-class Colombians, instinctively appreciated the unique quality of the pot the doctor had provided. The Indians who had given it to them probably said: "This is what the Americans like." The storied gold of Santa Marta, the legendary blond — Long had seen it before, but never anything so fresh. The pot had just been cured. Reed took one look at the stuff and said: "Allen, these are the guys."

Rolling a couple of joints, the two smugglers strolled down to the beach.

It was a clear, cloud-free Caribbean night, the kind of night on which rank amateurs were inclined miraculously to fathom the mysteries of celestial navigation. The air was cool, the heavens were clear, the ambient starlight was uncontaminated. It was a night that summoned images of snipers and Phoenicians. They sat on a log that had washed ashore, and there in the darkness they smoked. They fired up the dope — "delicate, flavorful, and smooth-smoking," in the description of the experienced pot smoker, unequaled when it came to inspiring mirth — and soon the marijuana had them laughing, philosophizing, and carrying on. Long, doing nothing more than looking at Reed, who sat there scouring the coastline as if he held a lease on the place, became dangerously entangled in the throes of his own merriment. His glee ran out of control. Eyelids fluttering, mouth stretching across the occlusion of cheerfully buzzing teeth, he snorted paroxysmally, laughing without benefit of his vocal cords, his outburst entirely sibilant, his facial musculature drooping like the jowls of a Virginia bloodhound, his grin so idiotic it was sublime.

"I got stoned that time," he said.

Reed was studying the joint in his hand, twirling it between his fingers, as if searching for a set of instructions. A man who embraced the cannabis plant as the gift of a benevolent God, JD Reed viewed every leaf as if it had his name on it.

"I can go anywhere in the world, and I'll find a connection," he said. "They'll come to me. I don't care where it is. I can go anywhere, and get the best deal."

They had been in Colombia not even thirty-six hours. And what they had was what everyone wanted. Everyone wanted Colombian Gold, and very few people could get it. There on a beach in Santa Marta, they howled at a starlit sky, convulsed with belly laughter, Allen Long and JD Reed high on grade-A dope and on the consequences of their score.

To Long the prospects were thrilling.

"If these people have access to thousands of pounds of pot like this? And we pull this thing off? Man, we're going to be rich," he said.

And at least within a small circle of American renegades, more.

"We're going to be heroes."

As expected, the Americans never saw Moisés, the taxi dispatcher, or his two friends, again. They were gone, cut out of the picture. They had been paid off and told to go home.

The next morning Miguel appeared at the hotel with discouraging news.

"I'm sorry, sir," he said to Long, "Dr. Cepeda wishes me to tell you that he cannot take you today. The army is patrolling in the area, searching for the *guerrilleros,* and traveling will not be possible."

Reed spent most of the rest of the day burning Santa Marta Gold. Long went for a run on the beach. Wearing emerald green nylon, split-sided jogging shorts — as goofy an outfit on any hombre as the locals were likely to see — he hit the beach in front of the hotel and ran toward Rodadero, sun-worshiping central in Santa Marta, by far the most popular beach resort in Colombia. Approaching along the waterline, he was brought up short by the presence of a group of teenage girls gathered at the edge of the surf. One in particular captured his attention, striking him in such a way as to throw him awkwardly off-stride. A Colombian, not yet twenty, with dark hair, green eyes, and almost nothing in the way of a bathing suit, she caught sight of him and smiled. She whispered something to her girlfriends, who checked Long out and giggled. Long smiled back, recovered his stride, and ran on without its ever occurring to him that they might be making fun of his outfit.

"Man," he told Reed, when he returned to the hotel, "I saw the most beautiful girl in the world today. And I think she liked me."

"Far out, man. Here, have a hit."

So much for love in the time of gold.

The following morning Long and Reed set off along the coast with Dr. Cepeda and his young associate in the doctor's Toyota Land Cruiser. Their destination, the village of Camarones, lay ninety-three miles to the east. Fifty miles into the journey they hit the Río Palomino. A large billboard greeted them there. It carried a U.S. State Department advisory notifying American citizens that the area beyond the river was considered extremely dangerous. U.S. passport holders were not prohibited from entering the badlands, the billboard merely served to warn them that once they crossed the river they were on their own.

Crossing the Río Palomino, the smugglers entered the Guajira.

Dr. Cepeda raised an imaginary pistol. "Boom, boom, boom," he said, turning to smile at the gringos. "La Guajira. It is . . . ruled . . . by the gun!"

At Camarones they left the paved surface of the highway, and followed a dirt track into the village. There they abandoned the Toyota. Joined by several more Colombians, all of whom carried handguns, they climbed aboard a pickup truck driven by a man introduced as Ernesto, who seemed to be in charge. Appearing to be about forty years old, wearing a straw cattleman's hat and stockyard boots, Ernesto would say little that day, and when he did speak, would speak only to the medical student, who translated for the Americans.

The truck, following near-invisible dirt tracks and bouncing through arroyos, penetrated the backland on a journey of a type with which Long would become familiar, a bone-jarring ride over washboard trails at speeds generally reserved for highway travel. Colombians, he would learn, did not slow down simply because the road ended. In the future, as now, whenever Long infiltrated such terrain, he would do so as part of a crowd. There would always be about fifteen guys, invariably armed, tagging along for the ride, none of whom spoke English. He did not know what to expect of them. Fifteen weapons, fifteen strange, indecipherable smiles — he did not know which way these characters were going to jump. Eventually he would come to understand that they were there to protect him.

After twenty-five minutes the truck came to a stop, the smugglers bailed out, and the expedition proceeded on foot. They were deep in the brush now, and every quarter of a mile or so an armed Indian wearing nothing more than a loincloth — "a guy in his underwear with a .45 pistol," as Reed later described it to the pilots — popped up out of the scrub, smiled, and dropped back down. About a mile in they came to what could loosely be called a clearing. There, under military tarp and camouflage netting suspended from trees, stacked ten feet high and twenty feet square, stood about 30,000 pounds of marijuana.

This was a classic Colombian *caleta*.

The word *caleta*, literally a hole, or hiding place, could be applied to a stash of any kind, including certain large caches of money, and was used to describe those mobile camps or staging areas where large supplies of marijuana were held in preparation for shipment.

As Long and Reed entered the *caleta* from one end, a burro train, kicking up dust, was entering from the other. The burros were slung, about seventy pounds on either side, with farm sacks containing loose marijuana, cured in the mountains and ready for market. On the edge of the clearing, mounted on sawhorses, stood large, square, steel mesh screens in wooden braces, and onto these screens the sacks were emptied. Two workers shook the screens until loose seeds, small stems, powder, and dirt fell through. Removing the larger sticks by hand, they then dumped the culled pot onto a canvas tarp spread over a table. From the canvas, the pot was scooped into a burlap bag that hung from the hook of a farm scale. In measured loads the pot was poured from the bag onto the bed of a screw-driven baling press, where it was compacted into rectangular bundles before being wrapped.

The smell of the place was overwhelming.

"This is it, Allen. These are the guys. Give 'em the money."

Reed spoke as if he had been there before, if only in his dreams.

"These are the guys," Long said.

Back in the truck, bouncing down more, barely discernible trails, the smugglers traveled to a tapering neck of shoreline that hooked out into the Caribbean like the acuminate beak of a parakeet, a topographical congruity from which the place took its name: Perico. The truck pulled into a clearing, and everyone aboard jumped out. Long hiked up his jeans, stretched his legs, and, brushing dust from his hair, stood waiting for whatever came next. Reed directed his attention to the tracks in the dirt at their feet.

Long looked up, incredulous.

"This is it?" he said.

The soil ran rough with tread marks.

"This is the strip? They're landing airplanes here?"

As fossil evidence the traces were incontrovertible: the unmistakable tracks put down by aircraft rolling in. The tires that had left the largest tread impression were easily as large as those of Reed's DC-3.

Walking the strip from the touchdown point, just above the tideline, and following it to the trees, Long paced it off. He estimated the length of the runway at about 1,800 feet, substantially shorter than Hatfield had told him was necessary.

Reed said, "It'll do."

Miguel, taking his lead from Dr. Cepeda, assured Long that large aircraft of every kind had safely landed on and lifted off the strip.

"Come with me," he said.

He led Long and Reed into the brush. There, under a tarp, in 55-gallon drums, were more than a thousand gallons of flight fuel. The fuel was green — gasoline, not kerosene — and as determined by

Reed, who checked it for rust and found none, it was fresh and uncontaminated by water.

Long found himself thinking, okay, now I'm impressed.

Everyone boarded the pickup, and Ernesto pushed through the sandy backcountry to a tiny fishing village on the coast just north of Perico. There, Long and Reed, parched, overheated, and covered with dust, were ushered into a one-room adobe, the door and windows of which were nothing more than openings in the brickwork. They were followed through the doorway by Dr. Cepeda, Miguel, and Ernesto and as many of Ernesto's subordinates as could fit, no doubt in descending order of authority. Children from the village gathered and hung on the sills, leaning in from outside the windows, remarking on the presence of the gringos. Apart from a few stools and a couple of crates upon which the men took seats, the interior was empty of furniture but for a pale blue, propane-fired Kelvinator refrigerator. Opening the refrigerator door, Ernesto asked the medical student to ask if the gringos would like drinks. Long and Reed saw that the refrigerator was filled with nothing but cans of Heineken beer. They exchanged glances, said yes with no hesitation, and one more time it crossed the minds, if not the lips, of the two Americans: "These are the guys."

Convinced that others before them had been entertained here, Long and Reed were nonetheless curious. Plainly, this was more than a pit stop. It was apparent that the Colombians were waiting for something. Before the second can of beer, Miguel cleared up the matter.

"You are satisfied with what you have seen, sir?" he asked.

Long said yes, he was.

Miguel nodded his head, conveying reciprocal satisfaction on the part of Dr. Cepeda. Taking his lead from the doctor, he said: "Now, you will meet the man."

A smile commenced its journey across the surface of Long's face, lighting it up like morning sunshine bleeding across a blanket with the opening of a bedroom blind.

Don Julio was maybe sixty years old. He had a full head of white hair and a heart condition. He was overweight by about thirty pounds, carried in a paunch appropriate to his stature, and he fit Long's preconception of "the man" perfectly.

He arrived in a cloud of dust at the wheel of a new Ford Ranger. Bouncing around in the bed of the pickup were two armed men on his payroll, and riding with him up front in the cab were two eighteen-year-old prostitutes. The young women remained outside, and his two henchmen followed him into the hut.

He wore blue jeans and a new pair of ostrich-skin boots. The brim of a tall white Stetson shaded his weathered face from the sun, and holstered to his gunbelt were two pearl-handled six-shooters. Every Colombian present stood and offered Don Julio his seat. Selecting a packing crate opposite Long, he sat, removed his hat, ran a hand through his hair, popped a nitroglycerin pill, and smiled.

"So, you are Allen," he said. He unholstered one of the revolvers, and placed it on his knee. "I am Don Julio."

Long nodded his deference.

"You have seen the runway?"

"Yes."

"The merchandise, the marimba. You are happy?" Don Julio asked.

"Yes. I am very happy."

Marimba, a slang reference to marijuana, was in common use among Colombian traffickers, but never really caught on with Americans. It was taken from the name of the resonating xylophone popular with Caribbean musicians — its etymology unclear to Long — and those who played the marijuana game, like those who played the instrument, were known as *marimberos*. As a veiled reference to pot, like the Spanish words for merchandise and material, the expression was abandoned by Long and his Colombian associates, along with other formalities, as soon as trust was established. They just called it marijuana and left it at that.

"I am glad you are such a happy man. Now I will tell you," Don Julio said, "about another happy man who came here."

With Miguel translating, Don Julio proceeded to tell Long the story of another American who had recently visited the village. The

American had looked very much like Long, and had asked to see all the same things.

"He asked to see the *mercancía,* the strip, the gas . . ."

Don Julio threw up his arms, and with genuine laughter explained to Long that they had shown the American these things only to discover that he was a policeman, and had come there intending to arrrest them. The other Colombians nodded as one, and laughed with Don Julio at the memory. It was very sad, Don Julio declared, shaking his head, smiling at the folly of it all. At any rate, he continued, it had been necessary to kill him. Here Don Julio raised his eyes, and looked directly into Long's.

"You look like a nice man, Allen," he said. "I hope we do not have to kill you."

Long granted Don Julio the concession he sought: an acknowledgment of his understanding that he was now in very deep. Staring into the wise and matter-of-fact gaze of the old man, he said: "I am not a policeman, I am a *contrabandista.*"

Don Julio jumped to his feet and smiled.

"*Bueno!* I am glad," he said, explaining that he would greatly lament the need to cut off Long's head.

Don Julio holstered the revolver, shook Long's hand, and left. He disappeared in the pickup with his henchmen and his whores, and Long never saw him again.

The deal Long struck with the Colombians represented something of a first on the Guajira. He wanted nothing but Santa Marta Gold, he said, and made it clear that he was willing to pay for it. And he wanted to pay the Colombians enough per pound to guarantee its availability on subsequent trips. The difference in price made little difference to him — what were a few dollars more, he figured, if he were going to sell the product with a 650 percent markup. Ernesto told him that the marijuana he wanted grew only in select parts of the Sierra Nevada, and further, that the region produced only a limited amount every year.

"But I will get it all," promised Ernesto, when the deal was finally struck.

Long would pay the Colombians $50 a pound for the pot, a total of $250,000 for a first load of 5,000 pounds. He would accept a few bales of *punta roja,* if the Colombians ran short on weight. He would pay the Colombians in three installments. He would return immediately with the first installment, a $60,000 down payment. That would be sufficient to cover the cost of holding the load.

(The Colombians would be paying the farmers between $10 and $12 a pound for the pot. And the farmers had to be paid. The difference between the $12 the Colombians paid for the merchandise and the $50 for which they sold it covered, in addition to profit, such things as security, the cost of the airstrip, and the price of fuel. The budget line for security included bribes paid to police and military officials. A fee of, say, $10,000 might buy a four-day window in which to operate; delays, typically due to weather, and more commonly associated with the arrival of boats, could therefore be costly.)

The Americans would deliver another $65,000 when the airplane arrived in Colombia, bringing the total paid out before distribution to $125,000, or one half the value of the deal. The other half would be paid to the Colombians, in a third installment, after the pot was sold. That money would be delivered within a couple of weeks of the load's arrival in Ann Arbor, optimally on a second flight down, along with a $125,000 down payment for a second load. And so on.

Santa Marta's newest hotel was Puerto Galeón. Situated on a private beach about five minutes from the airport, the resort was celebrated for its first-class suites and conspicuous for its restaurant, which was housed aboard the replica of a sixteenth-century Spanish galleon. Adjoining the ship was a casino, and that night before he left for the States, Long hit the blackjack tables, accompanied by Miguel.

Reed remained at the Irotama, kicking back with a stash of dope, having suffered his share of gambling joints as a resident of Las Vegas.

It was in the nightclub attached to the casino at Puerto Galeón that Long's Caribbean expedition was temporarily blown off course, driven from the predictable sea of a Herman Melville novel and fetching up on the uncharted shoals of something by the Brontë sisters.

On the patio outside the club Long was struck by the sight of a young woman in white. She was tall, about five-feet-nine, with bright eyes, full lips, and hair the color of mahogany. She was becoming in a way that was almost electrifying, and it was clear as she stood there in the darkness, surrounded by friends both male and female, that she had long since arrived at a level of comfort with the fact that others were naturally drawn to her. Radiating sophistication and at the same time an angelic innocence, she held special appeal for someone like Long. Here in a vessel of physical beauty was the promise of that treasured attribute so highly prized by American men, the attribute they find so alluring in the plainest of Latin American women, so elusive in women at home: subservience.

Like Saint Paul on the road to Damascus, Long was blind to everything but her light. Unable to take his eyes off her, he inevitably drew her attention his way, and reading in her glance what he took for an invitation, he made a pointedly casual approach, coming on to her with a pickup line that was as unimaginative as it was disingenuous.

"Do I know you?" he asked.

Not until she smiled at him did he realize that the answer was yes.

And she remembered him. She had seen him the day before. He was the gringo running along the beach, she said, in the "sexy" green *pantalonitas.*

They danced the night away.

Her name was María, she was nineteen years old, and according to Miguel, everyone in Santa Marta knew her as "a flower ready to be picked."

"Be very careful with María," he said.

In one way it was a little bit late for that. The young woman had stolen Long's heart.

"Qué sueñes con los angelitos," she whispered, when she and Long said good night, "May you sleep with the little angels." She addressed him as *lindo,* pretty boy, invited him to give her a call, then lightly touching his face with her fingers, she left.

With or without the angels, he would be unable to sleep that night.

Miguel, a true romantic, could not have been happier for his new friend. But he told him again to be careful. And then he told him why.

"She is the niece of Raúl Gaviria," he said.

The name was unfamiliar to Long, but it would not remain that way. Raúl Gaviria was one of the more famous smugglers on the Guajira. He moved his loads by boat, shipping tons of commercial Colombian out of Bahía Profundo. He would make headlines in Miami three years later as part of a smuggling ring whose flamboyant U.S. component styled itself the Black Tuna gang. His brother would figure prominently in a U.S. magazine feature in 1978, exercising his power to close down the Santa Marta airport, mobilizing the local military to land and load large smuggling aircraft at night.

Long, quite prepared to be careful, looked forward to his next trip to Colombia.

On the Guajira, Pablo Cepeda had asked how soon the Americans would return with the airplane. Long replied through Miguel.

"Tell the doctor I will call next week, and arrange with him to deliver the money. After that, the airplane will come. We have done it this way many times. And he has done it, too. Tell him the airplane is ready."

"I don't care what it takes! You have to get down there and see to it! I want you down there now!"

Long, standing at a pay phone in Richmond, Virginia, had reached out to touch Will McBride, who was encamped in a hotel room for which Long was paying in Marina Del Rey, California. And the news that Long received was not the news he had called to hear — the DC-3, for which the Colombians were waiting, was currently lying in pieces on the floor of a hangar in Long Beach.

A delay at this point in getting the operation airborne could blow the entire deal, and Long believed that given that prospect, McBride and Hatfield, assigned to move the job along, were having too much fun. Long envisioned their lounging poolside, fishing for flight attendants, a large, transient population of which bathed the city of Marina Del Rey in its singular brand of cultural sunshine. Long wanted his pilots off the party circuit and on the scene in Long Beach, where he expected them to make life as miserable for the airplane broker as Long was prepared to make theirs in the face of any further delay.

McBride and Hatfield assured Long that assembly of the airplane was on schedule. Promising that it would be in Richmond, ready to go, in a month, they departed for Long Beach to pressure the broker, and Long, in Virginia, turned his attention to putting together a ground crew.

There are over 10,000 airports, from large metropolitan airfields to small grass strips, within the borders of the United States. All of them are listed, detailed, and diagrammed in the *Jeppesen Airport and Information Directory* — from O'Hare International in Chicago to all the triangle strips, most of them county airports, built as part of the nation's civil defense at the time of the Second World War. Hatfield and McBride, to make the pickup in Colombia, could take off from almost anywhere. (They chose Fayetteville, North Carolina.) Where to land the load upon their return was a decision that required some research. Using the *J-AID*, they selected a municipal airport at West Point, King William County, Virginia, about thirty-five miles east of Richmond. McBride spent a couple of nights observing the field, and saw that nothing happened there after dark. He and Hatfield would be bringing the plane in under a full moon at midnight, when the airport was deserted.

On the night of the flight Long would be on the beach in Colombia manning a ground-to-air radio. He could not leave communications to chance. Everything depended on the use of codes and the fallback to special frequencies; any confusion caused by the language barrier, and the entire operation could go sour. From the beach he would be in contact with Reed, who would be aboard the DC-3, the one man aboard the airplane who knew the exact location of the strip. Reed would have been the logical choice to serve as chief of the off-loading crew at West Point. With him in the air and unavailable, however, the open position had to be filled.

Orchestrating routine ground operations — the off-load, conducted by cover of darkness, as the airplane came in heavy from

Colombia — eventually, and somehow inexplicably, took on the proportions of staging a grand opera. To run the job, Long came up with a guy named Hathaway, who owned a storage facility in Virginia. Long had used him in the past, paying him a dollar a pound to warehouse pot that came in from Nevada. Long admired his organizational skills and deliberative turn of mind, but not even Long was prepared for the professionalism that Hathaway eventually brought to the task.

Hathaway actually prepared and issued a ground operations manual. The ring-bound booklet was indexed with tab dividers in three colors. Instructions and contingencies were covered under separate headings for each phase of the operation: "Pre-Flight," "Off-Load," and "Post-Delivery," respectively. The booklet provided maps showing how to get into the area, how to get out, what lay to the east, what lay to the west, where to find a gas station, and the location of the nearest pay phone. It stipulated what to wear, what not to wear, and when to be there wearing (or not wearing) it. It contained instructions on how to proceed in the event of a breakdown, and detailed various ways to exit the area in the event of a bust. It included a checklist.

In addition to Hathaway, the pickup team would consist of three men recruited out of Virginia by Long and two of Reed's men from Las Vegas. There would be six men, two trucks, and a car. They would use a fourteen-foot U-Haul, a pickup with a snap-top camper over the back, and a sedan. The U-Haul would accommodate the entire load, but Long had made the decision to throw the first 1,000 pounds into a pickup, enabling him to get a half-ton off the scene while the larger truck was being loaded. In the event of a bust, he figured, he would have a thousand pounds on the road. The sedan would be used as a scout car. Hathaway allowed twelve hours for the drive from West Point to Ann Arbor.

"Hey, buddy, can I give you a hand?"

Allen Long was walking the street, shopping for a pay phone in midtown Manhattan, when he ran across a comedian. The guy was in his forties, well dressed and drunk. He was standing in front of a church with a credit card in his hand.

"Says 'Jesus Saves,'" the guy told Long. "I thought it was a bank." Stepping back several feet to take in the building's architecture, he reached into his pocket for a handkerchief, wiped his nose, and said he should have known. "Bank doesn't have that kind of money."

Long wished him luck before moving on and told him to go easy on the blow.

Long had arrived in the city that morning and was leaving the following day, but not before suffering a certain nostalgia for the kinds of things a man runs into only on the streets of New York.

The phone booth on Lexington Avenue had been decorated to rival a subway car, its translucent panels rendered festively opaque. Aerosol spray paint in primary colors had been applied to give it the visual flavor of something as funky as the No. 4 train — brushed aluminum and corrugated steel, sealed windows of newly stained glass, rolling into the gray air beneath Grand Central like a floral bouquet from Latin America. Long loaded the phone with quarters, and called Myerson in Ann Arbor.

"Hey," he said, "let's talk."

"Where are you calling from?" said Myerson.

"I'm at my mother's house."

"Where's that?"

"Let me spell it."

"Go."

"T-O-T-E-C-E-O-F-O-F."

"I'll call you back."

Allen Long, like everyone who violated the conspiracy statutes at a professional level, adhered to a security protocol governing the use of the telephone. Communication was conducted over public phones, never private lines.

Call it the American way.

Authorities in various other parts of the world seldom concern themselves with evidence, circumstantial or direct. They lock you up or waste you in accordance with the prevailing folk wisdom, maybe the direction of the wind. The American system of justice is more sinister. In the United States the government, in quaint deference to due process of law, subpoenas your telephone records, then cracks you for collusion, for conspiring to get away with what you easily have gotten away with, or simply intend to get away with. Outlaws, gangsters, racketeers, pirates, bandits, their respective lawyers, and desperadoes in general are by nature cloak-and-dagger freaks, and the domestic conspiracy laws impart a certain legitimacy to that aspect of their collective behavior which very often appears foolish to the weird minority of the population that can safely be called law-abiding.

Everybody has his communications procedure, and Long's was one he and Reed had developed over the course of their moving Mexican loads. Receiving a call at home, the conspirator would be given a code containing the number of the pay phone to which the call was to be returned, then go to a pay phone himself and return the call from there. Various codes had been established by Reed, and each consisted of a ten-letter word in which none of the letters was repeated, the letters corresponding in sequence to the ten telephone digits. The words presently in use were "cornbasket" and "motherfuck," and a caller would signal the code by saying something like, "I'm sending a cornbasket," or "Call me at my mother's house." (Using "cornbasket," where C is zero and T is nine, the area code for Manhattan, 212, would be given as R-O-R.) Later, the smugglers would add an alternate procedure, signaled by use of the word "Roger." If a phone number was given accompanied by any variation on the commonly used radio phrase — the expression "Roger that," for instance — one knew to transpose the number's area code and prefix.

Since leaving Barranquilla, Long had been on the phone to Colombia several times. He would call Miguel at home from a public booth in Virginia, telling the young medical student that he was sending a cornbasket. He would end the conversation with a series of letters corresponding to the number of a second public phone, where, at a specified time, Miguel, with Dr. Cepeda at his side, could reach him from a secure phone in Barranquilla.

A nighttime station-to-station call to Barranquilla from the United States cost $9.75. Long would always resist explaining this to the overseas operator who was handling the call, patiently allowing the operator to look up the charges.

Long's side of the subsequent exchange generally went something like this: "No, ma'am, it's not a credit card call . . . I see, well I have some change here, let me look . . . Why, yes, I just happen to have it . . ."

Long, holding a roll of quarters, would then interrupt the operator's calculations.

"It's thirty-nine," he would say. "I'll start now."

By the time he started doing business in Colombia, Long had achieved a level of proficiency whereby he could fire thirty-nine quarters into a pay phone in approximately thirty seconds, and that included pausing three times, as the coins, maxing out the telephone's capacity, were collected in three-dollar increments. Long would continue to better his record, achieving a per-quarter personal best in good weather in 1978 on a call from New York to Caracas.

On those occasions when getting through to Colombia proved virtually impossible, which was often enough, owing to an antiquated phone system and a limited number of lines, Long would present himself to the overseas operator as a pediatric cardiologist, a volunteer with Save the Children. Fabricating a medical emergency and an unfortunate Colombian infant, he would ask that the call be expedited to his colleague in Barranquilla.

"How is the little girl," he would ask when put through to Miguel.

"She is stable, sir, but she must be transported to your country very soon. Do you know when this can happen?"

Alexander Graham Bell, patron saint of conspirators everywhere.

Over the course of numerous phone calls, a meeting was scheduled with the Colombians. Long would fly to Venezuela to hand over the $60,000 down payment. He would deliver the cash in Maracaibo, about a hundred miles southeast of Riohacha, the capital of Guajira department. At the meeting the smugglers would also work out details of the flight — the date and time of arrival, and any other contingencies that needed attention. In Maracaibo, Dr. Cepeda would be waiting to meet Long at the Del Lago hotel.

Standing on Lexington Avenue, taking his callback from Myerson, Long asked if Myerson had confirmed his flight.

"I'll meet you tomorrow," said Myerson.

"Pan American."

"JFK. I got it."

"Caracas."

"Yeah, Caracas. I'll see you tomorrow."

Long did not travel to Maracaibo alone. Jake Myerson, whose money was scheduled to change hands, went along for the ride. But it was more than the money that prompted his doing so. The trip represented Myerson's share in the adventure. Action, excitement, X-rated entertainment in exotic locales — getting out of the house and getting down with the boys was a large part of the attraction of being an outlaw. It was very much like golf in that way.

Long and Myerson, flying into Caracas on Pan American, hopped a domestic flight the following day from there to Maracaibo. They checked into the Del Lago hotel wearing aviator shades and dark business suits, each man carrying a briefcase containing $30,000 in cash.

It was a bright, beautiful, hot afternoon on the Gulf of Venezuela, and within minutes of their arrival the two Americans were hopelessly stoned on the dope they had brought along with them. Myerson's observable universe, a motion picture projected in Technicolor at an equable twenty-four frames per second, had commenced to reveal itself to him intermittently, like a 35 millimeter slide presentation: (snap) . . . (snap) . . . (snap). It was a psychedelic entertainment Myerson was condemned to enjoy in the privacy of his own head. Long was slipping slowly into something like stage-three anesthesia. His voluntary muscles had seized almost entirely, and in another few minutes, if he did not consciously exercise it, he would lose the power of speech.

The two quickly changed into their bathing suits and headed poolside for some piña coladas. They navigated the beach chairs, convinced that they blended nicely with the tourists lounging there, each wearing nothing but a bathing suit, each of them having demonstrated the presence of mind — and the simultaneous absence of any connection to reality — to carry with him a large, black leather briefcase. Not until they were sufficiently drunk did they realize how stoned they were, and not until the *federales* showed up did their condition, the nature of their mission, or their idiotic appearance engender in them any measure of paranoia.

The first military helicopter touched down about sixty feet away. The soldiers aboard hit the ground running, armed with automatic weapons, and quickly secured a perimeter within the boundaries of which the two Americans sat. The effect on the smugglers' cocktail hour was predictably dramatic — like some pleasant Atlantic crossing interrupted at that moment at which the stowaways run out of Dramamine.

Myerson's search for excitement seemed to be paying off. His face turned a cadaverous white, the blood supply to the tissue there suddenly draining away, abruptly reversing itself like a man accidentally swinging into an autopsy room.

A second Sikorsky touched down. The soldiers aboard were accompanied by personnel armed only with what appeared to be a red carpet. It was from the third and last helicopter that Venezuelan President Carlos Andrés Pérez emerged, stepping out onto the aforementioned carpet and following it and a plainclothes security detail into the hotel.

El Presidente was there to attend a meeting. The smugglers' briefcases, so conspicuously and laughably out of place, escaped examination. Andrés Pérez did manage, however, to send all American businessmen a message. Within a year he nationalized twenty-one oil companies, mostly U.S. subsidiaries.

Long would attend his meeting with the Colombians alone. Myerson's meeting them was not even discussed. Injection of a stranger into the transaction would serve to unnerve the Colombians, but that was only a part of it. Just as Myerson would never introduce Long to his buyers, neither would Long be expected to introduce Myerson to his suppliers. The dope business was no different from any other business that way. One's connections, whether sources or markets, were like intelligence assets in the business of espionage — one did not readily share them if one wanted to *stay* in business.

Long's phone rang at seven P.M.

"Hello, sir, this is Miguel."

The young medical student invited Long to his room. He was alone when Long arrived.

"Where's Dr. Cepeda?"

"Pablo could not be here," answered Miguel.

And now, suddenly, Long, who was carrying $60,000 in cash, was unnerved.

"Maybe you need to call him."

"That will not be necessary, sir."

"I have money for him, Miguel. I don't know if it's right to give it to you."

"It is all right."

"I need to talk to Dr. Cepeda."

"Sir, maybe I should tell you —"

"I think you should get Dr. Cepeda on the phone."

Miguel, assured that Long would not part with the money until he spoke to Cepeda, dialed up the excitable doctor in Santa Marta and put him on the phone with Long.

"*Sí! Sí!* Yes, it is okay," Dr. Cepeda finally told Long, after the two had waded through a blend of broken English and Spanish.

"Okay," Long said, and hung up the phone. But before handing Miguel the money, he pointedly asked the young medical student, "Do you want to explain this to me?"

"Yes, sir," said Miguel politely. "I should tell you, it is I, not Pablo, with whom you are doing business . . ."

Long did not have to hear what came next to know what was going on. But he did hear Miguel say it — and this time it was true.

". . . You see, Allen, *I* am the man."

8 PICKUP AT PERICO

Long's outburst of laughter was infectious. Miguel laughed along with him. Once Long got himself under control, Miguel told him a story.

Miguel was not a medical student. His degree was in engineering, a degree he had received in the United States. All Miguel's life Pablo Cepeda had been his friend. Pablo was indeed a doctor — a doctor of veterinary medicine. When Long and Reed were in Barranquilla, Pablo had received a call from his cousin Moisés the taxi dispatcher. Pablo had then come to Miguel, mentioned the Americans Moisés had found, and asked if he thought Miguel's father would agree to do business with them.

Miguel explained to Long that his father was a man of great importance on the coast. Miguel Sr., a native of Santa Marta, was the first man ever to send marijuana from Colombia to the United States; that is, the first ever to do so commercially. A legend on the Guajira, he had pioneered the growth of the industry there.

"And I am the one," Miguel said, "who knows Ernesto and Don Julio and all the people in the villages. I used to go always with my father when he was doing his business there, and now it is my business."

It had been a year, Miguel explained, since his father had started doing so much cocaine that he had become unable to function.

"He thinks only about women and his *pinga* now."

Long said he was familiar with the syndrome.

Long had been witness to a charade orchestrated for his benefit. The deception was Miguel's way of throwing off suspicion in the event that Long was not who he claimed to be. If Long and Reed were DEA, Miguel was not "the man." Impressed by Miguel's cleverness, Long would see him demonstrate it repeatedly over time. The young Colombian would prove to be an invaluable resource, he and his good friend Pablo — they were equal partners, and between them could get anything done that needed doing in Colombia.

Miguel and Long, in the months to follow, would talk a lot about Miguel's father, a man who personified the origin of what would one day become the most lucrative black market in criminal history. In the story of Miguel Sr. was the story of the creation of Colombia's narco-economy. It did not start with marijuana, and it did not start with cocaine, nor did it start with the emeralds for which Colombia was equally famous, the country's geographical borders delimiting a natural repository of 80 percent of the world's supply of the gem. In Colombia it started with coffee, and it came about by accident, not by design.

Some ninety miles off the coast of the Guajira lay the island of Aruba, a Dutch free port where Colombian coffee fetched a far higher price than the impoverished Colombian farmer could realize selling his crop to the national cartel, the Colombian Coffee Federation. Outlaws like Miguel's father made their living trafficking in contraband between Aruba and the South American coast, shipping coffee in one direction, moving black-market Scotch and American cigarettes in the other.

Of course, smuggling was not new to coastal Colombia. *Costeños* had been trafficking in black-market goods since the imposition of government there, since the moment there were trade restrictions to violate. Marijuana cultivation on a limited basis began in the 1930s. Cocaine had been around much longer. On a smaller scale than in Bolivia and Peru, indigenous Colombian Indians had been growing and chewing coca for 2,000 years. But neither marijuana nor cocaine in Colombia enjoyed a significant market outside the country until the mid-1960s, when citizens of the United States started getting high on dope on a regular basis.

When the 1960s rolled around, and a boat captain with whom he worked told him that American merchant sailors in Aruba were in the market for marijuana, Miguel's father moved his first pound of pot. As Miguel explained it to Long, it was soon thereafter that the first commercial shipment of Colombian marijuana left the country bound directly for the States. The load, five pounds of pot in a suitcase, was delivered in a skiff by Miguel's father; he raised it to the porthole of an American merchant vessel anchored in the harbor in Santa Marta as the freighter took on a load of coffee destined for New York. The seaman who took delivery was one of several who inevitably followed. Soon a boat arrived that was there to pick up neither coffee nor anything other than that which had been stashed in the suitcase. Miguel's father sent the boat back loaded with 500 pounds of weed. And the face of the Western Hemisphere changed.

As April approached, there was a lot of worry in Ann Arbor. It had been two weeks since Miguel had been paid and still the airplane was not ready. How strict would the Colombians be? How much longer would they wait? How long would they honor the agreement, Jake Myerson wanted to know. Long had told Miguel he would be ready in a couple of weeks, and now it looked as though he would be lucky to be ready in a couple of months.

"Don't worry, sir, your money is safe," Miguel said, when Long finally put in the call. "You can come in two weeks or four weeks, but two weeks would be better."

Three weeks after that call, some five weeks after the meeting in Maracaibo, Hatfield and McBride ferried the DC-3 to Richmond.

The final briefing took place in a motel room in northern Virginia about ten miles from CIA headquarters. While Hathaway handed out copies of his booklet, Long read aloud from a list he had prepared. It had been decided that public relations would be well served if the Americans landed in Colombia not only carrying the money they owed, but also bearing gifts. Loaded onto the plane with the $65,000 in cash, he announced, would be Levi jeans, Nik Nik brand polyester shirts, Adidas running shoes (in what seemed to Myerson to be sufficient supply to outfit the entire Indian population of the Guajira), four cases of Heineken, a case of Marlboros, and a gross of Swiss Army knives.

This variation on the American CARE package, which seemed like a good idea at the time, would set a regrettable precedent, leading to ever longer lists of requests on the part of its Colombian recipients. Subsequent flights would carry patent medicines, tape players, and Seiko wristwatches. On one flight down, Long carried a twenty-three-hundred-dollar gold Pulsar watch to be presented to the commander of the local military garrison. A later flight arrived in Colombia carrying a seventeen-foot inflatable Zodiac with a 70 horsepower Johnson outboard and a brace of pedigreed German shepherd puppies.

It was flights such as these and those of other smugglers that accounted for the proliferation on the Guajira of the Sony Trinitron as a status symbol — in homes that received no television signal and many of which enjoyed no electricity. Within three years of Long's arrival, one could visit the most humble adobe in the smallest of villages there, cut off from power and running water, and find the latest in high-end audio equipment stacked steep against a wall inside and a late-model four-by-four, its high-gloss paint reflecting the sunshine, parked on the hardscrabble outside. Within that time, impoverished local Indians would come to occupy dwellings assembled with parts salvaged from out-of-commission airplanes — a wing here, part of a fuselage there, a tail number over the door. (On a trip to Perico in 1979, an elder of the nearby village reintroduced Long to his DC-3, the nose cone, complete with windshield glass, serving as a makeshift solarium on his humble sheet metal home.) By then, with America's appetite for dope as well established as its appetite for coffee, Colombia would account for more than 70 percent of the marijuana reaching the United States from abroad, and between 30,000 and 50,000 farmers along the coast would have come to depend directly on its cultivation for their livelihood. Another 50,000 Colombians would make a living from it. Local food production would decline as tens of thousands of hectares were converted to marijuana farming, producing unprecedented prosperity and a degree of economic stability never before enjoyed on the Guajira.

"Bullshit!" said JD Reed.

Reed's legendary cool evaporated when he beheld the ground operations manual that Hathaway had prepared. Leafing through the printed matter as a citizen would a mug file, Reed grew red in the face.

"This is bullshit!" he said, slamming it down. "Lose this fucking thing!"

Reed's argument was persuasive. If the document fell into the wrong hands, police would be waiting for the plane when it landed. If the publication were to come to light later, even several years down the road, it would win a contest, hands down, for Exhibit A in a conspiracy prosecution. But more than that it was just bullshit.

"I've done this twenty times," Reed said, "and I've never had a book like this."

"This is professional," countered Long, holding the document aloft, extending his evaluation to apply to the operation in general.

Reed grabbed the booklet, and got to his feet. He looked Hathaway in the eye, scrutinizing him as he would a phone book, as if Hathaway were some manner of urban directory that wanted tearing in half.

"There's only one thing I want to know," he said. "I want to know are you gonna *be* there. I don't care if you have this book with you or not. You better fucking *be* there. That's what's important — you're *there*, man."

Reed, who on more than twenty occasions had met planeloads of pot from Mexico, had only one rule when it came to off-loading: Stay there until the plane shows up. Do not set a time. Too many things could go wrong. Just *be* there. You sit there until you hear something. It had once taken one of his pilots three days in Jalisco to fix a flat tire. Reed, with no means of communication, had just stayed where he was, waiting right there where he said he would be. The airplane showed up on the fourth day. He had once sat alone in the middle of the desert, he and five trucks, waiting for his DC-3. He sent everyone else on the crew home. The plane, scheduled to show up at midnight, arrived at three P.M. the following day carrying 5,000 pounds of pot. "No communications," he said, and he had managed to get the job done. "Just tell 'em what you're gonna do and stick with it. A basic warrior tactic." He had never lost a load.

"Be there, motherfucker," he said to Hathaway, and yielded the floor to Frank Hatfield.

Hatfield said, "We leave Fayetteville at five P.M., fat with fuel, we fly low over the Piedmont and head south until we hit Jacksonville. We enter the normal flow of air traffic, and bear about thirty degrees southeast making for the Bahamas. No lights, no radio contact, no radar transponder. At Great Inagua we turn south, which will take us over the Windward Passage, around Cuban airspace, and up over the Haitian mountains. The Maracaibo beacon will bring us in just east of Riohacha. We fly southwest from there, and follow the coast. JD will bring us into the airstrip. We arrive at eight in the morning, and we're about two hours on the ground. With the manpower they have down there, it'll take only about thirty minutes to load the plane, but we have to pump a lot of fuel, which is going to take a couple of hours using the equipment they've got. Coming back, our airspeed's cut. Over the Bahamas we fly low, we drop down to lose radar, maybe fifty feet off the water, then pick up an airway, joining the weekend traffic coming out of the islands into the States. We rendezvous at midnight. We kick out the load at West Point, take the plane and park it somewhere. Round-trip, we're looking at over thirty hours of work, nonstop."

He asked if there were questions. There were none. The briefing ended. Long and Reed worked out the radio codes and frequencies for the rendezvous at Perico. One week later, Long was in Colombia, and the DC-3 took off.

"Once you've been a smuggler, you know it's not Murphy's Law, it's Murphy's Law times ten. When you talk about contingencies, you don't know what you're talking about, until you've done a smuggling trip. Because not only anything that *can* go wrong *will* go wrong, things that *can't* go wrong will go wrong. If there ever was a true story about, 'How I was captured by aliens and forced to submit to torture,' it's the story of some smuggling pilot, who it really happened to. And nobody will ever believe him. And they took all the dope."

It was just after seven A.M. Allen Long was crouched in the morning light, hugging a low dune that sloped away from the Caribbean to the edge of what passed for a runway on the northeast coast of Colombia. And his heart was racing. With him, hidden in various places in the vicinity of the airstrip, were about twenty-five people — Miguel, Pablo, Ernesto, and others — a ragtag assemblage of personnel whose faces had filtered in and out of his consciousness over the preceding several weeks and whom he had come to view collectively as "the Colombians." Long was the only gringo on the scene and the only man not carrying a gun. Even the mild-mannered Miguel was strapped. He was armed with a .45.

In the bush, about twenty yards off the runway, hidden, stood a truck stacked with two and a half tons of high-grade Colombian weed. Delivery of the marijuana had been handled by the Colombians without any help from Long. Whether coffee going out or cigarettes coming in, it was something that had been done on this coast for a hundred years. It was what they knew how to do — being mustered at two o'clock in the morning, or noon, or eight at night, to jump in the truck or jump on the donkey and go off and do this stuff.

The Colombians, ready for anything, were in a sufficiently serious mood, and Long was in a condition that boiled down to barely repressed hysteria. Counter to his confident self-portrayal — the assurances he had given the Colombians that he knew what he was doing, that he had done it numerous times before, that he was a capable, experienced professional — the truth was that he really had no way of knowing whether the plane would ever make it. This was all new to him. He was ripe with anxiety over the possibility that his partners might not show up. He knew that they had *left*. He had called the States at midnight, and no one there had heard from them. The plane, he had to assume, had taken off on schedule.

All he had now by way of control over the flight was a hermetically sealed, hard-sided case about six inches deep, sixteen inches wide, and twenty-two inches tall. Crouched on the beach, he checked his watch, and releasing the clamps on either side of the case, removed its cover to expose the workings of a ground-to-air radio. Manufactured by Narco Avionics and purchased by Reed, the radio came recommended as the latest in high-end aviation equipment, engineered specifically for ground-to-air communications. Long tuned it in to monitor an air-to-air frequency.

Hatfield, once within range, would be transmitting on a frequency designated to carry air-to-air traffic. The smugglers did not want their voices picked up on a frequency that was used, by international standard, for transmissions between control towers and incoming craft: a pretty dead giveaway that a man on the ground was nursing an airplane into a strip. On the radio frequency the smugglers were using, they would be taken for a couple of pilots conversing cockpit-to-cockpit, like interstate truckers discussing highway conditions over their dashboard citizens band radios.

With the pilots coming down the coast, the first move was to burn a tire and bring them in with smoke. If still unable to locate the runway, the pilots would use the plane's direction finder to home in on a radio signal transmitted by Long. Popping on headphones, they would tune to his frequency, pick up the transmission — the simple repetition by Long of a monotonous syllable, *bah, bah, bah* — and the unit's receiver would bring them in on his position.

But none of that should be necessary. The pilots had the strip's coordinates, they had maps and charts, and more than that they had JD Reed aboard. Estimating a fifteen-hour flight, they had timed their takeoff to insure that they not arrive before daybreak, when they could pick up the runway visually. Whatever happened, Long's job now was simple: monitor the frequency to which the radio was tuned and await their first transmission.

An hour earlier, side by side, Long and the Colombians, all of them, had walked the dry, hard-packed clay of the runway, moving from one end to the other, clearing it of the burrs of a local thorn that flourished near the strip. The burr, about four inches in diameter and spiked in such a way as to resemble the head of a medieval mace, exhibited spines up to an inch and a half long, which could very easily puncture a tire.

It was just after seven A.M., and even at seven the air temperature on the coast of Colombia will make you think twice about building your dream house there. Long, in a knit, short-sleeved shirt, was dressed pretty much the same as the Colombians — some wore chinos, some wore jeans, as he did — the difference being that where he wore sneakers, they wore shoes or sandals. Some of the Indians were barefoot. The heat had not yet reached the point where it might typically induce perspiration, but Long was sweating nevertheless. He had a planeload of grass, and it was ready to go. He was excited, expectant, he was apprehensive. He was out to beat the government. His adrenaline was pumping at the redline. He was sweating like a movie cop defusing a bomb. He was even sweating the small stuff.

Everything looked different to him all of a sudden. The colors were richer, the textures more diverse. It was like looking at the world with a new set of senses. And so, like the protagonist of a popular novel, at the appropriate and perfectly predictable point in a particular brand of narrative, Long chose that moment to inventory his natural surroundings, to conduct a personal inspection of earth's physical plant: soil stratification, atmospheric phenomena, botany. He gave the world a good going-over. Angles of incidence of visible light, the presence of wildlife, the absence thereof — he noted things like that.

Crouched five or six feet from the water, he had a chance to look at the Caribbean through different eyes. He noticed the interesting mix of aquas and cobalt blues, all the different species of jellyfish that floated on the surface, the color of the sand. And the color of the clay bank reminded him of Albermarle County, where he had grown up in Virginia, the same red clay, which sent him off on another thought . . .

Which one is behooved to let him entertain alone.

And now it was eight o'clock.

Long that morning had been awakened at five A.M. by loose fragments of thatch falling upon his face. Asleep in a hammock that was strung between two of the poles of an open-sided hut, he had passed the night in the tiny village down the trail from the runway. A crescendo of jungle sounds had risen with the moon. "Love talk between the animals," Miguel had observed, drifting off to sleep nearby. Between the hammock and the moon, unknown to Long, hidden in the thatch above his head, were the cables, batteries, hoses, and pumps that would be used to fuel the airplane. As Ernesto's men were retrieving them, the thatch was disturbed, and the pieces spilling on Long's face awakened him.

Easing back into sleep, Long was startled by the sensation of something crawling through his hair. He bolted upright, slapping his head furiously, fearing the presence of a scorpion. Opening his eyes, he heard giggling, and turned to see two five-year-old girls standing behind the hammock. They had sneaked up to feel his hair. He laughed and started carrying on with the curious pair, encouraging them to resume running their fingers through his curls, of a color the Colombian children had never seen before.

It was not until ten o'clock that morning that Miguel expressed concern.

"Sir, do you think you should call them on the radio?" he said.

"No, Miguel, I'm listening for them. There's no reason to call," said Long. "It could only attract attention to us. They're only on one frequency."

Beyond that, he had nothing to say.

Periodically, individually, the Colombians, over the following hour, approached and asked him what was happening. What they did not do is point out the obvious: There was a truck over there loaded with two and a half tons of marijuana. The pot was good to go. There was another mounted with drums holding more than three tons of fuel. They had mobilized a couple of dozen people who had to be paid for the morning's work. They simply wanted to know what was happening.

It was a question to which Long had no answer.

At eleven-thirty the plane was more than three hours late. There were few things that could have accounted for that, none of which Long cared to imagine. The flight was not the typical shakedown cruise. It was a long haul over blue ocean, and it was inconceivable to him that the crew had put the plane down anywhere. The only reasonable answer to the questions he was getting was that the pilots had crashed it. Of all the plans the smugglers had, they did not have a plan for that.

Long vacillated between anger and serious worry. Pablo Cepeda appeared to vacillate between a nervous breakdown and whatever came next. It was hard to tell with Pablo. Dysphoria was a condition the high-strung Colombian constantly walked the verge of.

"Where's the plane?" he wanted to know.

And he was asking the question with increasing frequency. He approached now, and he stood there as though under a cloud, his eye-glasses so uncompromisingly thick that his countenance favored that of an albacore, the melancholy he embodied so eminently turbid as to be observable even to Long, and asked the question one more time. It was one time too many.

"Okay, that's it, they're not coming," said Long. "Let's wrap it up."

Not a decision JD Reed would look upon as "a basic warrior tactic."

With little complaining the Colombians demobilized. Long headed to Santa Marta with Miguel and Pablo, and from there he called the States.

"You hear from JD?"

"Not yet," said Myerson.

"Neither have I."

"You're kidding."

"No," Long said. "Did they leave on time?"

"As far as I know. They'd have called if they didn't, right?"

"I guess. Yeah, they should have," said Long.

But he was not really sure of that.

At about four P.M. Long and the Colombians stepped through the door of Miguel's house in Barranquilla, and they were inside no more than a matter of minutes when the call came from Riohacha.

"Sir," said Miguel, hanging up the phone. "Sir," he said, his eyes receptacles of resignation and wonder, "the airplane has come."

"What?"

"It is there. In Riohacha."

Well, not exactly. It was not there any longer. It had *been* there. It had been there, loaded up and left. Slowly, as though on a rheostat, Long's eyes brightened. The corners of his mouth inched upward, and his face opened like a chrysanthemum. It took him a second to shake off his confusion, throw up his fists and cheer. Wavering between elation and incredulity, he was not sure what to think. He felt shameful for not having been there, but as terrible as he felt, he felt a hell of a lot better than he had a few minutes before, under the weight of his responsibility for the lives of the crew, when the plane had not come at all. But how the hell had they done it? No radio, no pot, no fuel, nobody there on the ground. And why were they running so late?

The installation of auxiliary fuel tanks in the wings of the DC-3 was referred to by Hatfield as the Pan Am conversion, initially performed by Douglas, as he explained it, to increase the aircraft's range for Pan American World Airways' commercial operations in the Pacific. The adaptation was a feature of various military configurations of the plane. The tanks, however, while legally installed, had been officially decommissioned. Rigging them for use, as the smugglers had, without securing a waiver, was against the law.

So what else was new?

As JD Reed had it figured, the fuel gaskets in the auxiliary tanks had dried out in the desert, in the government graveyard at

Davis-Monthan. Not having needed the tanks until now, the pilots had never tested them. According to McBride, the tanks *had* been tested. And having been tested, they failed. And the problem had been corrected. With fuel found leaking through a dumping valve, the bladder tanks had been drained, and the plane had been flown on its main tanks from Long Beach to Virginia, where the leak had been repaired.

Or so it had been assumed.

When the airplane was being fueled for the flight to Colombia, gasoline poured out of the tanks. The problem was traced to a feeder line. But diagnosing it meant replacing the fuel gaskets, and in the time it took to remove and replace them you could have undergone brain surgery. It required disassembly of the wings. The wing rivets had to be removed, and once the new gaskets were finally installed, all those rivets had to be replaced. And then the fire department had to be called in to wash down the runway.

"Puttin' heat on us," Reed maintained.

The DC-3 left the States five hours late.

When the pilots reached the Guajira, they failed to pick up radio contact. There was no smoke in the vicinity of Perico. Reed, standing in the cockpit, leaning over Hatfield, directed him to the location of the strip. When the airplane came in over the beach, the runway was deserted. The stillness, the emptiness — they were something you could feel. Words were absolutely unnecessary. Nothing that passed through anyone's mind was as memorable as what happened in his stomach.

When it came to the conduct of business, JD Reed would have been the first to admit that he was not much of a talker. He left the back-and-forth to others, to people like Allen Long. He let others do the talking, let others negotiate the deals, and let others worry, usually unnecessarily, in advance of what transpired. He was a worker. He liked getting out in the middle of it. Working with people who knew what they were doing, he exercised his right to remain silent. But at those moments when he saw that nobody else knew what to do, a change came over Reed, a change that was physically measurable. At those moments Reed took charge. At those moments, Reed was suddenly the one who knew exactly what to do. Forced by circumstances to act, he did. And nobody challenged his authority. It was not his imposing stature, but something in his tone of voice, his absolute, unequivocal certainty at those moments that made questioning his decision unthinkable.

Reed contemplated the jungle.

"That way," he said.

He directed Hatfield over the treetops.

A mile and a half inland, he said, "There. Back there."

He had sighted the camouflage netting. Beneath it, the last time he had looked, had been 30,000 pounds of pot.

Hatfield buzzed the *caleta*.

Activity in the staging area came to a halt as the DC-3, dipping its wings, roared in over the trees. Hatfield circled the plane. He made a second pass. He dropped in so low the mules shied and the flyers could read the astonishment on the faces of the Indians processing the merchandise. When the DC-3 turned and made for the airstrip, Ernesto was chasing its shadow, speeding below in a jeep. Pulling up at the runway, he waved the smugglers in, and Hatfield landed the airplane.

"Espera aquí!" wait here, shouted the Colombian, when he saw Reed emerge through the cargo door.

Jumping back into the jeep, Ernesto sped off, and reappeared moments later at the head of a rushing motorcade carrying pot, fuel, and personnel.

The first bale of marijuana had not yet been hoisted aboard the plane, when Reed turned to Ernesto and asked him, "Where's the stuff for the pilot?"

Reed had been on the ground not much more than a minute, and he was looking to roll a fat one. And Ernesto, who instantly provided the dope, wanted to know why. Which, in turn, astonished Reed. Here, thought Reed, was Colombian marijuana's very own Juan Valdez, and he could not understand why Reed wanted to light up?

Not smoking marijuana never even suggested itself to JD Reed. It was not something that ever would. Not even haphazardly. Reed needed his energy, as he was quite willing to tell you, and coming from Reed, it was something even a Colombian could try to understand.

In Latin America, to the native speaker, the adjective "macho" simply means male. "Machismo," a noun derived from it, is a modern social-sciences construct, and it enjoys little currency south of the border, especially among those alleged to exhibit the behavior specified by the term, which is defined in American dictionaries as "strong or assertive masculinity, characterized by virility, courage, aggressiveness, etc."

Commonly ascribed to Latin American men, almost always pejoratively, machismo is used rather conveniently to bootstrap a variety of qualities that have less to do with gender than they do with human circumstance. In parts of Colombia, those parts where life is cheap, acquaintance with danger comes with the turf; acceptance of violence and violent death is neither masculine nor particularly Latin. On the Guajira, where life is *really* cheap, risking your life, as often as not, is part of earning your daily bread: eking out a hardscrabble existence, taking bare subsistence from the land, straining literally to put bread on the table.

On the Guajira, in the time of the Americans, "courage and aggressiveness" were what it took to get by. Machismo, if you want to call it that, was born out of desperation, the way of the desperado in all its nuances of meaning. These were the badlands. And carrying a gun, when it actually came to doing so — illegal everywhere in Colombia — came with understandable indifference to everything but the money it cost to buy it.

With large quantities of merchandise and money lying about, possession of a weapon was mandatory among marijuana traffickers in Colombia, serving them in a way not intuitively obvious to the average American.

"It is not to protect the money, Allen," a young *guajiro* explained to Long. Nor, he added, were guns necessary to fend off the police. "In Colombia, when a man takes from you, yes . . . ?"

"Yes, if he steals."

"If he steals from you, he must also kill you. If he does not kill you, he will walk forever with *culebras* in his back."

"*Culebras.* Snakes?"

"*Sí.* He knows that you will find him, that some day you will kill him."

"In English we call it revenge."

"In English and Spanish the words, I think, are the same. In Colombia we call it *justicia.*"

"Justice."

"Justice. Yes. It is what must be done."

Carrying a gun on the streets of Riohacha was like carrying a gun on the streets of Tombstone, up in Deadwood, or maybe Dodge, there and in other mining towns and cow towns of nineteenth-century America. Nor were the names of these places unknown to the smugglers of the Guajira. The image of the American West was as familiar to the average Colombian as to any moviegoer anywhere in the world. It held a special place in the heart of the *guajiro.*

And JD Reed was its embodiment.

Reed was the receptacle of every Colombian Spaghetti Western fantasy of the American frontier, nothing less in the eyes of the typical *guajiro* than a personification of gunfighting myth. He was Wyatt Earp on steroids, the inner outlaw in Wild Bill.

And so it came as a big surprise to Ernesto when the first thing Reed did was fire up a joint.

Ernesto said, "You are a burro?"

"A burro? You mean like a donkey?" said Reed.

In Colombia, Ernesto explained, a man who smokes marijuana is referred to as a burro. "The Colombian people," he said, "they do not smoke this, only the lazy ones." Acting the part of such a man, Ernesto rolled his eyes, dropped his head, and rocked forward in imitation of a junkie on the nod. "He smokes, and he is like the donkey."

Earlier, Allen Long had been told this by Miguel. Long had laughed when he heard it, and nodding enthusiastically, explained to the Colombians gathered, *"Todos los gringos son burros,"* all gringos are burros. And lucky for him they were. Lighting up, he sucked in smoke, showed his teeth and waved his head, and he cracked the Colombians up, braying: "Hee-haw, hee-haw . . ."

There was another drug the Colombians associated with animal behavior. They called cocaine *perico*. It made a man chatter like a parakeet. Long did not have to do any acting to pull that imitation off. The Colombians got it without the clowning.

When Reed handed Ernesto the suitcase containing the $65,000 in cash, refueling was underway and the Colombians were overloading the airplane.

"Colombians, same as the Mexicans," Reed later told Long. "The more they put in, the more they get paid for."

The standing rule for smugglers — "You always overload" — held for almost any decent military aircraft on a decent runway. On a marginal field, such as the strip at Perico, pretty rugged and too short to start with, one had to consider the fact that the DC-3, carrying an added two and a half tons of fuel, was pushing the military-maximum overload hauling any significant amount of cargo.

"Let's try it," Hatfield said.

The plane never got off the strip. On takeoff it hit the high brush at the end of the runway and stayed there.

Hatfield, knowing he would never catch air, chopped the throttles and hit the brakes about a thousand feet downfield. The wings took the worst of it. The crash ripped the aluminum and tore away the petcocks fitted to drain water from the fuel.

For the second time in twenty-four hours gasoline was leaking from the airplane.

Reed, the first man off the plane, stepped through the cargo door carrying his survival gear, prepared, pending assessment of the damage, to take up residence in Colombia. He circled the plane, inspecting the wings. It was McBride who stepped up and stuck a finger in the hole from which most of the fuel was leaking. Reed pulled out his

Swiss Army knife. He cut branches from the standing brush, whittled them into shape, and with fuel pouring down over his Stetson, he plugged the holes where the petcocks had been. Ordering the Colombians to commandeer a tractor, he and the pilots set to work applying duct tape to the torn aluminum.

By the time a tractor arrived, it was no longer needed. The twenty-five men on hand had muscled the 26,000-pound airplane out of the trees. Reed ordered the unloading of almost half the pot aboard. The fuel that had been lost was replaced.

"Okay. Once more, with feeling."

And now the operation was running another two hours late, a total of seven.

Once the DC-3 had cleared the trees, Reed left the cockpit, climbed up onto the bales in the back of the plane, and started smoking. The pilots had assumed that Reed, who had flown a number of airplane trips, would be a relatively competent, interim pilot, that once the plane was in the air they would be able to take a break. Both of them. But as soon as the plane took off, Reed rolled himself a large spliff. And he sat there on top of the bales, smoking and talking to God, all the way back to Virginia. On the one attempt they made to hand the plane over to him, "it did things in the air that planes aren't designed to do," said McBride, who blamed it on the pot, informing Long that, "we had to relieve JD of command."

The plane did not fly up the Chesapeake Bay under cover of darkness. With the seven-hour delay, it flew up the Chesapeake Bay in broad daylight, roaring over the heads of fishermen who had been working on the water since dawn. Over the Oceana Naval Air Station at Virginia Beach, over Portsmouth and Newport News, over the nuclear fleet at Norfolk, it came in over the express lane to, if not on the doorstep of, the Pentagon.

"The Distant Early Warning system and all that stuff, forget about it," Hatfield said. "If you come in low enough and slow enough . . ."

A hundred feet off the water, a large military aircraft with no markings except indecipherable, three-inch tail numbers, came roaring in over the trees. The loggers on the James River had never seen any-thing like it. At West Point crop dusters were landing and taking off. Private aircraft were being fueled. The runway the smugglers were using, one of three 5,000-foot runways, represented the leg of the tri-angle farthest from all the activity. It was partially obscured by trees. Observers on the ground, while unlikely to be alarmed, were never-theless sufficiently mystified to take note of what they saw. They saw a big cargo plane touch down, and disappear behind the trees for only a few minutes before taking off.

Equally mystifying in that moment was what the smugglers saw.

". . . the curious incident of the dog in the night-time."

"The dog did nothing in the night-time."

"That was the curious incident," remarked Sherlock Holmes.

Hatfield brought the airplane about. McBride handled the talking.

"Where the fuck are they?" he shouted.

By "they" he meant the ground crew.

"Stay where you are," said Reed. "I'll unload it."

The pilots shouted questions as Reed retreated to the cargo deck. Reed shouted back, yelling over the roar of the engines.

"Forget about the pot," he said. "We've got to save the airplane."

The pot was easily replaceable, the airplane was not.

"I'll unload it," he shouted, "you get out of here."

He threw open the cargo doors, and started throwing out the mar-ijuana. There were more than fifty bales aboard at around eighty pounds apiece, and in six minutes Reed had the airplane empty. He jumped to the ground, McBride slammed the doors, and Hatfield released the brakes.

"Motherfuckers!" Reed said.

There was no one to hear him say it, he stood on the tarmac alone, but to say that Reed said it "to no one in particular" would be to over-look the six particular people Reed had in mind when he said it.

The marijuana stood in a small mountain, stacked as close to the tree line as Reed had been able to throw it from the cargo deck of the plane. He opened one of the bales, grabbed about three pounds of dope, which was as much as would fit in his knapsack, stashed it, and started walking. He hiked through the woods away from the airport until he hit blacktop, and hitched a ride into town.

Passing a roadside diner, Reed spotted a familiar assortment of vehicles parked out front, and instructed the driver to pull over.

"I'll get out here."

Inside the diner, seated at the counter with their backs to the door, members of the ground crew were enjoying breakfast. Reed, entering, walked up behind them, started throwing them off the counter stools onto the floor, and, calling them worthless shitheads, told them they had work to do. He sent them scrambling out the door, took a seat at the counter, ordered bacon and eggs, and ate his first meal in forty hours.

"Excuse me, ma'am. Nurse. Excuse me. Your royal highness. I asked for a *quart* of water. Thank you."

Long had started celebrating within minutes of his learning that the plane had made the pickup at Perico. He and the Colombians spent the night drinking, and early the next morning he caught a flight out of Barranquilla.

In Miami, standing at a pay phone in the airport, Long heard what happened in Virginia. That was where he heard everything these days: standing at a pay phone in some airport, or standing at a pay phone somewhere. And all the pay phones and kiosks eventually became one. There were retail clerks in various cities who knew Long rather well, but did not really understand him — all he ever wanted from them, as he came strolling into their shops off the street, was a roll of quarters. "I'll pay you eleven dollars for a ten-dollar roll of quarters . . ."

What happened in Virginia was this:

After finishing his breakfast, JD Reed headed for West Point. And so did the county sheriff.

The sheriff got there first.

Nearing the airport, Reed, on foot, was intercepted by a member of the ground crew, and was informed that numerous police cruisers had arrived at the airfield in advance of the trucks.

The load was busted.

At that moment the sheriff of King William County was having his photograph snapped, sharing the frame with the impressive stack of contraband he had seized. Posing before the bales of pot that Reed had off-loaded, he told reporters he had no suspects, and speculated quite matter-of-factly that what he had was probably the result of a "flubbed pickup."

The next day it took him and his deputies six hours to burn the load and bury the ashes.

Not even Reed could have smoked it that fast.

9 AUTOMATIC PILOT

All the planning, all the training, all the checklists and charts — all that, and the crew had ignored the only instructions that mattered: Do not leave, no matter what. Stay where you are. "Just *be* there," as Reed had said. Had they waited, the newspaper accounts confirmed, they could have easily unloaded the pot and nobody would have seen them. The sheriff did not get the call until an hour and a half after the drop.

"Strange planes have been seen there numerous times," the sheriff said. "Really, no one pays a lot of attention to them. Anything or anybody could have come in there at night and nobody would know the difference."

Had they been there, even had they been seen, they could have been out of there before anybody had been able to stop them.

"Nobody lives down there," explained the sheriff. "It's strictly a wide-open area."

And had Long called from Colombia — to say the plane had come and gone, that it was running seven hours late — the ground crew in all likelihood would have been there. But no contingency plan existed for his doing so. No phone or radio contacts, no channels of communication, had been established for that purpose. Similarly, neither the pilots nor Reed had a number to call to announce that they were leaving late. Nor should that have been necessary. Not according to Reed. Long's one move from Colombia would have been to try to call a member of the ground crew, try to get lucky and catch him at home. He had had about six hours in which to do it, but like Reed he had believed it unnecessary.

"Somebody's gonna have to pay for it in one way or another," the sheriff speculated. "I'm reading the papers and keeping my eyes peeled. We'll probably have a body come out of the James River with no identification one of these days, something like that."

Something like that.

From the phone booth at which he heard the news, Long instantly called Ann Arbor. He told Myerson what had happened, told him not to expect the trucks, and said he would be back in touch in a couple of days. Arriving in Virginia, he sent Reed's crew back to Las Vegas, and immediately jumped aboard Reed's hobbyhorse to join him in blaming the failure of the operation on Hathaway.

A lot of people were pissed off. *Everybody* was pissed off. The pilots were pissed off at the ground guys, the ground guys were pissed off at Long. The Colombians were happy, but the Colombians had yet to learn what had happened. Long owed them a hundred and twenty-five grand. He owed Myerson two hundred and fifty. And he had to lay it on somebody, so he laid it on Hathaway. He was out, that was it, Hathaway was done. They were looking for a scapegoat. Long did not like owning up to the fact that he had made a mistake. But the truth was he had neglected to call from Colombia to say that the plane was running late, or anyway had neglected to try. It was *his* fault. His trip, his fault. Now *he* was the man.

And there was only one move to make. Double-up the bet. He broke the news to the pilots, told them there would be no payoff on the load.

"All we did, we did for nothing," he told them, "unless we go down and do it again."

Pushing the proposition, he said, was the only way to go.

"I'll fix it," he promised the pilots.

They agreed to fly a second trip, and he told them to prep the planc.

Reed needed no such assurances. His faith in Long and the operation was exceeded only by his belief in the crusade.

"Call me when you're ready," he said, before he headed home.

To get ready Long needed money. There were airplane maintenance and fuel to pay for. There were payoffs he had to make. Reed's crew would have to be flown back in, everyone's expenses covered.

He flew to Detroit with a pound of the pot that Reed had salvaged from the load, and said, "This is what we could have had," knowing it was a pound of the best marijuana Myerson had ever seen. "All we have now is the airplane," he said, by which he meant to say they should use it. Everything was up and ready, he reported. Reed would be on the ground this time supervising the off-load. And the pot was all set to go.

"The Colombians will front us the next load."

Long expected Myerson to say no. But his business partner surprised him, agreeing that they should try it again.

"Why pull back now?" was his answer. "I have faith in you, I believe you can do this." Before Long had a chance to dance out the sales pitch he had prepared, Myerson went into his pocket. "I'm in, do it," he said, and coughed up the necessary cash.

Three weeks after talking to Myerson, Allen Long was standing on the tarmac at a general aviation facility in North Carolina, and Will McBride was telling him that the airplane "occasionally fires up. It catches fire when you turn it over. So you stand here with the fire extinguisher, and when we start it up, you spray it real good . . ."

It catches fire. Terrific.

Long was undergoing this drill in response to a simple arithmetic problem. Flight operations required a third man in the DC-3, and with

Reed now running the ground crew (in the arithmetic problem, call him the subtrahend), the flight crew was reduced, by process of simple subtraction, to a remainder of two. Someone (yes, an addend of one) was needed to make up the difference. Allen Long, for the first time in his smuggling career, was about to go seriously airborne. Long, on the threshold of a deepening romance, was about to consummate an affair with the DC-3, and his palms, like those of any young suitor, were sweating.

Long was scared to death of the airplane. First of all, he knew the wing rivets had been put in by hand, and he fully expected to see them come popping out while the plane was in the air. The reassembled plane was thirty-four years old, commissioned in 1942, and some of its parts came from aircraft that were — God knew how old they were or what condition they were in.

In fact, the airplane, as part of a class, was as safe as airplanes get. Douglas manufactured more than 14,000 of them, in one variation or another, both civilian and military — it had undergone more conversions in forty years than the government of Italy — and there was no greater testament to its safety record than the fact that so many of them were still flying. Everywhere. Douglas shipped them all over the world. The DC-3 was ubiquitous in the sky during World War II, over Burma, over Normandy. The U.S. government was still flying them during the war in Southeast Asia. The DC-3 ushered in modern, economical air transportation in 1936, and civilian airlines would still be flying them after the turn of the century.

The plane was more than an antique. It had a personality and a presence of its own. It was a tail dragger, and everywhere it showed up, pilots came out to admire it. It was not something you could hide. Long, despite his misgivings, took great pride of ownership in it. The plane had now become his close friend. But as with all close friends under pressure, he was waiting for it to break. He was looking for the chinks in the armor.

Planting season in North Carolina is never uncomfortably warm, but seldom is it especially cool. Tobacco country enjoys a temperate climate. Spring weather tends to be mild. And so Long, confronting the terror of flight, had all the more reason to sweat, laboring as he was under the weight of three layers of clothing.

Long and the pilots had shown up at the airport dressed the way pilots dress: in the navy blue trousers, visored caps, and crisp white shirts with epaulettes favored by commercial aviators, the doormen of pretentious nightclubs, and bell captains of the world's finer hotels. In any position short of parade rest, they looked the part they were playing, flyers ferrying short-haul cargo. Once aboard the airplane, however, the smugglers had stripped off the uniforms, and geared up for the flight they were making. Beneath military-surplus flight fatigues, they wore warm civilian clothes, and beneath the civvies thermal underwear. At 14,000 feet, which was the altitude the plane would have to exploit to make the long haul to the coast of Colombia, the air temperature in the DC-3 would drop by almost 50 degrees Fahrenheit.

In the thin air above 10,000 feet the crew would have to suck oxygen (after dark they would do so above 5,000 feet, the altitude at which hypoxia begins to devitalize one's night vision). McBride, familiarizing Long with the aircraft, directed his attention to the location of the O_2 supply in the cockpit. One of the lengths of rubber tubing running from the tank would serve the purpose of an oxygen mask. Long was to place it in his mouth and breathe through it if he wished to remain conscious at high altitude.

Mandatory only if he were flying the plane. The guy in the back could pass out, he would learn — and soon be happy to demonstrate — he did not need to stay awake.

In the cockpit, behind the captain, the smugglers had installed a first-class cabin seat salvaged from a Braniff Airways jet. A stretched-canvas cot on a collapsible frame was set up in the cargo bay behind the flyers. Separating the cockpit from the cargo bay was a firewall, and running from the firewall the length of the plane were tracks rigged for cargo netting. Long would spend the first few hours of the flight lining the cargo bay with Visqueen, using duct tape to attach the edges of the green plastic tarp to the bulkheads, elevating the vertical face of the liner three or four feet off the floor. The tarp would keep the airplane clean, preventing seeds and stems — or evidence, as the latter were viewed forensically — from collecting in the cargo area.

Once Long was instructed in how to accomplish the various tasks assigned to him, which included opening and closing the cargo doors on the port side of the aircraft, the pilots went through their pre-start check.

You do not start a DC-3, it has been said. Instead, you wake it up. Hatfield, manually, pumped up the brake and hydraulic pressure, before he cracked the throttles. With his left hand on the magneto switch, using his right to operate the primer, the booster coil, and the starter switches, he watched the left prop turn six blades, and then he fired the magneto. The engine yawned and snorted, and erupting in a distinctive blend of sounds, smells, and vibrations, the airplane started its day. Hatfield then fired the starboard engine. Long jumped aboard carrying the fire extinguisher, strapped himself in, the plane received clearance from the tower, and before the admiring eyes of those pilots who had come out to watch the takeoff, the old DC-3 lumbered down the runway.

The plane's tail wheel came off the ground. The plane leveled off — it felt more like an airplane now — and Long, unable to help himself, unstrapped his belt, stood with his hands on the shoulders of the pilots, and watched. At just over sixty-five knots the plane achieved flight. Catching the air, steady and slow, it lifted off, and with a couple of hurrahs from the flight controllers, sailed away, as smoothly and as slowly as only a DC-3 can.

Long would remember experiencing a rush of exhilaration unlike anything he had ever felt. There he was, truly embarking on a life-or-death enterprise. He was doing it for the money, yes, but no amount of money would replicate the experience. They were off, on their way to Colombia, searching for some clandestine runway, there to meet a bunch of machine-gun-toting desperadoes who would load them up with contraband. And Long and his partners, manning the cockpit, would fly it back against all odds. It was *Treasure Island* and he was Jim.

Over the Carolinas they flew relatively low, maintaining an altitude of under 10,000 feet. Overflying Savannah, Georgia, they came up on

Jacksonville, Florida, and banking southeast from there, they joined the normal flow of air traffic headed for the Bahamas. Under FAA regulations an aircraft leaving the United States must file an international flight plan. The smugglers left the country illegally. Being required by the same and other regulations to report to Customs upon reentering, they would render that particular infraction inconsequential some thirty hours later.

With the sun setting behind them, they made for the dark blue of the night, rumbling out over the Atlantic. They picked up the twinkling lights of Freeport. And soon they were flying by moonlight. Hatfield took a break. While Long, taking left seat, flew the airplane, McBride acquainted him with the navigational instruments, various radio frequencies, and other things they were not using. The radar transponder was disengaged. They maintained radio silence. They were flying with no lights.

The plane settled into a rhythm. There was the steady, hypnotic hum of the engines pitching against each other, running in sync for a moment or two, then slipping out, like a pair of joggers whose strides fall apart, then come together again. The course the smugglers followed took them south from Great Inagua over the Windward Passage, circumnavigating Cuban airspace. They were sucking oxygen when the mountains of Haiti passed below the fuselage of the aircraft. As they broke through the clouds hovering about the peaks, the incandescent glow of Port-au-Prince came into view on their right. Before them, invisible, lay the Caribbean. Below them everything was black. In the distance, through scattered clouds, they could see fast-moving formations of thunderheads drifting away. High above blinked the lights of commercial airliners, their pilots talking to Houston, Caracas, Nassau, Miami, one of them advising that his radar had picked up an aircraft but he could see no lights.

Long was really enjoying himself now.

There was a beauty to flying an airplane at night. He instantly came to appreciate why pilots so quickly grew addicted to flying. There was a solitary beauty up there. At one point, up in the cockpit, flying all alone, he took a few, long, lazy S-turns just to have some fun, canted the airplane to starboard and back to port, just like a kid on his bicycle.

Hatfield was unable to sleep. He took to the cot, but with every shift of the plane, he would ask if everything was all right. Long and McBride were having a good old time, yakking away and flying the airplane. And then McBride took a break. Hatfield returned, and Long, taking the right seat, flew with Hatfield for a while.

They had picked up the Maracaibo navigational station and were following a VOR radial that would lead them in on a magnetic course over the easternmost tip of Colombia. At five-thirty the sky brightened. The breaking dawn vaguely illuminated the South American coastline. Streams of sunlight, penetrating the clouds, hit the glaciers high in the Sierra Nevada. You could almost hear the explosion of light. Spiring in the sky, reflecting the sun, the mountains shone like a beacon in the morning, burning with the intensity of a star. As the sun ascended the heavens, the daylight broadened and flattened out. The diffusion of light diminished, and the geography came into higher relief. The foothills became clearly discernible. The shore and the plain came into focus. The smugglers could see coastal freighters plying the waters below. Picking up a visual of the coast, Hatfield banked the airplane. He tuned the VOR receiver to the Barranquilla frequency, and activated the plane's DME unit to get a fix on their position.

They were flying southwest along the coast, maybe a hundred miles from Riohacha, and it was starting to warm up. Off came the flight suits. The three men were a bit haggard, but at the same time they were excited, and none more excited than Long, for only he had serious reason to wonder what the next couple of hours would bring.

At 2,000 feet off the water, Long was no longer worried about the plane. He had another, more unstable variable to confront. Long, that morning, was the one man aboard the DC-3 who knew that, contrary to what Myerson and the pilots believed, not everything had been taken care of. He knew he had not worked things out with the Colombians.

The Colombians knew nothing about the seizure at West Point. They were expecting Long to return with their money. He owed them $125,000. And here he was coming back empty-handed, bluffing it out, assuming that they would be satisfied with less, with something else entirely, guessing that maybe instead of the money, these guys would go for the smoke he was going to blow up their ass.

The possibility at this point that the airplane would crash paled by statistical comparison with the probability that the three men aboard would be shot.

The pilots did not have a clue.

McBride and Hatfield were flying to the Guajira expecting the second load of pot on the arm — fronted by the Colombians, pending distribution in the States — putting the Americans in position to pay for the load and also pay for the load that had been lost. The pilots would not have agreed to the trip had they thought the load was a "maybe."

The Colombians expected the plane to land carrying not only the money the Americans owed, but a down payment on the pot the Americans were there to pick up. From the Colombian point of view, the plane, when it landed, would be — to the penny — a quarter of a million dollars short.

The thought that the Colombians might kill them right there as they stood on the beach for showing up empty-handed would have been that much more discouraging to the pilots.

All three men were playing light, but only one of them knew it.

By unofficial agreement in the dope business, the impact of a seizure like the one at West Point is absorbed evenly by buyer and seller. By tradition, if a smuggler can show the loss to be legitimate — providing a police evidence sheet, for instance, to prove that he is not actually stealing — the loss is split down the line, usually at the farmer's price. The farmer gets paid in full, and the traffickers share the hit. Long assumed the protocol to be standard, but never having worked with the Colombians, was not sure they observed the convention.

One way or another, by raising the issue beforehand, he jeopardized his shot at a second load, or so had been his reasoning. He was presenting the Colombians with a fait accompli, judging it a way to improve his odds. Apart from Long himself, only Reed knew he was running a con.

"You'll do it," said Reed, when Long laid out the plan. "You can talk 'em into it, Al."

But even now, a hundred miles from touchdown, Long wondered what to say. He wondered how he was going to handle it. He knew only one thing for certain. For whatever it happened to be worth, he knew he could count on Reed. He knew he could trust JD to be there, waiting for the airplane, no matter when it got back.

If it got back.

"White to red. White to red."

"Red to white. This is red, sir. I read you five-by-five."

Loud and clear. No static. No interference.

They flew in over Riohacha at 1,500 feet. Below them, a fishing boat tied to the pier was tossing in the waves. Indian dugouts were motoring up the coast, powered by the small Volvo gasoline engines ubiquitous on the Guajira. At 1,000 feet the temperature in the cockpit reached 90 degrees. It was probably 95 on the ground. The mist had burned off the jungle. At the mouth of the Río Camarones, children played in the tide.

"Red to white. Red to white. We have you. We can see you."

Hatfield did a flyby of the airstrip, circled north, and brought her in. Banking in on the northeasterly sea breeze, he put the airplane down.

Boom, they were on the ground.

Soon it was *abrazos* all around. The tail wheel was hanging on the edge of the ocean, the pilots were shutting the airplane down, and Long was exchanging hugs with the Colombians, when the truck hauling gasoline pulled up. While greetings were still underway, the Colombian crew pumped fuel. On one wing they used a hand pump, on the other an electric unit hooked up to a 12-volt battery. Behind the fuel truck came the reefer.

Long had not seen these bales. They had been selected by the Colombians. And so he spent the next hour and a half, the time required to refuel the plane, inspecting the load for quality. He borrowed a knife, cut two sides of a triangle in the face of each bale, peeled the wrapper back and removed a bud. He crushed and smelled a sample taken from every bale that went aboard the airplane. He rejected fifteen bales. The remainder of the load was strapped down, and the refueling was just about done, when Miguel reminded Long of the money.

"Sir, we forgot something," he said with a laugh.

"No, Miguel, I didn't forget," said Long, walking his Colombian friend away from the airplane. "And I think now you need to call Ernesto."

"Ernesto?"

"Yes, call Ernesto over here. And Pablo, too."

Long told Miguel what had happened.

"Oh, sir," Miguel said, shaking his head.

"It was the seven-hour delay," Long explained.

"You do not have any money?"

"No."

"This is a big problem. This is a very big problem, and I don't know what is going to happen. I don't know what we can do."

"You have to tell Ernesto," said Long. "And he has to make this decision."

It was Miguel's deal. To Miguel the setup owed its existence. It was he, as his father's son, whose word had been good, he to whom everyone finally deferred. But while it may have been Miguel's deal, it was Ernesto's operation. He ran the camp where the pot was processed. All the men on hand worked for him. The logistical work, the organization, Ernesto controlled the show. In every way that mattered, it was Ernesto's marijuana. A former employee of Miguel's father, it was he who had to answer for the pot. Long knew that no matter what Miguel thought, it was Ernesto who would make the call. However reasonable the young engineer might be in the face of the "problem" before them, its resolution rested with the man who approached them now toting a submachine gun.

Long and Miguel were standing about sixty feet from the aircraft, where no one else could hear them, when Ernesto and Pablo walked over. Long took from his pocket a newspaper clipping that he had cut from a page of the *Richmond Times-Dispatch*. He opened it up, and he showed Ernesto the photograph that had been snapped the day of the bust, the picture of the county sheriff posing with the confiscated bales. Ernesto studied it for a moment, pushed back the brim of his hat, and placed his finger on the photo.

"Mis bultos," he said, identifying the bales. He recognized them as his own.

Confounding to many a casual observer of the international traffic in dope is why anyone involved in the trade, why any *contrabandista* in his right mind, would do something so incriminating as to personally brand his product. Yet it is done all the time, just as ranchers brand their cattle — or rather, in Ernesto's case, brand someone else's cattle. What Ernesto identified in the photograph were markings that he himself had affixed to the burlap in which the bales had been sewn up. Marijuana sent to a runway might originate with three individual farmers. The bales are labeled to indicate which farmer's merchandise constitutes which bale. Each farmer is compensated according to how many bales of his product make it aboard the plane. (In certain cases, depending on how a particular operation is structured, the brands are affixed by farmers, who sometimes bale the pot themselves.)

Examining the photo, Ernesto grew indignant, remarking that it was clearly a policeman standing with his foot on the bales.

"Quién es este hombre?" he wanted to know.

Long told him who the man was.

"Hijo de la gran puta!" he said.

He asked what happened, and Long told him.

"Yo no tengo dinero," I have no money, said Long.

Ernesto squared his shoulders, looked at Long and narrowed his eyes.

"No dinero?" he said.

Life on the Guajira was tough, Ernesto was a very tough character, and eye to eye with him now, Long suspected he was younger than he looked. He was a short, rawboned, rope-muscled man. His features were sharp and weatherbeaten. His sunburned skin was like leather. The devil-may-care smile of the adventurer had just disappeared from his face, and his eyes looked like jacketed nine-millimeter rounds that had just been chambered.

"Sí," said Long, shaking his head. *"No dinero."*

Yes, we have no bananas.

Ernesto inhaled deeply. He had to think this over. This was a grave situation, and one he had never had to grapple with — not using anything more than his trigger finger, or so it appeared to Long, who wondered how many others, having lost a load, had ever had the temerity to return.

"I'm here," Long said, "because I intend to come back and pay you. *Yo regreso aquí con dinero.* Not just for this one, but for the first one that we lost. *If* you will give me this one. But I have nothing to pay you now."

He told Ernesto he would come back with the money or die trying. He had planned to say that. It was the extent to which he had come up with anything to say in rehearsing for the showdown — it was as far as he had gotten. From here on, he would be winging it.

"Nada?" Ernesto said. Nothing? Not even a piece of it?

He wanted to know what Long had. Long gave him the entire inventory.

"I have . . ."

He paused, and continued in labored Spanish.

". . . *Yo tengo solamente mi avión . . ."* he said, gesturing to the airplane. And then grabbing them, he said, ". . . *y mis cojones."*

I have only my airplane and my balls.

Ernesto stepped back when he heard this. It took a moment for the words to sink in. For just an instant, as he locked eyes with Long, it seemed that almost anything could happen. His pupils appeared to close down about the equivalent of four F-stops. The barrel of his submachine gun rose. Long's temperature dropped like the price of bad livestock. And slowly the corners of Ernesto's mouth turned up. He raised the weapon into the air, screamed and started firing.

"Okay!" he cried. "Okay, *ándale!* Go, Allen! Go!"

He grabbed Long's hand and wrapped him up in a vigorous embrace.

He said, *"Adiós!* Go. Good luck, my friend. Go, *bandido!* We will wait for you."

Miguel released the breath he had been holding, and heaving a sigh, broke into uncontrolled laughter. So touched by the whole thing was the unpredictable Pablo that he broke into tears.

Long would look back on the moment as consecrating the birth of a brotherhood. These were men with deep wells of sensitivity, who at the same time could kill you without breaking a sweat. They would do so with sincere regret — "I'm sorry, my friend, but we have to kill you" — then bury you where you fell. It was a joyous moment for Long, and his spirits were visibly elevated as he leaped aboard the airplane.

Hatfield, revving it up, asked him, "What was that all about?"

"I told them we didn't have the money, and they agreed to give us the pot."

The silence rolled in like thunder.

"You didn't straighten that out?" McBride said. "You told me you straightened that out."

"If I didn't, would you have come?"

"No fucking way," said Hatfield, spinning around to face Long.

"Well, now we're on our way. Let's go. No need to worry."

But Hatfield was breathing fire.

"I trusted you, man!" he said.

"Well, Frank, your faith has been validated."

"Bullshit! We could have been killed."

"I asked you if you had the balls."

"Don't give me that shit. Coming down here, we could have crashed. Anything could have happened. On a trip that wasn't worth the risk."

"Yeah, but it worked out okay."

"Motherfucker, no, it is not okay. This is not okay with me. I'm pissed."

McBride said, "Let's get her out of here."

The revs were up, the brakes were on full, and the propellers were straining. Hatfield let her go, and as the airplane bounced down the runway, the Colombians waved their guns in the air, following alongside in their trucks. The plane cleared the trees, banked out to sea, and dropped to forty feet over the water. There was no more to be had out of the engines.

"What do you think," said McBride, "should we throw a couple of bales over?"

"No!" said Long, "we're not throwing anything out."

An hour later they were flying at 400 feet.

At 400 feet they were not shark bait. The plane was running like a young thoroughbred, they had forty-eight hundred pounds of the world's best marijuana aboard, and Long had just been imbued with a rainstorm of faith by a guy named Ernesto for whom he would ever maintain admiration. He had stood eye to eye with this man who was from a culture very different from his, and the only thing they had understood at that moment was that they had to place faith in each other. Otherwise, there was no future to their enterprise. It was going to end right there. Long could not go home empty-handed and come back and try it again. And if Ernesto did not give Long the pot, he could not get paid for the first load. A lot of people would have cut their losses right there.

"But I looked at him," Long told Reed, "and it was one of those moments in my life, JD. I discovered I have this ability: I can get people to believe in me. I can lead people. And that's what happened. I promised him I would die trying to do this rather than fail."

And so Allen Long, leader of men, the General George S. Patton of pot, breathed a sigh of relief, climbed back into the cargo bay, opened a bale, and rolled himself a bone.

"Oh, no," said McBride, "not you."

"Hey," said Long, "I'm not JD. I can still fly the plane. But I'm smokin' some of this stuff. Don't worry, bro', I ain't gonna roll one no bigger than a donkey dick."

Long's adrenaline had been pumping for hours. As it dissipated, he proceeded to get buzzed on the variety of ingestibles aboard the plane. Near the airstrip at Perico was a processing lab, and there, just off the runway, stood several 55-gallon drums of cocaine. Long, seeing a lid being removed from one of the drums, had said, "Hey, can I have some of that?" Ernesto emptied out a Marlboro pack, scooped it into the drum, filled it with flake, and handed the pack to Long, who tucked it into the pocket of his flight suit. Halfway to Haiti, Long opened the pack, removed a rock about the circumference of a dime, chopped it up and shared it with the pilots. And then he broke out the beer.

There was no head aboard the aircraft, not even a relief tube, just a bucket containing blue toilet liquid and lime. Whether it was alleviation of a lot of the anxieties of the trip, or all the beer and cocaine with which the Americans celebrated their safe departure from Colombia, the bucket, which they called the honey pot, got a good workout on the way home.

Drinking Heineken, sucking oxygen, snorting coke and smoking pot, and flying back to the USA with some two and a half tons of blond — this for Allen Long was perhaps the finest moment of the trip. Pulling the trip off was not *all* about money. It was also about the achievement. It might have been the *only* good moment had there not been money waiting at the end of it. But right now nothing else seemed to matter except what he had just done. Getting the load into the country, getting the pot to market, and finally getting paid for it did not seem like much of an obstacle compared with what he had already accomplished.

Long, fast in reverie, was flying right seat when he spotted below him, rising out of the blue of the Caribbean, an island that did not exist. Or had not existed until that moment. No more than a strip of sea floor, ringed by coral, it was probably listed on the charts as a shoal. A sandbar. But for now, for one instant, it was an island, a piece of the

Caribbean upon which no soul had ever set foot. And Long let his imagination put him there. Nothing could change the inevitable now. They would touch down safely, or maybe not. Maybe upon landing they would be busted, but in a way, that was out of their hands, too. He was overcome by a feeling of calm. He had faith in the airplane — he was no longer waiting for the rivets to come popping out of the wings. The plane was on time, flying just fine. And JD was on the ground waiting. There was no worry about anyone's not being there.

The plan was to land in northeastern South Carolina, on the dragstrip at Darlington International Raceway. Lookouts were posted at all access points within five miles of the track. Reed was equipped with wire cutters, and nothing short of a buffalo gun was going to stop him from going through the fences. Darlington was one of three potential landing sites, a triangle of strips within fifty miles of one another. They were coded A, B, and C. The pilots would communicate with the ground crew within an hour of the plane's arrival — a good hour out they would be in radio range — and if the rendezvous were compromised in any way, the crew would have a decent head start in getting from A to B.

Reed had used a chartered plane to ferry his men into the region. Flown in from Las Vegas and Virginia, they had not known where they were going, and even now did not know exactly where they were. Reed had them bivouacked in a hotel somewhere near the state line, waiting for night to fall, waiting to begin the slow, steady progression to Darlington. There were eight men on the crew, two lookouts, three loaders, and three drivers, one of whom was Reed's father.

Reed would use two pickups fitted with snap-top campers to haul the load to Ann Arbor. At Darlington there would be a third such truck, a backup to be used in the event of a breakdown. The trucks were not new, but in perfect running condition, and were made less conspicuous by the exterior-mounted tool boxes and aluminum extension ladders they carried. They looked like the trucks of working men, whose vehicles were an established presence on the nation's byroads early in the morning.

As he did on every airplane trip, Reed had scouted the landing strip exhaustively in advance. Once Reed had located a strip on a map, it was his practice to park far away, walk to the location, and securing a nearby vantage point, sit there and watch it all night, using an infrared scope, and all the following day. After the off-load, he would assign a lookout to remain at the site, parked nearby in a motor home. The lookout would wait twenty-four hours, staying to see if anyone came to investigate the night's activities. In that way Reed would know if he could use the strip again. A nightwatchman's appearance would not scuttle a trip — Reed would already have selected a tree branch to cut to break the telephone line.

The same motor home that would remain at the strip that night would be serving another purpose as the DC-3 came in for a landing. Reed's father, at the wheel of the vehicle, would be parked some distance away with an open bottle of whiskey.

"His job is to run people off the road, a cop or whatever," Reed said, assuring Long that from the time the DC-3's wheels hit the ground to the time it was airborne again, it would take only six minutes to off-load it. "For those six minutes, I need somebody I can trust, and that's my dad, the only man I know who has the nuts to drive over and ram into a cop."

Long had reacted with amusement to the notion that Reed would be bringing his dad along as a member of the ground team. He found it rather quaint. But that was before Long knew much about the elder Reed. Once he finally met him, his amusement would evaporate, to be replaced at least temporarily by something like stone horror. Only later would he appreciate just how much of JD Reed, how much of who he was, had been inherited from his father, and given what his father had to offer, how lucky it was for Reed that he had not inherited it all.

The DC-3 crossed Haiti at mid-afternoon. After passing over Great Inagua, as the plane approached Eleuthera, Frank Hatfield initiated a series of evasive maneuvers. At that point the plane had come within range of mobile radar stations along the Florida coast, and was showing up as a blip on the screens of U.S. Coast Guard vessels patrolling the Straits. Appearing north of Haiti, it could be taken for almost any aircraft, a passenger plane, for instance, flying from Port-au-Prince to the Bahamas. At the southern tip of Eleuthera, as though bringing her into the airport there, Hatfield took the airplane down to forty feet off the deck, hugging the ocean for about fifty miles, taking cover of the island's land mass. At the northwest tip of the island he climbed, bringing the airplane up from below radar as though it were taking off, one of countless aircraft leaving the Bahamas for the States. He ascended to 5,000 feet, headed to Freeport, Grand Bahama, and beyond it to Florida, setting a course for Palm Beach.

10 SMOKE AND MIRRORS

The plane entered the United States in daylight, at about five in the afternoon, with all the air traffic from the Bahamas. On radar screens that were lit up like the Milky Way, it showed up as just one more aircraft, an unidentified blip. It entered U.S. airspace not at 25,000 feet, not at 300 feet, but at 5,000 like all the others. It came in at Palm Beach, Florida, but its crew, unlike those of other flights, would not report to Customs upon landing.

Coming out of the Bahamas, homing in on the Palm Beach directional beacon, Hatfield had known that within fifty miles of the Florida coast he was going to get a call from air-traffic control instructing him to switch on his radar transponder.

They had been calling for half an hour when Hatfield flew directly *over* the airport. He could not have been more conspicuous had he come in upside down.

"Unidentified aircraft, you are requested . . ."

The smugglers maintained radio silence.

"Please turn on your transponder and switch to . . ."

They did none of it. The tower ordered them to land.

". . . execute a turn to the south, descend to twenty-one hundred feet and prepare to . . ."

They just kept flying.

"Please announce your intentions . . ."

They were overloaded, fighting a slight headwind, and Long, who spent no measurable stretch of the trip not stoned, had become fascinated by the movement of automobile traffic below. The cocaine, acting chiefly as a motor drug, did not interfere with the immaculate marijuana buzz he managed to maintain. He took note of the fact that many motorists were in fact traveling faster than he. The plane had been holding even with one red car that continued to occupy his attention until, finally overtaking the DC-3, it disappeared out of sight.

Hatfield climbed to 12,000 feet, picked up an airway, and headed northwest, pushing through central Florida. They were sucking oxygen again, and the cockpit was cold, when over Lake Okeechobee, Long took the left seat, relieving Hatfield, who needed to rest up for the landing later that night. Exhausted now by twenty-four hours of flying, Hatfield, unlike his second officer, had not been shoveling cocaine for the past eight.

The plane was on a heading for north Georgia, where the Blue Ridge and the Great Smoky Mountains converge. The smugglers planned to disappear from radar for a while, running in and out of the valleys there, and check to see if anyone was following, before swinging around to Darlington. They were about fifty air miles north of the Everglades when in the top left quadrant of the windshield they picked up a massive storm front coming their way.

"What do you think?" said Long.

"Hey, Frank?"

"Where are we?" said Hatfield, leaning into the cockpit.

McBride said, "I think I saw Sebring back there."

"Give me the map."

Moving southeast, and moving fast, the thunderstorm presented the DC-3 with fewer options than enjoyed by other aircraft. The storm was too heavy, it was carrying too much turbulence, to go through or attempt to go under, and the DC-3, with a service ceiling of about 20,000 feet, was unable by design to achieve the necessary altitude to go over it. Going east would get the smugglers safely around the formation, but constituted a collateral risk Hatfield was unwilling to take. Advancing in that direction, the storm could very well push them back out over the Atlantic.

"We can't gamble that kind of fuel," he said.

And there, even with sufficient fuel, they would have to beat the U.S. border a second time. The odds on doing so were not prohibitive, but considering that and considering what the move might cost them in fuel, Hatfield figured why go up against the percentages. To circumnavigate the storm, the smugglers took the better odds, choosing the only course left to them. They went west, into the clear sky over Tampa. And into the restricted military airspace surrounding MacDill Air Force Base.

"Cool," said Long.

"Wake me when it's over."

Allen Long's equanimity at this point in the trip could be explained quite conveniently by the parts-per-milliliter of dope in his blood. But viewing it that way would ignore the very elements of his personality that accounted for his being where he was in the first place. The trip was far from over, the deal was far from done. With Reed in charge of the ground crew, there was reason to be confident that the off-load would go smoothly, but as a source of potential danger it still could not be ignored. All that lay between Darlington and Ann Arbor, not to mention what still lay between Florida and Darlington, could be evaluated quite rationally in the light of how much could go wrong. And yet, as he sailed around the thunderstorm, Allen Long was way past worrying about anything. Whatever is gonna happen is gonna happen, he reasoned. Now he was just having fun.

If one examines the overworked principle that cops and criminals are flip sides of the same constitutional coin, one might arrive at an appreciation, if only superficial, of Long's nonchalance. The average well-adjusted individual is programmed by nature to recoil from danger, to avoid it, and, failing that, to flee. Cops are trained to run in its direction. Their fitness reports, like those of firemen and military officers, measure their ability and their eagerness to do so. Their careers thrive on confrontation and their willingness to initiate it. Allen Long and other outlaws come by this trait not by formal training, but by a combination of natural temperament and experience. Crime's rewards reinforce their antisocial behavior. The syndrome sometimes expresses itself as an addiction to action. JD Reed described himself as an "an adrenaline junkie," and readily admitted that in the absence of confrontation, he felt the need to scare it up.

"I got to go wrestle a mule or have somethin' thrown at me to keep that life going."

There is nothing particularly profound in this. It is nothing new, or even strikingly novel, and it is not unique to outlaws. The same character trait can be found in a variety of law-abiding soldiers of fortune and, to one degree or another, in the typical downhill skier. It is a quality that propels certain people to become cops and firemen in the first place. Indeed, in Allen Long's case it was one of the more innocent manifestations of a psychological profile the darker side of which revealed itself in other ways. But it helps explain why in the air over Florida, facing a constellation of negative prospects, probably the least of which was a prison stretch, Long could ignore everything but the upside of the proposition and all the fun he was having. He was high on reefer and luxuriating in an almost unlimited supply of coke, he had an oxygen hose stuck in the left side of his mouth, a cigarette stuck in the other, he was holding a Heineken between his legs, he was flying that airplane, and he was having the time of his life.

That is what makes guys like Allen Long different from you.

"Hey, what do you think those are?" he said, turning to McBride.

He directed the co-pilot's attention to four black dots, appearing like pencil points in the distance, forming a diamond in the sunlight off to the west. In the time it took Long to turn his head back, the fighter jets had closed the gap, coming in on the smugglers at about 200 knots. They made a deafening pass over the DC-3, roughing it up. Air Force F-4 Phantom jets. The cockpit shook as the tactical fighters roared by,

Allen Long in 1975

Cherie Harris in 1977. This was taken during a photoshoot set up by Allen which led directly to Cherie being represented by the prestigious Wilhelmina Agency

the explosion of jet wash, hitting the fuselage, rocking in with the shock of a breaking wave.

"Hmm," said McBride, "were you speeding?"

The fighters came back around, and the formation pulled alongside.

"License and registration."

A traffic stop in the wild blue yonder.

Throwing on all the brakes — gear down, flaps down, flying at a high angle of attack — the Air Force pilots were unable to slow their craft sufficiently to pace the DC-3 for more than seconds at a time. One of the flyers, hanging on the edge of the stall envelope, holding for as long as he could on the smugglers' left wing, looked Long and McBride over and checked out the cockpit. The weapons system officer, flying rear seat, tapped the edge of his helmet, over his ear, signaling Long to get on the radio.

Long raised his mike with a shrug and a series of idiotic gestures understood by international standard to mean: "Radio's busted."

Total platform kill. Sorry, man.

Over the cockpit radio the smugglers heard MacDill tower trying to raise them on the override frequency.

". . . Douglas eight-six-four . . . ordered to exit military . . ."

The tower eventually gave up. And then, over their UHF receiver, the smugglers heard the F-4 reporting to MacDill.

"Probably just another weed smuggler. And that is not our business. Tango flight is departing the area."

No threat to national security, just some dumb, severely stoned citizens flying a planeload of drugs. The F-4 pilots raised their gear, hit the burners, and were gone.

Long raised his Heineken in a farewell salute.

"God bless America."

"The arsenal of democracy," McBride volunteered.

"Let's have some more of that coke."

Just before sunset, as the shadows below were lengthening and house lights were switching on, Hatfield took over. Running up the Smoky Mountain valleys, he dropped the aircraft to 1,000 feet, and disappeared from radar for a while. They were about five hours from touchdown when darkness fell, and the plane came out of the mountains flying with no lights. All three men were exhausted. It was time to shave and clean up. At some point the pilots would have to step off the plane to face the personnel of some general aviation facility. By then the plane itself would have to be cleaned up. There was still a lot of work to do.

The DC-3's extended range, thanks to the auxiliary tanks, was of significant advantage to the smugglers, enabling them as it did to land as far north as Virginia and the Carolinas. The distance between Colombia and the U.S. border was a good piece of what put so much heat on Florida. And made Darlington such a good bet.

They were a hundred miles out when they raised JD Reed on the radio. He and Long, over an air-to-air frequency, gave the impression of two pilots shooting the breeze, Long transmitting not from Douglas 86459, but Cessna 4603 Zulu, on a putative flight from Hilton Head to Spartanburg.

"Yeah we can see you over there, what are you flying?" said Long.

"This is Piper Cherokee four-six-seven-three India," responded Reed, transmitting from the dragstrip. "I see your lights. You at about eight thousand?"

"I'm at eighty-six hundred, descending into Spartanburg now. Golfing was great at Hilton Head. Are you the guy that operates the fleet of planes out of Middleburg, Virginia?"

"Affirmative," said Reed.

"What was the weather like over Spartanburg?"

"Everything was just fine, you're going to have a fine landing, shouldn't be any problems."

"Fine. That's an A on that then?"

"Yes," Reed said. "That's an A. I'd give conditions there an A."

Meaning Darlington, coded Landing Site A, was secure.

Hatfield navigated visually, carefully studying the landmarks below. As he closed in on the dragstrip, he started looking for a signal.

"I hear you. Yeah, I see your lights," said Reed. "I sure can. I see your lights. Can you see mine?"

The headlights on the pickup trucks flashed at the end of the dragstrip. Hatfield in response flashed the landing lights of the DC-3. Hatfield buzzed the runway, came back around to land, and Long was working the cargo doors when the airplane hit the ground.

The trucks pulled up, Reed secured the hatches, and Long started throwing bales. McBride, eager to be airborne, stepped back into the cargo bay and heaved bales along the fuselage, throwing them in the direction of the door. It was then, as the rhythm picked up, that one of Reed's crew, a guy named Billy, took a bale in the side of the head, momentarily knocking him cold. Reed, without missing a beat, picked the unconscious crewman up, and threw him into the back of the truck along with the cargo as if he were one of the bales.

"Don't say it."

"I wasn't going to say it."

"Yes you were," said Reed. "I could tell."

"I wasn't," said Long.

"Yes you were."

"Can I say it later?"

"I'll think about it."

After a quick consultation with the pilots, in which McBride confirmed that he could clear up the Visqueen by himself, Long decided that there was no need for him to go on with the airplane. The DC-3 took off without him. The plane lifted off in one direction and the trucks took off in the other. Before jumping aboard the blue Chevy Suburban in which they would follow the pot to Ann Arbor, Long and Reed, both patting themselves down for a match, looked at each other and simultaneously asked:

"Got a joint?"

The smugglers, facing each other, turned like the two halves of a French door swinging closed, and watched the trucks disappear into the distance with 4,800 pounds of weed.

The pot was aboard two covered pickups, one driven by Reed's father, the other by the crewman Billy, who had been knocked unconscious for only a minute. Long and Reed, using a CB radio to stay in touch with the drivers, followed a half-mile behind in what they were prepared to use as a crash car. If a truck were pulled over by police, the driver would report it over the CB. Long and Reed would slow down, allow the trooper to advance toward the truck on foot, then rear-end the police cruiser at about sixty miles an hour, just take it right off the road. The cop was not going to care what happened to the truck at that point, he was going to bust Long and Reed for reckless driving.

Long had been up now for almost two full days. Awake at six A.M. the day of the flight, he had not slept in forty-two hours. His system had been subjected to a lot of heavy sensory input — a significant share of emotional and psychological stress — and a lot of psychotropic substances, without benefit of solid food. He had been forcing fluids, but his liquid intake consisted exclusively of Heineken. He was a bit removed from the situation. He had ceded control of things to Reed.

They ran due north, avoiding the Interstate, up through Asheboro and Greensboro, North Carolina, to Roanoke, Virginia, cutting northwest from there, taking to the backcountry, and circling through the hills around Beckley, West Virginia, where Reed had been born and his father had been reared. It was somewhere in the West Virginia hills that Long and Reed lost radio contact with the trucks. And Long, in his compromised spiritual condition, found himself wondering just how terrible it would be if he never saw them again. It occurred to him that he did not know how to reach Billy in Las Vegas, and he had never laid eyes on Reed's father. Reed was his only contact with these guys. What if they just decided to dump him, wondered Long, who had been doing drugs for two days now. When they broke out of West Virginia and still were unable to raise the trucks on the radio, he turned to Reed and casually asked him, "What does your dad do for a living?"

"Oh, he's a hit man," Reed said.

Long laughed. "No, really," he said, "what does he do?"

"Oh, no, I'm not kidding," Reed said. "He's a hit man. I can't tell you the number of times I've gone with my dad to throw a gun out somewhere in the desert. Police have been to my house plenty of times with warrants for my dad's arrest."

Still, Long did not get it.

"For what?"

"Murder for hire, mostly. But he's never been convicted."

Indictments by the dozen. No convictions.

"Really," said Long.

"No witnesses." Reed's dad was old-school. "Yeah, he's not allowed in any of the casinos in Vegas. But he does a lot of work for them."

"Like a collector?"

"He does jobs — dirty jobs for the mob and people like that — an independent contractor."

Luther Reed, a confidence man, rip-off artist, and killer for hire, had been doing contract murders all of JD Reed's life. The seventh son of a seventh son, Luther had gone to war against Hitler as a teenager, and killed his first civilian for the operator of a Biloxi casino. He was a cornucopia of sound advice — "Don't carry a gun" — and bad example. He had turned his son on to cocaine as early as 1967, when the latter was sixteen years old. Instructing his family to rent a motor home and meet him in Death Valley, the elder Reed alighted from an airplane there carrying two suitcases filled with coke he had picked up in Ecuador. A few years after Long met him, Luther Reed's latest indictment would result in his first conviction, on charges of operating a bootleg Quaalude factory outside Las Vegas. Under surveillance by drug agents, he was convicted, he explained to his son, only because "you can't kill a video."

And this guy now had a truckload of Allen Long's pot.

"JD, I hate to ask you this, but what happens if your dad decides he's gonna keep the weed?"

"My dad wouldn't do that. No, he'd have to talk to me about that."

Which Long found only marginally consoling.

They found Luther and Billy waiting, as instructed, at a motel off Interstate 94 in Ann Arbor. The trucks were parked outside. The two men had checked in about an hour before. It was Long's first look at the elder Reed, a robust man with bone-white hair, shorter than his son. Looking into the eyes of an animal that evinces no response to seeing you is precisely what it was like for Long to meet and look at Luther. He had dead eyes, Long decided, eyes Long would never forget.

Long and Reed took the trucks from the motel, and not far away they met Myerson.

"Follow me," he told them.

They followed him to a farm he owned, where they backed the trucks into a large, brightly lit Quonset hut. Champagne, cocaine, and caviar awaited the two smugglers when they pulled in. After a brief celebration, five men wearing gloves and dust masks started unwrapping the pot.

The industry-standard wrap for bales of marijuana is three-fold. The bales are first wrapped in brown paper, which is sealed with masking tape. The layer of paper is necessary because the merchandise sweats. Much like a haystack gets moist and hot in the middle, this too is organic material. And even well cured, the product needs to hold moisture if it is to maintain any level of quality. If it were wrapped in plastic alone, it would decompose as its natural juice heated up and tried to evaporate. It is wrapped in paper to absorb the moisture, then wrapped in plastic to make the bale waterproof, to protect it not only from rain and seawater, but from contamination by crude oil and bilge. The plastic is taped, and then the bale is wrapped in a burlap bag that is sewn up on the open end, making the bale easy to handle — smugglers can grab the burlap by the corners and throw the bale around.

While the bales from the first truck were being unpacked, Long and Reed drove the second truck out of the building and dumped its load in an open field. Wearing burlap bags over their heads, they posed arm-over-shoulder in front of the mountain of Santa Marta Gold while somebody snapped a couple of photographs.

"Powerful stuff . . ." said Long, from inside the burlap.

"You're going to say it, aren't you," said Reed, speaking in the direction of the camera.

Long said, ". . . It goes right to your head."

Myerson gave Long the cash necessary to pay off the ground crew, and Long and Reed returned to the motel. Handing Luther Reed $25,000, Long detected the hint of a smile, but saw no change in the hit man's eyes. With his forefinger and thumb, Luther Reed pantomimed a gun, pointed it at Long, and said, "Al, you're a good guy to work for. You know, if you ever need anything done . . ." he let his thumb fall ". . . give me a call." He walked out the door, stepped into his truck, and drove away.

The $25,000 that Long paid each member of the ground crew was more than the going rate. In many cases, half that would have been sufficient to cover the cost of the job. Throughout the industry, off-loading, driving, and similar activities were very often handled by otherwise law-abiding citizens, working men with mortgages to pay and families to support. Many of the workers Long recruited fell within that category, and he paid them well, believing they deserved it. It changed the lives of some of them, and not always for the better — once they got a taste of that kind of dough, they decided they wanted to be scammers.

With the drivers on their way back to Las Vegas, Long and Reed celebrated late at Mr. Flood's Party, the bar on West Liberty being a mandatory stop for any visiting troublemaker, and that night they settled into Weber's Inn to await the payoff on distribution of the product. The 4,800 pounds of dope that arrived in Ann Arbor was by far the best available there, and Myerson found himself able to sell it for an average of $325 a pound. But before any profit could be taken on this, the first successful load, the loss on the previous trip had to be swallowed. Myerson had about a quarter of a million in start-up costs to recoup, most of which had gone into the purchase and outfitting of the airplane, and the smugglers were in arrears to the Colombians for $79,000 on the busted load.

Paying the Colombians for the busted load, which Long had promised to do on the airstrip, was unnecessary and highly unusual, according to Myerson, but even had Long not promised to do so, Myerson would have insisted on it. It achieved its intended effect, substantially raising Long's stock with the Colombians. With an unspecified number of bales being thrown off the overloaded airplane at Perico, the first flight had left the airstrip in Colombia carrying only 4,080 pounds — according to the sheriff of King William County, who weighed the load — hence the balance of $79,000.

Once all the numbers were crunched — an additional $240,000 had to be deducted to pay the Colombians for the pot that had just been distributed — the load generated over $900,000 in profit. Under the original terms of the deal, this was to be shared by the principals according to a formula that left the pilots with about 30 percent less than Long. If the trip was anomalous to begin with, considering all the necessary deductions, the decision to change the formula, once the money was finally counted, made it that much more irregular.

McBride and Hatfield had flown two trips, they had seen no money at all, and right now the pilots were probably asking themselves whether they ever would. They had risked their lives, invested their faith, and they had done it all on a maybe. McBride knew what it was like to make money on pot but had never done so on so large a scale. Hatfield, for his part, a man who had never before earned an unlawful dollar, had no idea what to expect.

To minimize carelessness and the influence of greed, Long had led everyone including the pilots to believe that they were doing business with the mob — the "boys in Detroit" is how he referred to Myerson and his pot-smoking pals in Ann Arbor. On one occasion Myerson had even been cast to play the heavy in person. Long put him in a trench coat, handed him a cigar, and had him mug it up for the benefit of Buddy Blanchard, using Myerson to impress upon the Richmond lawyer the importance of discretion. Jake Myerson: Murder Incorporated.

Long had shown on the second flight down that he was willing to let the pilots believe anything. The pilots, when it came to their end of the deal, could be excused for thinking, "I'll believe it when I see it." And so once the Ann Arbor money came in, the second thing Long had to do was get back to Richmond to take care of them. The first was to talk to the others involved and propose a juggling of the arithmetic, a one-time deviation from the formula governing the split. They agreed it was the right thing to do — the pilots this time would take a share equal to Long's.

"A plague upon it when thieves cannot be true one to another!"

This is as close as Falstaff comes to the subject of honor among thieves. And while thievery may not be entirely accurate in defining the smuggling operation in question, its correlative can probably be found there if one ransacks the conspiracy's ethical character.

Criminal endeavor, in general, flourishes in a behavioral no-man's-land between questionable ethics and no ethics at all. Smuggling as a criminal subcategory boasts situation ethics, at best. In any case, when you stop following the established rules, you have to make up your own. Seldom in any criminal conspiracy do the rules undergo codification, and almost never over the long haul do one man's rules remain consistent with those of his fellow conspirators. The greed of the typical capitalist manifests itself earlier in the outlaw simply because the ethical train has been running without brakes from the start. Greed and self-preservation — turning on your accomplices when your conduct gets you in trouble with the law — inevitably afflict even the most collegial conspiracies. Until that time, you just do the best you can. And call it honor if it makes you feel good.

This conspiracy would be no different. But in the beginning it sported attributes that reflected a surprising measure of sophistication on the part of Long and his partners. And it featured a strain of goodwill that was unique to its place and time. It was not honor so much as enthusiasm that gave the enterprise its special quality. In the early days of the marijuana trade there was so much money to go around — the numbers just came up so big — that Long and his partners were in a position to discover that generosity was good for business. Overpaying the Colombians for the merchandise, paying members of the ground crew higher than the going rate, kicking in as they did for the pilots — cutting the pilots in for a percentage in the first place — all of this promoted the success of an enterprise that would soon generate so much cash that eventually, rather than count it, the smugglers would simply weigh it.

Long delivered the money to the pilots in two $400 leather briefcases that he purchased for the occasion. Neither man knew exactly what his cut was going to be, but imagined it was going to come in at around $100,000. Long took great pleasure in toying with their expectations, and was exuberant in his willingness to take credit for the benefaction when he handed them $150,000 each. Giving them a handwritten record of accounts showing all the operation's expenditures, he did everything but take a bow.

The pilots should have been speechless. Instead, Hatfield hit Long with a question, Hatfield, for whom everything up to that point had been a maybe.

He said, "When are we going to do it again?"

Frank Hatfield was now a believer.

Long's biggest one-time score up to that point was the $25,000 he had earned on the Mexican load he and Reed had sold Myerson the previous fall. Now, on the Colombian trip, he hit for $150,000. And the next flight would be worth almost twice that. "He now starts havin' money," as Cherie Harris would later explain to a friend, introducing an attribute that would be colorfast in the character of the man others came to know. From then on, no one who met him would mention meeting him without mentioning the money; failing mention of the money, Long's character was inexpressible.

Long was not alone in flashing his newly acquired wealth and undergoing the numerous changes that came with it. McBride bought a house. Hatfield bought a plane, a cabin-class, twin-engine Cessna Titan. And Reed — "I never been extravagant" — moved onto a small ranch in Las Vegas that he "got cheap, four acres on a corner, $54,000," next door to singer Wayne Newton. (History does not record what "Mr. Las Vegas" made of the camouflage gear, the shotgun, and the dogs with which Reed routinely patrolled the grounds, nor the fatties laced with hash oil hanging from the laundry line outside the kitchen.) Jake Myerson's fortunes were largely unaffected. The money he earned was insufficient thus far to alter a lifestyle already influenced by what might be called very tall bank. Soon, however, at least for a while, Ann Arbor would become known as the place to score the best Colombian pot in the country, and as Myerson's reputation as a distributor of it grew, his business would grow along with it.

Long and Cherie had been together on and off for several months when he told her he was going to "do this other thing." It was no different from running liquor, he told her. In a few years marijuana would be legal, and he would be in the forefront of the industry. Because she did not want to appear unsophisticated, also because she wanted to appear somewhat aloof — reinforcing the notion that they were keeping the relationship casual — Cherie acted cool, as if what he was proposing were no big deal. Now, with another year or so having passed, the relationship was more than casual, and the pot business was a big deal in ways that Long had merely dreamed of.

Wealth's effects on Long were nothing if not predictable. The money and the cosmopolitan air it encouraged him to adopt made him attractive, he found, to a much greater range and variety of women, and he adapted to the change accordingly. Dating Cherie, whom he had fallen for when he did not have money, he started to see a lot of other women who were available to him now that he did. It was getting complicated. At least for him. Cherie was beginning to find his infatuation with himself a little bit stifling anyway. When he gave her the I-need-my-space routine, she was neither surprised nor especially chagrined. When he announced his intention to return to New York, she looked forward to having her own space back. Or so she told herself. When he subsequently asked her to go with him, she readily quit her job and made arrangements to go. Only after she had cut her ties did he announce that he had changed his mind, that he wanted to go without her. Cherie's response to the breach of promise — "Send me to Europe and I'll forgive you" — was a measure of her current commitment to the relationship. Long bought her off with a two-month trip.

If and when Long moved to New York, Cherie would not be the only one he was leaving behind. Tom, his twenty-one-year-old brother, estranged from both sides of the family, and finding himself pretty much adrift, had needed a place to be, and Long, who had not been there for him for the past ten years, had taken him in. Having no real direction at that point in his life, Tom, benefiting from his brother's prosperity, decided that what he wanted to do was work with him in the marijuana business. Long turned him down. That he himself might end up in prison Long relegated to the realm of the metaphysical. The prospect of his little brother's landing in jail was a hypothesis he found unbearable.

The same prosperity that enabled Long to look after his brother, had other, less salutary effects on his behavior. It was more than the money itself that made him difficult to deal with. He was loaded in more ways than one. Through his friends in Colombia he could buy cocaine for two dollars a gram. Which was just about for free. Street cocaine in the United States sold for exactly fifty times that. Long could pick up pure in Colombia, and at that price he could pick up weight. And with all the money he was making, he could easily pick up what he needed at U.S. retail when he ran out. In Richmond he started spreading so much blow around, and doing so much of it himself, that his wealth had come to be attributed to it. The misperception was part of the reason he considered leaving town. "I'm not a coke dealer, I'm a marijuana smuggler," was not the kind of protestation of innocence a judge was inclined to look upon favorably.

By now Long had a cocaine jones that was the envy of every junkie in America. If, as has often been said, a cocaine habit is God's way of telling you that you make too much money, Allen Long was the word made flesh. And he was way ahead of the curve. It would be a couple of years before the rest of the country caught up.

"Most I could do," JD Reed would say, "was three days. Third day I was done, I couldn't do it again for a month. I knew guys who went weeks without sleeping. Yeah, guys like Allen."

Of gringos in the marijuana business virtually all were marijuana smokers, and many were on the cutting edge of cocaine use. The dope smugglers of Long's acquaintance, like dope smugglers and dealers in general, tended to be prodigious in their use of a variety of drugs, but few matched Long's appetite for cocaine. More interesting, however, is that none of them, Long included, mixed business with obsession, at least in the early days.

As Lee Carlyle understood: "The two don't go together, coke and pot, you can't mix the two in business." Pomeroy and his partner had proved it in Marin when they stashed twenty-two pounds of cocaine in the safe in the Mill Valley house. Pot smugglers like JD Reed explained cocaine as a different vibe, "a different business altogether, out of harmony with what we do."

"Try explaining *that* to the Colombians," Long told him.

It was on the third flight to the Guajira that Ernesto approached Long with what seemed to be a very reasonable question. Why come with such a big plane, when he could come with a small one, load it with cocaine, and make more money? As Long well knew, Ernesto had plenty of coke. Moreover, Ernesto said, he knew people in the States who would buy it, Long would not have to find a way to distribute it.

"My nose says yes, but my mind says no," answered Long.

This of course made no sense to Ernesto. It required an explanation. And so Long, whom the Colombians had come affectionately to refer to as "El Piloto Loco," favored Ernesto with a tutorial on karma.

The two men were squatting in the shadow of the airplane just above the beach, and Long fell back on the use of a visual aid. He picked up a rock and drew two stick figures in the sand. "If I take cocaine and give it to this man," he said, drawing an arc in the sand between the two figures, inscribing a vector from left to right, "this is not a good thing for this man. This is bad for him. And karma will come back," he said, inscribing a reverse arc, "and hurt me. Something very bad will happen to me."

Ernesto pondered this for a moment. Cutting to the heart of the problem, he jumped up and pushed Long aside. Long tumbled to the dirt, and his ears rang with the sudden report of Ernesto's submachine gun as the Colombian emptied a short burst of nine-millimeter rounds into the sand, obliterating the hieroglyphic.

"Allen, if this Karma comes back to hurt you, I will kill him for you," Ernesto declared, smoke rising from the barrel of his Ingram.

Allen Long sincerely loved the Colombians, and this was one of the reasons why.

It was a pot smuggler named Tom Forcade, founder of *High Times* magazine, who was credited with saying, "There are only two kinds of dealers, those who need fork lifts and those who don't," and it would be a few years yet before a proposition such as Ernesto's held any appeal for the former. In 1978 Lee Carlyle would still be able to say with authority, "Coke does not generate the flow of cash that pot does." He would look upon the days when pot smugglers made millions as "the days when coke smugglers were making peanuts." There was just not a market for cocaine in the United States that came anywhere close to the market for pot. It took muscle to sit on a hundred kilos of coke for the month and a half required to move it. It was a dangerous game. The only people with that kind of muscle were guys like Vito Genovese and other heavies in the rackets. When the market for cocaine did open up, which it did shortly thereafter — with the suddenness of an artery hit with the blade of a knife — it would not be Americans who benefited most substantially from it.

11   FIRE IS THE TEST
OF GOLD

In advance of the third flight, Long paid a visit to his Colombian part-ners. He traveled alone to Barranquilla as a houseguest of Miguel's. But he was there to do more than pay the Colombians the money they were owed. It was apparent that if, before each flight, he did not select the marijuana personally, he would not get loads consisting exclusively of Santa Marta Gold. If half the load were of even slightly lower qual-ity, it could mean a difference of at least a hundred thousand dollars in Ann Arbor.

Miguel had married his childhood sweetheart, and they and their two children lived in a large house in suburban Barranquilla, with his mother, his mother-in-law, and two female servants. The house was surrounded by a seven-foot concrete wall topped with fragments of broken glass. As an architectural statement, the security feature, a deterrent to the common criminal, was pretty typical of upper-middle-class residential construction in Colombia. With all the women in the house waiting on them, Long and Miguel were served lunch, a typical *almuerzo*, or noonday meal, of rice, chicken, and salad, followed by flan and immediately thereafter a siesta, during which all the residents of the house slept off the meal and the midday heat.

Long's first order of business after paying Miguel was to select pot and oversee its packaging. The size and weight of marijuana bales were anything but standardized; every farmer and trafficker baled the product differently. Long would instruct the Colombians to limit the bales to between thirty-five and fifty pounds of what he referred to as semi-press. If the pot was compressed too tightly, if the buds were crushed, the quality of the product suffered. In addition to affecting the pot's cosmetics, crushing the buds crushed the seeds, the oil from which permeated the pot, imparting a bitter taste. Long was carrying $50,000 in hundreds against unforeseen expenses, portions of which he intended to pass around when necessary to whet someone's appetite for the rest of it. In four packages, each of which was less than half an inch thick, the cash was stashed in his boots on either side of each leg.

Nailing down a load of high-quality pot was his first priority. The other was to see María. "Sometimes love is a matter of the special chemistry between your skin and hers," he had been advised by an Italian fashion photographer to whom he had confessed his infatuation with the beautiful young Colombian woman. But it was the memory of María's eyes that Long could not get out of his mind, the look she had given him, her parting touch when she whispered *"lindo"* that night at Puerto Galeón and told him to call. The closer he got to Santa Marta, the more irresistible the memory became.

Before making their way inland to the town of Aracataca in the Sierra Nevada foothills, where 5,000 pounds of *mona* were being held for Long's inspection, he and Miguel would stop in Santa Marta, but not to see María.

"We must go there," Miguel said, "to get Armando."

Long knew Armando well. Rarely did he see Miguel, in fact, without seeing the reticent, soft-spoken mestizo lingering somewhere nearby. Short, dark, and thick-bodied, loyal, fearless, and efficient, Armando, about forty, former bodyguard to the younger man's father, now worked for Miguel. And really worked for him. Armando was ever-present on the smuggling side of Miguel's life. When something needed handling, Armando was the guy who handled it. Traveling deep into the foothills carrying $50,000 in cash, Miguel and Long would travel with Armando, who would travel with a gun.

Arriving in Santa Marta late in the afternoon, the smugglers pulled up before a modest house where a woman in her late twenties, holding one naked child in her arms and dragging another along behind her, responded with a shake of her head when Miguel inquired after Armando. Miguel thanked her and drove off.

"We must go to the home of his wife," he said.

"That was not his wife?" said Long.

"Yes."

"Yes, that was *not* his wife?"

"No."

It was like an Abbott and Costello routine.

"Armando has many wives," Miguel pointed out.

Many wives, and he had children with each of them.

Long's limited experience in-country had shown monogamy, or more precisely marital fidelity, to be the exception not the rule among Colombian men. Of the Colombians Long had met, most were married men, and most of them had girlfriends, many had more than one, and as often as not their girlfriends bore them children. But where monogamy was unusual, polygamy was rare. Armando, in that way, was eccentric, compelled as he was by honor to marry every woman he fell in love with.

"He is called the hardest working man in Santa Marta," Miguel said, smiling. "We say that you can always find Armando on the road to his house."

They found him that day speeding by in his truck.

"Observe," said the young engineer.

Hitting the brakes when he saw Miguel's car, Armando turned the truck around and pulled it up alongside.

Miguel asked, "Where are you going?"

"Home to my family," Armando replied.

Miguel nodded his head, then turned to smile at Long.

"Q.E.D."

They followed Armando "home," and from there, an hour later, the three set off for Aracataca.

"Do you know the book *Cien Años de Soledad*, Allen, written by Mr. García Márquez?"

Long told Miguel that he had read it.

"This is his home, sir, Aracataca. This is where he was born."

Gabriel García Márquez and his masterpiece, *One Hundred Years of Solitude*, were a source of understandable pride to Miguel and his countrymen. And the citizens of Aracataca took equal pride, Miguel explained, in the eccentricity ascribed to them by the author.

"Where we are going is Macondo," he said.

Macondo, the fictional village in which the book is set, is not imaginary, it is Aracataca. It was a town, Miguel said, where everything ran contrary to nature, where yes meant no, where bad fortune was cause for celebration, and the rivers ran uphill.

The tropical foothills of the Sierra Nevada, emerging out of the sea, rose toward Aracataca curving like the prop roots supporting the trunk of a bald cypress. They ran rich with banana trees and fast with the rivers and streams that irrigated the marijuana that Long had come to see. Aracataca lay hidden in the hills a hundred miles from the coast. The smugglers arrived at nightfall. Buses were still running, and the central plaza was busy, the marketplace alive with local people doing their shopping. Miguel, skirting the activity downtown, made for the old section of the city, site of the original village.

There on a cobblestone street, awash in the glow of lanterns, the smugglers entered a small house illuminated by candles. They were greeted by an elderly woman whose skin was wrinkled by age and weather. She wore a peasant dress and sandals. She ushered them to a table, and sat them down in the shadows. Filling a clay bowl with a loose handful of yellow buds, she set them afire. She leaned into the curling smoke, and cupping her creased hands, swept the fumes into her nostrils. She inhaled deeply, opened her eyes, favored Long with a smile that featured no more than three teeth, sighed and said,

"Buena." With outstretched fingers she urged the smoke in his direction and invited him to do the same.

Long, moved to poetry by the color of the buds alone, did so eagerly, discovering to his satisfaction that *"buena"* did not come close.

"You are happy?" said Miguel.

"I am happy," Long said.

"You have a question?"

"I have a question about something else."

The walls of the room, reflecting the light of the candles, had galvanized Long's attention. They were papered with U.S. currency, decked in a splendid array of one-dollar bills.

"These, Miguel, where did they come from?"

Miguel inquired.

After conferring with the old woman, he turned to Long and said, "Years ago an American paid her this money for marijuana. One suitcaseful, she says."

Miguel did not translate the obvious follow-up question. Asked by Long *why* she had used the money to paper the walls, he simply smiled at his American friend.

He said: "Because it is Aracataca."

Before leaving the old village, Miguel walked Long across an ancient stone bridge.

"Look," he said, "see the river? This is that river, sir."

And viewed from the bridge the river appeared to be flowing uphill.

"In Aracataca," Miguel said, "the people think everything goes the opposite way. We call them the yes-no people. When they say yes, they mean no, and when they say no they mean yes. All Colombian people know this to be so. It is one of the things that we love about our country, one of the many things that make my country so interesting."

The next day Long and the Colombians drove high into the hills to meet the farmers who had grown the pot he had sampled that night. The fields Long visited were blond — acre upon acre, nothing but pale yellow covering the side of a hill. The plants were eight to ten feet high, all female, packed with buds. It was what Ernesto in Riohacha had wanted Long to see. Ernesto was not going to move the pot unless it met with Long's approval.

The farmer who owned the crop led Long to a small outbuilding and showed him thirty-five bales ready to go.

"I need five thousand pounds," Long told the farmer, and said he needed it right away.

"*Bueno,*" the farmer said.

If Long paid now, $10 a pound, the farmer would guarantee its delivery.

Long instructed him not to pack the rest of the pot so tightly. He pulled out the $50,000 he was carrying and handed over the cash to the young farmer.

Back in Santa Marta, with Miguel's help, Long found and was once more bewitched — willingly and that much more helplessly — by the headstrong, eager María. They swam at Bahía Profundo, ending the day in a coconut grove, where for what might have been the first time in his life, even as her bathing suit came off, Long denied himself indulgence in the exercise of immediate gratification. It was the first time he was able to recall, and it would be the last time for a while, that his racing libido was impeded by common sense. He feared that in taking what he assumed to be her virginity he would be taking an irretrievable step. This was Latin America, where casual behavior carried ceremonial freight, and he was unwilling to make the promise inherent in what she proposed. She was Raúl Gaviria's niece, and he was not yet prepared for the consequences of summarily breaking it.

Before leaving Colombia, Long received a visitor at the Irotama. A stranger, he appeared at the hotel unannounced with an endorsement of the soundness of Long's instincts. The man was tall and slim, easily as tall as Long, with fine European features. His hair was black, recently barbered, thick and apparently oiled, exhibiting the bright reflective properties of a carefully Simonized fender. He wore cotton slacks, a fitted silk shirt, no smile, a platinum wristwatch, and made-to-measure shoes. Just under forty, elegantly mannered, he struck Long as a cross between a classic matinee idol and a member of the recruitment arm of some Ivy League business school. Around his neck, he wore a thin gold chain, suspended from which was a piece of black coral carved in the image of a fish.

He said, "I am Raúl Gaviria."

His English was perfect and the black coral fish was a tuna.

The visit was extremely cordial, the conversation for the most part casual, and where formal, pleasantly so. Asked what kind of smuggling he did, Long described the airplane. Gaviria talked about boats. His visit lasted about twenty minutes, and then it was time to go.

"María is my favorite niece," he told Long. "I would hate to see anything happen to her." To see her heart broken, her sanctity violated, "This would be bad," he said.

Long was left nodding his head as Gaviria turned and let himself out.

"You fellas are lucky sons of bitches," the old-timer at the airport said. "I'm gonna help you this time, then I want you to go. And I don't ever want to see you back here again."

The sun was high in Georgia when Frank Hatfield and Will McBride returned to the small municipal airport west of Atlanta to discover that the DC-3 had been moved. The fixed-base operation was a one-man facility, and the seasoned FBO operator who was staring them down had a piece of advice for the pair.

"Next time you set down," he said, looking around, and seeing no need to lower his voice, "you clean up that plane."

Running a hand through his crew cut, he pulled a bent cigarette from his pocket, patted himself down for a match, and with the tip of his ring finger removed a trace of particulate matter from the corner of his brown, or left, eye. Batting his lids, he huffed air through his nose, evacuating his sinuses in passable imitation of a steam locomotive, massaged the side of his face, aimed his blue eye at the pilots, and said: "Bird's a mess."

They had landed the plane at about two-thirty that morning after dropping a load at Darlington, called a cab from the pay phone, and, exhausted, had checked into a nearby motel. They did not wake until noon. The FBO operator, an ex-military mechanic, had come upon the airplane when he showed up for work. He found palm fronds hanging from the air intake, opened the plane up, saw seeds and stems all over the cargo deck, towed the plane behind the hangar and vacuumed it out.

"You get yourself some more gaffer's tape, and do a better job of sealing the tarp. She'll fly another forty years, you boys keep her out of the trees."

And with that they were dismissed. Just one more good old boy with a hustle, they figured. But even in the absence of a scam of his own, which explained his not calling the law, his reluctance to turn them in would have come as no surprise. They had seen it happen before. After landing the busted load at West Point the previous spring, a friendly FBO operator in Virginia had obliged them, no questions asked, when they said, "You got to put her in a hangar." He did pose a rhetorical question: "So, I wonder what you guys are up to." As expected, the feds showed up inquiring about a cargo plane like the one seen landing at West Point. "I seen a plane like that," the FBO operator told them, "a couple of months ago. Never seen it since." As he spoke, the DC-3 was parked right there, behind the locked door of an aviation hangar no more than a few yards away.

Long attributed such acts of defiance to a protective instinct, a feeling of brotherhood among pilots that extended in varying degrees to the aviation community in general. He believed that all pilots had a similar streak. To say that all might do something similar is definitely stretching the point when the something in question is smuggling dope. That all pilots might be able to see themselves doing it is probably true. What every pilot can probably imagine himself doing is manning a cockpit with his life on the line in support of some wild adventure, going up against the odds with the success of the operation riding on him. Or her.

Nobody has ever tried to fly who does not know how to dream.

On the third flight of the DC-3, moving the blond buds he bought in Aracataca, Long earned some $300,000. After that trip, he moved back to New York. He sold his two-year-old BMW, bought a new one for cash — a 3-liter sedan, top of the line, loaded, $17,000 — and rented a two-bedroom, corner apartment, facing southwest, on the twenty-seventh floor of a luxury building on East 68th Street in Manhattan. Convinced that he was smarter, sexier, and better-looking now than when he was the same guy without a half a million bucks, he was a lot of fun to be with. Women, he decided, loved him — he had a bag full of coke, a pocketful of money, and he had plenty of time to spare, time to sit there and listen to their life stories.

But Long, for all his erotic adventuring, was nonetheless susceptible to the seduction of true love. Because neither was likely, any time soon, to find anyone quite so troublesome to be with, it was only a matter of months before he and Cherie were back together. Long's pot was selling in Ann Arbor for $350 a pound, and as Cherie discovered when she moved in with him, he had really learned how to spend money.

"I could just point to stuff in the window, and he'd get it for me," she would recall.

And sometimes for everybody else.

Long's visits to Tourneau on Madison Avenue had taken on the flavor of religious duty. He dropped in with regularity, the way other Catholics dropped into church. One trip was memorable for its piety. He was there to buy Cherie a Rolex, a Lady Day-Date President in 18-karat gold, an elegant product of what might be thought of as the school of applied jewelry, a variety of ladies activewear that addressed the simultaneous physics of precious metals and explosive decompression, tasteful, endlessly feminine, and certified accurate at up to something like thirty atmospheres. While Long was pondering the purchase, another Oyster Perpetual caught his eye, a Datejust for men with a rotating bezel in gold and stainless steel.

"And I'll take a dozen of those," he told the jeweler, picking up a thirty-eight-hundred-dollar watch for every member of his team.

The loss of the load — call it physical evidence — on the DC-3's maiden voyage was more than an inauspicious beginning in the operational life of the airplane. It was the beginning of the end. People at West Point remembered what they thought to be a DC-3 landing that day. There was nothing to tie it to the pot that had been found, but as an investigative lead it was sufficient to go on: a DC-3, no name and a tail number too small to read. (The registration number of an airplane, which might appear among other places on the tail of the aircraft, is sometimes called its N-number, the N designating an airplane of U.S. registry. At three inches high, the digits of the DC-3's tail number satisfied FAA regulations for aircraft operated at speeds within its limit.) Over the ensuing weeks FAA investigators and federal drug agents visited airports in the vicinity of West Point. The plane came under suspicion when they pulled its N-number off a refueling receipt that had been issued at one of them.

Shortly after their run-in with the FBO operator in Georgia, Hatfield and McBride were practicing touch-and-go's on a deserted airstrip in Florida, when the airplane was surrounded by squad cars, bringing it to a halt. Calling the pilots out of the plane, police threw them to the ground, put shotguns to their heads, and told them not to move. They opened the plane up and found nothing. Neither pilot had drugs on him, not a joint, not a gram. The two men were clean. They were thrown into the back of a patrol car, and sitting there, unattended, they listened to the radio — the police radio — over which the officer in charge, seated in another car, was querying the feds. Patched through to the government, he described the behavior that had raised his department's suspicions — an old cargo plane, a deserted runway — and reported the DC-3's N-number.

"Yeah, well they're suspected of smuggling," came the official reply, "but if there's nothing in the airplane, there's nothing we're interested in. You're free to let them go."

The DC-3 went on the FAA hot list.

The pilots, on purpose, had been bouncing the plane around the country. Georgia, Tennessee, Florida — it was based no place in particular, and rarely did it show up at the same place twice. The cover story everywhere was pretty much the same: ferry pilots working under one contract or another. It was in Knoxville, Tennessee, after the Florida incident, just before their fourth trip south, in the fall of 1976, that Allen Long discovered what it meant to be on the FAA hot list.

With a load waiting in Colombia, Long traveled to Knoxville to rendezvous with the plane. When he arrived at the general aviation terminal at Knoxville Metropolitan Airport, wearing a uniform that smacked convincingly of commercial aviation, the DC-3 was parked there, cargo door open, chocks up under the wheels, gassed and ready to go. He stepped inside the office, where McBride and Hatfield were waiting, dressed exactly as he. Also waiting, ostensibly for the arrival of some private flight, were three men in civilian clothes, outfitted as concordantly as the smugglers. All had military haircuts, all wore black shoes, dark pants, and white, short-sleeved shirts.

"Will, what do you think?"

McBride said, "They're narcs."

"Frank," Long said, "those are feds."

"No question," said Hatfield.

And they could not have been friendlier.

"Nice little airplane," said one of them. "What are you fellows doing?"

Long gave the man the cover story McBride had come up with. They were ferrying rebuilt mining machinery parts between Knoxville and West Virginia.

"How long have you been doing that?" the man asked.

We know what you're fucking doing, pal.

"Oh, about six months."

"Interesting," the man said.

We're on to you.

He wished Long luck.

The atmosphere at the airport that day was pregnant with legal authority. At the end of the runway stood two nondescript Dodge sedans, idling with the doors open, and the two guys who stood beside the cars snapped photos of the smugglers' takeoff.

"Very nice," came word from the Knoxville tower as the DC-3 caught air. "A lot of people are interested in you guys today."

There it was again, the aviation fraternity.

"You're looking fine. High, wide, and handsome."

The airplane was running beautifully.

"Best of luck."

Before boarding the plane, Long had called Ann Arbor to tell Myerson the feds were watching them. They would have to abandon the plane after this flight, he said, bring it back, land it, unload it, and find somewhere to blow it up, maybe set fire to it, claim it was stolen.

That was the plan when the smugglers hit Colombian airspace the following morning. And Miguel said: "Sir, it has been raining here."

THE
LORDS
AND
THE
NEW
CREATURES

12 DISPOSABLE BIRDS

By the end of 1976 smuggling aircraft were beginning to stack up over the Guajira like commercial flights over JFK. In the 130 miles between the Palomino River and Portete Bay, northeast of Riohacha, there was always an airplane somewhere. (Within a couple of years, traffic in the skies east of Santa Marta would take on the scope of the Berlin Airlift.) Vessels of all kinds, from oceangoing sailboats to heavy freighters, were being loaded every day at docks along the coast. And every day the Colombian government sent air patrols aloft to spend the drug-interdiction money it received from the United States on something that looked like drug interdiction. In its endeavor to cooperate with traffickers, the government expected at least a modicum of effort on the part of smugglers. Leeway was not unlimited.

Allen Long, sitting on the beach at Perico with the DC-3 undergoing cannibalization behind him, had a couple of hours at most to get his ass out of there. He and the pilots. And with any luck, the pot. On the beach, so that Long would have somewhere to put the ass in question, the Indians had placed the first-class cabin seat ripped from the cockpit of the plane. But Long was not going to be comfortable no matter how much legroom he had. At that point, not even a complimentary cocktail would help. The humidity, holding in the wake of the rain, along with the escalating heat of the day — the same atmospheric conditions that had deprived the DC-3 of the lift necessary to clear the trees — conspired to make sitting in the sun just about unbearable. Looking out to sea now, Long was not studying the interesting mix of aquas and cobalt blues; he was not marveling at the rich variety of jellyfish. Not this time. Right now, he was wondering.

"What the hell am I going to do?"

The question, echoed by McBride, had gone without an answer for more than an hour, and Long's assertion that he was "working on it" was growing impoverished of the force of persuasion.

Well. Time to get classical.

Deus ex machina, literally translated, means "god from a machine," small *d* in *deus*, small *g* in *god*. The term is defined as: *1. A deity in Greek or Roman drama who was brought in by stage machinery to intervene in a difficult situation. 2. Any unexpected, artificial, or improbable character, device, or event suddenly introduced to resolve a situation or untangle a plot.* Or, some dictionaries add: *3. Anyone who unexpectedly intervenes to change the course of events.* As a dramatic technique the device was employed sparingly by Greek playwrights Aeschylus and Sophocles, but came into common use with Euripides. A purely mechanical contrivance, judged an unnatural stage convention, it invited criticism soon after its appearance on the theatrical scene in ancient Athens. Aristotle was particularly penetrating in his argument against its use. Some modern scholars maintain that its employment in classical drama, rather than a sign of poor workmanship, was often deliberate and achieved striking effects. Contemporary writers are granted no such license. Its use today is unanimously deplored as a cheap, artificial trick or coincidence for conveniently resolving a story's action.

If Allen Long were a fictional character, that is how one would size up the fifty-foot bay shrimper that hove into view that morning while he was sitting on the beach. The boat came to a stop in front of him a few hundred yards offshore. As Long was trying to make sense of the vessel's appearance, over the side went a twelve-foot Zodiac, and into it a single crew member, who motored ashore, heading straight for the beach where Long was sitting. The man at the throttle was in his late thirties. He had black hair flecked with gray. Long took him for a Colombian fisherman. He came ashore, stepping out of the inflatable clad only in cutoff blue jeans, walked directly up to Long, stuck out his hand, and said, "You must be Allen. I'm Tony. I'm from Miami."

Out of nowhere, completely improbable — like the Virgin Mary utterly misused in a medieval mystery play.

"I buy this shit from the same guys you do," Tony explained, his pronunciation of English influenced by the phonetic habits of a Latin American Spanish that was different from that of the Colombians, abbreviated, more rapid, less self-consciously deliberate. His was the Spanish of the native Cuban. "They told me about you. You get all the good stuff. I ask them for the good pot, they say you have it all locked up. All the best marijuana, Allen gets that."

"Yeah, well, that's me," said Long.

Always nice to have a fan, he thought. But really, could this be happening?

Tony, anchored off Perico, had been waiting to load 20,000 pounds of commercial weed when the call came from the Colombians telling him to lie offshore for a while. The DC-3 was coming in. Waiting for his own pot to be delivered to the beach, he had seen the plane return with smoke rising from the starboard engine. He had been watching when it crashed.

"So, look," he said, consulting his watch, nodding his head in the direction of the wreckage, "you want a ride home?"

"Well . . ." This could *not* be happening. "Man," said Long, "I don't know. Let me get . . . I have to talk to my guys."

He did have to talk to his guys. His instinct was to say no. The trip was well over a thousand miles by sea. But by whatever means available, he could not deny his partners the chance to escape. He laid it out for the pilots, who were understandably skeptical. Seven days at sea in the vessel Tony was sailing, a carvel-built shitbox of wood plank and questionable vintage, was duty not even the heartiest mariner would readily volunteer for. Hatfield and McBride waited for Long to weigh in.

"This is what I think," he said. "That guy has a radio. He can call the Colombians to come and get us out of here." Long felt the best odds on their getting back to the States still lay with the Colombians. "Hitching a ride with this guy," he said, "we run the risk of dying at sea." In Colombia, he argued, they were not facing the prospect of being killed.

"Not immediately anyway," McBride observed.

To which theory Hatfield applied the wisdom of the tax accountant. "Defer."

They voted no on the boat, agreeing that the better bet was giving Miguel and Pablo the opportunity to make good on their word.

"What I *am* going to do," Long said, "is I'm going to give him the pot. I'll pay him a hundred a pound to deliver it to Miami. If he makes it, it's a good arrangement. We can make two hundred a pound on it."

A comfort, no doubt, to the pilots. Never could it be said of Allen Long that he let life-and-death decisions distract him from the deal.

Tony, waiting for his own pot to show up on the beach, happily took aboard the bales removed from the DC-3. Running Long's pot out to his boat in the Zodiac took him several trips. Writing his phone number on the palm of Long's hand, he said he would see him in Miami. Long wished him bon voyage.

Two dugouts manned by Indians had motored into sight, dispatched by Ernesto's people in response to Tony's radio call. The Indians picked the smugglers up off the beach and ferried them to a tiny coastal village just east of the airstrip, one of numerous fishing communities on the Guajira given over to the marijuana trade.

"Where do you think they're taking us?" asked a nervous Will McBride.

Long, who was just as nervous, felt compelled to assume the image of confidence. These were Ernesto's people, he answered. Ernesto would call Miguel. Once Miguel was notified, he and Pablo would take it from there.

"Are you sure they can get us out?"

"Absolutely," Long lied.

The boats pulled into a tidal creek. The Indians tied them down in the grass. It was only fifty yards from there to the village, which comprised no more than a dozen huts and might as well have been deserted. In the early afternoon heat, nobody was moving. An adobe hut had been cleared for the smugglers. The Indians put up hammocks, brought the Americans food, and asked what else they wanted.

"Cigarettes . . ."

They got a carton of Marlboro: a product of Virginia.

"Beer . . ."

A case of Heineken: brewed in Holland.

"Marijuana . . ."

A bag of it: grown in Colombia.

"Cocaine . . ."

Two bags: extracted in Peru.

"Women . . ."

The Colombians drew the line.

"Can't have any of our women."

The smugglers were settled in, and Tony was on his way back to Florida, when on the beach at Perico the DC-3, undergoing disassembly, was spotted during a routine government overflight of the area. The Americans were instructed to stay in the hut. They were not to step outside for any reason, they were told. There were military patrols in the air. There were soldiers in the surrounding villages asking questions. What had happened, the army wanted to know, to the people who had been flying the plane that went down? Where were the pilots?

"What now?" McBride said.

And as meaningless as Long's answer might be, the question did not surprise him. Ambitious, aggressive, a guy who kicked ass to get things done, McBride was very much like Long that way. He took poorly to having no control over his fate. The revelation was Hatfield. Long cast a glance his way. He had been entirely wrong about Hatfield. Of the three of them, he was the coolest. He had asked only one question since the plane went down. On the beach, reporting to Long on the progress the locals were making in their demolition of the airplane — "I think they're going to bury it right here," he observed — he had simply asked, "What's next?" When there were no instructions forthcoming, he had just kicked back and waited. He had asked no questions since then. Now he reclined, if not wholly relaxed, as fearless as one could be in the sinister circumstances, stretched out in a hammock, less like a pilot than an airline passenger.

As the day wore on, and collective anxiety turned inward, McBride gave voice to a question that had already passed through everyone's mind, a question that had taken up residence in the neighborhood earlier that day: Why, having come so far, had they been so stupid as to push their luck?

"We're rich, already, all of us," he said.

Hatfield just burst out laughing.

Long admitted his culpability, saying, "It was stupid to load the plane."

"It was stupid to come down here in the first place," said Hatfield. "If you hadn't been that stupid, we never would have done any of this. None of us would be rich. It takes balls to be that stupid. I got no regrets. I'm glad we did it. I'm happy."

And by now he was also drunk.

"I guess we learned a lesson," said Long.

McBride said, "You're right about that."

Hatfield nodded his head. The lesson was pretty clear.

He and Long said it together:

"What we need is a bigger *plane.*"

While the fugitives were exercising bravado, their Colombian partners were doing everything necessary to get them out of the country. The plan was to hold them in the village until nightfall, then move them someplace safe, someplace where the Colombians could deploy more muscle, where they could throw some more men and some more guns on the job.

By sunset the three men were strung pretty tight, the fear of capture exacerbated now by growing physical discomfort. They had been drinking and smoking, they had been snorting cocaine, and they had been unable to relieve themselves for a period of several hours, forbidden as they were to leave the adobe in the light of day.

They waited for darkness.

It came late.

"There's a man in the doorway," McBride said.

It was just before the sun went down that the Colombian soldier appeared. Neither particularly tall nor especially young, he was armed and impeccably tailored. His uniform was immaculate, his combat boots were shined, he wore a holstered semiautomatic pistol and the visored cap of a commissioned officer.

"Do you think he's grinning 'cause he's glad to see us?"

Overseas jails are not what popular fiction would lead most Americans to believe. They are significantly worse. The writer who has come closest to describing incarceration therein is probably Dante, who did it as early as the fourteenth century with *Inferno*. None of the three smugglers was conversant with the writings of the Italian poet, so each was entertaining his own particular vision of the hell he was facing when the soldier walked through the door.

He walked in carrying a battle rifle, and reached for Long with his left hand. His lips parted. His teeth flashed. And so did the jewelry on his wrist: a twenty-three-hundred-dollar gold Pulsar watch with a red screen and a push-button LED readout.

"Gracias para el reloj," he said, thank you for the watch.

Which Long had bought in New York and had delivered on the second flight down. The watch identified him as the commander of the local military garrison. From every flight of the DC-3 this officer and his soldiers had reaped benefits far in excess of the value of the timepiece. There in the half-light of their one-room quarters, their hammocks suspended over the dirt floor of the thatch-roofed hut, the *comandante* sized up the smugglers. It did not take combat infantry training for him to identify the fragrance fouling the atmosphere. He picked it up instantly. Adrenaline. The smell of it was thick in the air. The adobe walls ran wet with it.

"Don't be afraid," he said. "Everything will be good."

Soon Ernesto arrived, then Miguel and Pablo. Armando pulled up to the hut at the wheel of a jeep. The Americans climbed into the back of it, and were driven out of the village. At the Río Camarones highway bridge, a roadblock had been thrown up by the army. As the jeep approached, McBride, seated in the shadows behind Armando, saw the bodyguard's hand reach down below the driver's seat and grasp a .45 automatic. Standing at the checkpoint when the truck pulled up, in charge of the soldiers assigned to it, was the unit's commander, who inspected the truck himself, checking a twenty-three-hundred-dollar wristwatch as he passed the vehicle through.

Some forty-five miles west of the village the truck pulled onto a secluded piece of rural property on the banks of the Río Palomino.

"My *finca*," Pablo said.

Underutilized and overgrown, Pablo's *finca*, his country estate, was hardly magnificent. The property flourished on the edge of disrepair. But being isolated as well as unoccupied, it came highly recommended for safety. Hammocks were strung up for sleeping. The Americans were not to be alarmed, they were told, if they saw armed men walking by the windows. In the morning they could wash up in the river. They were warned against going near the Palomino at night, when local traffickers would be using the waterway to ferry marijuana down from the mountains.

Once the Americans were settled in, Miguel and Armando departed for Barranquilla. Long gave Miguel a phone number to call in the States — in the absence of notification Reed would never leave the strip. The smugglers turned in early. Pablo told them to check their shoes for scorpions before putting them on in the morning, then climbed into his own hammock and bid them good night. He told them to ignore the bats.

Against the eventuality of a problem, the Americans always carried their passports when flying to Colombia. Under any circumstances, it would have been insane for them not to do so. They were flying over maybe five sovereign nations. To put it in Long's words, and to say the least, it would "raise a lot of eyebrows" if a cargo plane with three

Americans aboard landed, say, in the Dominican Republic, and the pilots were found to be without passports: *Imagine our surprise! We were flying to Texas and somehow we ended up here!*

So the Americans were carrying passports, but the documents displayed no immigration stamps showing that the three men had entered Colombia, or more to the point, that they had entered Colombia legally. To exit the country, they first had to acquire the necessary entry stamps. Their passports, ex post facto, had to be officially stamped to show their arrival in order for them to leave. An international traveler with any experience would have told them that getting it done loomed as an undertaking of epic proportions, that pulling off something like that, even if it were legal, presented a bureaucratic mountain all but unclimbable anywhere in the world.

In Colombia it was like buying a pack of cigarettes. It just cost more.

A lot more. And it took some political juice. Miguel, of course, had money, and his money bought him plenty of influence, but neither would be sufficient to enable the government official in his pocket to pull off the trick more than twice, not without running the danger of exposing the trick altogether. Things were very tight right now, Miguel had been told. The DEA was pressuring the Colombians. U.S. drug agents were adamant — they wanted the pilots of that DC-3.

(A photo of the downed aircraft would show up in local newspapers two days after the crash. A couple of months later the surveillance photo would run in *High Times* magazine.)

"I can get only two," Miguel said of the stamps.

"What about me?" said Long.

It went without question that the pilots would be the first to reap the fruits of the bribery. Their passports would be stamped. They would go immediately. Of the operational ship that was going down, Long was clearly the captain.

"Soon," answered Miguel, assuring Long that once a couple of days had passed, and the heat had died down, getting the third stamp would present no problem.

In the morning food was supplied by women from the nearby village, which was located about half a mile away. The Americans ate well, bathed in the river, and spent the rest of the day drinking *aguardiente* and twelve-year-old Scotch and wallowing in the endless supply of drugs available on the Guajira. They had been given something to wear while one of the local women washed their clothes in the river. Among the clothing delivered to them were souvenir T-shirts, in limited circulation, imprinted with a smoking gun and the legend: SOY GUAJIRO, Y QUE!

Roughly translated, it meant "I am from the Guajira, you want to make something of it?"

They spent the next three days at the *finca*, McBride being the only one among them to show any impatience. One morning he watched a boy with a stick in his hand walking a small donkey in the direction of the sea. When the boy returned about three hours later the animal was covered with thirty-pound snook, to McBride's mind an excellent game fish, and the only tackle the smuggler saw was the sharp stick the youngster carried.

He said: "Next time I'll bring my gear."

The night Miguel returned with the passports, everyone at the ranch was wasted. They were sitting on the poured-concrete patio of the house with a campfire burning in the dirt nearby. Hatfield was so gone on coke, Johnnie Walker, and *aguardiente* that he was sitting on the edge of his chair leaning into a conversation Long and Pablo were having, serving in the capacity of a translator. Long spoke passable Spanish, Pablo slightly less passable English, and both of them were so loaded that they sat there nodding in agreement with Hatfield, grateful for the intervention of a translator who spoke no Spanish at all. McBride, staring at the fire as if in its flames there were dreams going up, was so drunk that had it not been for the coke he would certainly, and quite mercifully, have passed out by now. His condition was laboratory proof of the hypothesis held by many that cocaine's most pernicious effect on man is in promoting the effects of alcohol.

Miguel, handing their passports back, told the pilots: "You leave tomorrow."

It was late in the evening when Long, his natural bonhomie and volubility amplified, his rheumy gaze intensified, by the collective good cheer and his massive intake of dope, smiled at Miguel and said, "I have to tell you something."

Miguel's eyes were glassing over as he drank to catch up with the others.

"When we met," Long said, "I told you I had been doing DC-3s for years."

"I remember," Miguel said.

"I had never done one," Long admitted. "Ever. I was lying."

Miguel laughed. They all did.

"That's okay," he said.

Long smiled and said, "I'm sorry." And then he told the truth. "No, I'm not," he said, and laughed again. And everyone else laughed that much louder. Long was really stoned now. Miguel poured another drink.

He said, "You asked the same of me and Pablo. How many airplanes. No?"

"Yes," said Long, "I did." And now his smile began to fade. "'So many I cannot count,' you said."

Miguel looked at Pablo: "*Sí?*"

"*Sí,*" said Pablo.

Pablo, so buzzed on flake that he was grinding his teeth, had to close his eyes to make room for his grin.

Miguel turned to Long, and said, "We did not do even one."

"What?"

Pablo was in stitches, he was snorting with laughter, tickled with pride.

"Not one," said Miguel.

Long was incensed that Miguel had lied. The others found it hilarious.

Encouraged by their laughter and a nod from the beaming Pablo, Miguel carried his confession to its high-spirited conclusion. It was not simply airplanes that had been new to him, he said. Before Long and Reed showed up in Barranquilla, Miguel now revealed, he and Pablo had never smuggled marijuana at all. "My father can't do this, but we can," Miguel had answered, when Pablo approached him that day about working with the Americans. "I know all the people my father knows. I will do it." And he did. He did it never having done it before. And he had carried the charade a step further, engineering the appearance of Don Julio, a friend of his father's, who fit what he knew to be Long's profile of "the man."

"I don't believe it," Long said, his outrage giving way to admiration. "Don Julio?"

Yes, admitted Miguel. They had even fabricated the gringo policeman whom Don Julio had claimed to have killed.

"You made him up!" said Long.

Yes, Miguel said. He was as bogus as Don Julio himself.

Long, the object of everyone's laughter, surrendered to the beauty of it all.

"*Et tu*, Pablo?" he said.

Everyone was having a great time now. Perhaps it was in the spirit of brotherhood, or maybe it was the *aguardiente,* but Hatfield had something to say. He stared at his feet, a picture of penitence, everything but sackcloth and ashes.

"I said I'd flown 3s all over the West. I told you I had thousands of hours in 3s . . ."

"Don't . . ."

"When we left Long Beach, I had eight."

At midnight the pilots were smuggled off the ranch.

The immigration official on Miguel's payroll had warned him not to move the Americans through the airport at Barranquilla. In Santa Marta the following morning they boarded a domestic flight to Bogotá. They flew from there to Caracas and then on to Paris, before eventually catching a flight home. Unlike Long, McBride and Hatfield both enjoyed relatively stable relationships with the women in their lives. Before the two left France, they were joined in Europe by their girlfriends, and spent some of their money as tourists, returning to the States at the speed of sound aboard the Concorde.

It was in one of his more serene moments that the excitable Pablo Cepeda, who had come to be known affectionately as El Demonio to his pot-smuggling partners, tipped Long off to the fact that María wanted to see him. The two men were sitting in the darkness with a campfire going, twisted on Scotch and the latest delivery of uncut cocaine, when Pablo broke the news.

"She asks for you, she wants to be with you."

Long could not resist allowing the thought of it to carry him away. Here, at the heart of a true adventure, danger and romance had just converged. All of a sudden he was more than a smuggler, more than a pirate, he was a leading man.

"María loves you," Pablo said.

All of a sudden he was the handsome hero of some swashbuckling, bodice-ripping tale of derring-do.

"She has told everyone she is going to marry you."

All of a sudden . . . Hmm. Marriage was a prospect Long had not entertained. He did not remember bringing it up. This was the first he had heard of it. Could he have mentioned something like that? He did love María. He loved her, in a way. But what could he have said to her that she might have taken for a proposal?

Yeah. What was there in the longing of a young Latin American woman, the trusting, treasured daughter in a traditional Roman Catholic family, with whom a man had lain naked, whispering under the stars, that could possibly lead her to believe that a wedding was in the works?

"She looks for you," said Pablo.

When María had come to Pablo to ask where her lover was being hidden, Pablo had remained silent. Mindful of security, Pablo was also a realist in matters of the heart. The demon in Pablo Cepeda, the turmoil that had earned him his nickname, owed much of its intensity to the suffering that romance had inflicted upon him. Pablo was in love with his wife, a medical doctor, a career woman, whom he admired as much as he adored. More than anything he wanted her respect. And it was the one thing she was unwilling to give him. Pablo's wife was a *cachaca,* a native of interior Colombia, her conservative manner, her mode of dress, and her overall sophistication standing her in visible contrast to the typical *costeña.* She was unhappy and intellectually unfulfilled living on the coast. And with Pablo resisting repeated pleas that they relocate to the city, she had moved back to Bogotá without him. It had left him a broken man. Traveling to Bogotá regularly, he spent time with her and their children, but he could not, as a man, move in with her. They could not be seen to be living under *her* roof, his masculinity would not allow it. As it was, he had become a laughing-stock among his friends in Santa Marta, ridiculed on the coast as a man who could not control his wife.

It was Miguel, the romantic, who eventually gave Long up.

Armando was behind the wheel of the stake-bodied truck that pulled up to the ranch the last night Long was in residence. Miguel stepped out through the passenger door, and María stepped out after him. She was wearing a hat with the brim turned down and matching shirt and trousers of the kind associated with the stalking of missionaries, a beau monde rendition of the field khakis in evidence when Stanley presumed to meet Livingstone. Walking into the light of the fire, immaculate, beatific, like some fashion-forward vision of the Virgin, she removed the hat, her hair dropping like syrup poured from a jar and funneling in the region of her seventh cervical vertebra, and she threw herself into the arms of her intended. Long's excitement at seeing her was exceeded only by his incredulity, which was evident in the look he cast Miguel's way.

Miguel shrugged, spread his arms, and raised his hands palms-forward like a man submitting to arrest.

"She has asked her uncle to help us get you out of the country," he said.

And the look Long was giving him suddenly changed, Long's face assuming the expression known to speakers of every language to mean: Whoa, dude, back up.

He said, "I thought that was taken care of."

Miguel shook his head. "The situation is growing dangerous." They would not be waiting for the immigration stamp. "We leave tonight," he said.

María, the warmth of her eyes softening the urgency in her voice, said, "You will go through Sabana Rubia."

Again Long looked to Miguel.

There was a place in the mountains, Miguel said, where no gringo had ever been. Few Colombians dared go there. Not even he himself had been there. A valley in the Sierra de Perija in the Eastern Cordillera, it was known as Sabana Rubia. It was southeast of Villanueva at the southern tip of the Guajira. More marijuana was cultivated there than anywhere in Colombia. Long would be smuggled out of the country by way of the valley, up through the high pass, and into Sabana Rubia following routes controlled by traffickers.

"Raúl Gaviria," said Miguel, "has offered his help. He said, 'I will help Allen because I love María.'"

And now it was time to leave. Pablo's cousin Ricardo, who lived in Caracas, would have people waiting to meet Long at the Venezuelan border. They would lead him to Maracaibo. Ricardo would obtain the necessary documentation, the stamps and visas required for Long to fly home from there.

"It is far and the way is dangerous," Miguel said. "But Raúl Gaviria has sent his man ahead to Villanueva to meet us. He will know María."

"María? She can't go with us."

"Without me . . ." said María.

"You're not going. I won't allow it."

"Without me, Del Río will not take you through the pass."

Del Río: her uncle's man in Villanueva, said Miguel. It was he who would insure their safety.

"And now we must go."

He instructed Armando to collect any evidence of Long's stay at the ranch. Long and María were hustled into the back of the truck, where they lay on a blanket over a bed of banana fronds, under more of which they were hidden. For the next eight hours they remained there under the leaves, as the truck with Miguel and Armando up front wound along the coast and up through the backcountry, making for Villanueva, 170 miles away. They arrived at Del Río's house just before dawn.

Like Raúl Gaviria himself, his lieutenant Del Río was a man of Spanish blood, his complexion fair, his bearing aristocratic. His wife was Indian, his household alive with children, and staffed with men of indeterminate age who under indigenous costume carried nine-millimeter submachine guns. Long and the others spent the day at the house, setting out for Sabana Rubia just before midnight escorted by Del Río and two of the bodyguards in his employ. Following a dry riverbed, they drove up into the foothills of the Sierra de Perija. They abandoned the truck at three A.M., and leaving Armando behind, proceeded on foot for another two hours, until they reached the mule station from where they would stage their two-day journey across the mountains to Venezuela.

Like a stagecoach stop or similar outpost conjured up intact off the American frontier, the mule station marked the foot of a trail snaking out of the mountains, the first sign of life as one descended out of the clouds at the end of a day-long journey. Still hours from civilization, it was overseen by a man named Augusto, home to him and his family.

Augusto was in his late thirties, thickset and swarthy, his hair waved close to his head, his hands showing the calluses of a man who worked hard for a living. Under his wool *ruana,* the traditional Colombian poncho, he wore the off-white cotton pants of the native and a bright orange T-shirt old enough to qualify as one of those CIA give-aways that continued to haunt the Third World. His sandals had been fashioned from rubber tire treads and leather, and his smile was so big you could park in it.

"Five mules," Del Río told him. "Hurry."

But before leaving, the guests would meet the children, and there would be *arepas* and coffee served by Augusto's wife. Ordinarily there would be little sense of urgency at this point, but after leaving Villanueva, as they drove through the night, the smugglers had hit a roadblock. A four-thousand-dollar bribe had bought them passage, but was unlikely to buy silence. They had to assume that government troops would be on their trail soon. The mules were saddled, and the party set off, Augusto in the lead, followed in order of ascent by Miguel, María, Long, and Del Río. The Indian bodyguards made the climb on foot.

The distance from Villanueva, which they had departed six hours before, to the headwaters of the Guasare River, which rose on the Venezuelan side of the cordillera, was approximately fifteen miles as the crow flies — after the crow's altimeter started pushing 10,000 feet. Long asked how many hours they must ride before they reached Sabana Rubia.

"*Cuántas horas*, Augusto?"

Augusto raised an index finger, then pointed to the rising sun, and describing an arc from east to west, threw out a number in Spanish.

Long was confused, laughing more at himself than at Augusto when he told Miguel, "I thought he said seventeen hours."

"Pay no attention," said Miguel, smiling. "He does not own a watch."

The journey to the mule station at the southeastern foot of the trail would take exactly seventeen hours. And that would bring an end to the first day's ride. It would be almost sunset on the second day before they reached the border.

For seventeen hours they zigzagged up the mountain, moving from microclimate to microclimate, from the dry brush of the foothills into a lush, tropical rain forest, where monkeys and parrots flourished. Up from there through the high desert, they ascended into the coniferous range, where the path was strewn with pine needles and the air was thin. Across rock, snow, and boulder, they inched through canyons overlooking glass-blue lakes, in the still, icy waters of which were reflected the distant glaciers of the Sierra Nevada.

The trail in places was no more than eighteen inches wide, marked by a switchback every few feet. The mules moved two feet left, then two feet right, inching their way up the cliffs, turning to face back down the mountain even as they climbed it. Within inches of the mules' hooves were drop-offs of a thousand feet.

Periodically there would be the tinkling of a bell, and the ascending party would be forced to find a cutout and pull off the trail as a

burro train loaded with marijuana descended toward them. The burros, each one packed with more than a hundred pounds of pot, as
much as the creature could carry, crab-stepped down the trail, heading
for the mule station at Villanueva. Around the ridge would come the
first burro, then the next, and the next, hopping, sidling down the
slope, lashed together, the animals stacking up behind each other as
the trail narrowed and reversed itself. Long tried counting the burros
of the first train he encountered. He stopped counting at eighty, estimating there to be at least half as many more again. Well over a hundred burros — maybe 15,000 pounds of pot — all driven down the
mountain by one small boy with a switch.

Shortly before midday, the bodyguards detoured. Turning down
the mountain at a point where the trail divided, the Indians descended
into a river valley, leaving the other members of the party to continue
straight up.

Long asked, "Where are they going?"

"They are going where we are, sir," Miguel said.

"They're going the long way," said Long, watching them take
off downhill.

"They will meet us later."

The heavy weapons and ammunition necessary to defend the pass
were hidden somewhere below, and the bodyguards had set off to
retrieve the hardware, Miguel explained. Following an alternate route,
they would rejoin the party farther up the trail.

"They are going the long way," Miguel said, "but they will be
there first."

"How's that?" Long wanted to know.

"Because," Miguel answered, "they are much faster than the
mules. The mules have to rest, sir," he reminded Long, laughing. "The
Indians do not."

They rested the mules at noon. The temperature had reached
90 degrees on the high, arid plateau. They dismounted at the site of a
dry wash where mesquite, desert grass, palms, and other vegetation
sprouted in the absence of any evidence of water. And here for the
next two hours they would wait out the midday sun.

Augusto began digging a hole. He crouched on his knees, and using only his hands, he dug about two feet down, creating a depression in the arroyo that measured maybe a yard in diameter. He lined the hole with leaves from a banana tree growing in the creek bed. The indentation resembled the head of a drum in a Caribbean steel band. He stood up, clapped his hands clean, and walked off to take a nap in the shade.

About forty-five minutes later Long was roused from his siesta by the sound of the mules lapping water. The humans, as thirsty as the animals, joined the mules at the edge of the pool that Augusto had created. The water percolating into it was neither cool nor sweet. But it was pure and it was water, and everybody drank.

It was late in the afternoon when Augusto, leading the way up the mountain, stopped the mules again. He raised his hand, turned in his saddle to face the others, and pointed to the cliffs below. Long alone was surprised. An army patrol was climbing the mountain four or five hours behind them. Clearly, word had been passed that an American was on the trail.

"What will they do if they see us?" he said.

Augusto essayed a smile, exposing a wide and crooked array of gold teeth.

Del Río answered for him.

"They will make sure they do not catch us," he said.

And Augusto told Long why.

"Because," he said, when Long inquired, "we have more guns than they have."

"The army," Del Río confided, "has never come through the pass."

Long was unsure of what Augusto said next. Assuming it to be a statement of corroboration, he looked to Miguel for a translation.

"Augusto says if they entered it, they would never leave it," Miguel explained.

Perhaps more than Long needed to hear.

"We will kill them, they know that," Del Río confirmed.

Yeah. Thanks for spelling it out.

Long was unfailingly fascinated by what he heard and saw in the course of the journey. Finding Augusto to be a boundless source of information and entertainment, he was gratified by the chance to reciprocate, to reward Augusto's fascination, when Augusto rode up beside him to get a better look at his watch.

"*Es oro?*" Augusto asked.

"*Sí*," said Long, happy to confirm for Augusto that the Rolex was indeed gold.

"*Puro?*"

Yes, Long said, pure gold.

Augusto raised his eyebrows, favorably impressed.

"*Cuánto vale ese reloj?*" he asked, how much did it cost.

"*Diez mil,*" ten thousand, said Long.

"*Diez mil pesos,*" Augusto said, with a whistle.

"Dollars," Long told him.

"*Dolares!*"

"Yes, my friend."

This inspired an animated soliloquy on Augusto's part. Delivered in rapid Spanish, it had Miguel and Del Río laughing and Long entirely confused.

"Why is he so excited?" Long asked. "What did he just say?"

Augusto could not take his eyes of the watch, and now he was talking to himself.

"He is calculating," said Miguel. "He thinks perhaps it is worth more money to kill you and take the watch, than to take you over the mountain."

Now and then, in the course of the journey, Augusto, for Long's amusement, cast a surreptitious glance at the watch and narrowed his eyes, playing the part of a man doing arithmetic in his head.

At sunset they reached the pass, and to Long it was immediately clear why the army had never attempted to breach it. The trail passed through a canyon that ran for about half a mile, ten feet wide at its widest point, walled in by hundred-foot cliffs. From the far side of the canyon as few as three men armed with rifles could hold off a well-equipped military patrol, the ultimate body count limited by nothing more than the defenders' ammunition supply. Only by way of some high-performance, high-altitude parachute drop could an army penetrate such a stronghold. But marijuana trafficking would never be enough to justify trying, even if doing so were within the capacity of the Colombian military. Beyond a fundamental survival mentality on the part of the typical soldier, a characteristic reluctance would reveal itself. The Colombian soldiers on the trail were men from the villages. A guerrilla incursion was one thing — they would do what they had to do — but to pursue a difficult, determined mission that required their eradicating the sole source of income of people just like them was not what they had signed up for. They climbed the mountain. They did not enter the canyon.

Augusto, emerging from the pass, was greeted by an Indian holding an automatic rifle. Draped in a woolen *ruana* with a *mochila* slung over his shoulder — in the woven pouch indigenous to the region, he was probably carrying ammo — the gunman embodied a rather effective tourist office advertisement for the country's native handicrafts. The M-16 was imported. Standing with him, protecting the pass, were the two Del Río bodyguards who had detoured off the trail with submachine guns earlier in the day. Now, in addition to their Ingrams, they had six automatic rifles and enough ammunition to slow down the cast of a Cecil B. DeMille movie. Under the weight of the weapons and cartridges, the Indians, going the long way, and traveling there by foot, had beaten the mules to the pass by three hours.

As darkness fell, the party descended into the valley, a high, tropical grassland in which, Long had been told, farmers produced between four and five million pounds of marijuana a season. From the cliffs he could see, flickering below, the distant light of campfires spread out for miles. Still hours away, these were the home fires burning outside the huts of the pot farmers of Sabana Rubia. The party traveled until midnight. The air was cool when Augusto led the others into a clearing in the forest on the eastern slope of the range, to a small stand of thatch-roofed huts where several men sat surrounding a fire, drinking *aguardiente* and cooking a goat. Here the party would spend the night.

Long, dismounting after seventeen hours on a mule, had difficulty walking upright, and was far too tired to do anything but sleep. He and

María were handed blankets, a lean-to was cleared for them, and the weary couple expended the last of their energy trying to shake the blankets free of fleas. Walking off to relieve himself before turning in, Long, looking out over the valley, urinating into the clouds, was startled to hear coughing behind him, and turned to find his safety assured — it was Colombia, after all — by the presence of a bodyguard standing in the moonlight with an assault rifle cradled in his arms. Known as El Tigre, he was Del Río's man, and Long had a question for him.

"I am told there is marijuana everywhere," he said, zipping his jeans. "Can you show me where it is?"

"*Aquí*," said El Tigre, waving to indicate the forest. "It is here. There is marijuana everywhere."

"Yes, but I don't see it," said Long. "All I see is the trees. Where is the marijuana?"

"My friend," said Del Río, stepping out of the darkness, "it is all around you, the marijuana, everywhere you look. In the morning you will see."

And in the morning he did see.

The forest itself was marijuana, the jungle in which he stood. It grew to the height of trees, ten, fourteen, sixteen feet high, rising on stalks that were five inches thick. Everywhere he looked he saw it, choking the hillside, growing wild. He stood in the very shade of it. Flowering from the seeds that had been spilled over a decade as marijuana passed through the camp, shooting up coarse and fibrous, it grew undisturbed, a thriving profusion of *Cannabis sativa*. Visible beyond the camp, here in its natural habitat, the weed, propagating as part of the region's native vegetation, had been overgrowing the mountain for ages. The fact that it was all but unsmokable — growing untended, it was suitable only for hemp — made the sight of it nonetheless breathtaking.

"You've got to be kidding," he said.

"Come with me," said Miguel.

He led Long out of the clearing, walked him to the edge of the cliff, and waited for the clouds to move. Through the mist, as the clouds scattered, the valley rose into view.

"Look," he said.

And there it was.

Long had never seen anything like it. He had never dreamed it even existed. There in the valley, on terraced hillsides, as far as the eye could see, the red and gold of cultivated marijuana carpeted Sabana Rubia, from horizon to horizon. In every direction, the crop undulated, seemingly into infinity, its colors coming alive as it absorbed the light of the early morning sun.

"Yes, the other ridge, too," said Miguel.

The other ridge, five miles away — cultivation ran as far as the river, Del Río had told him.

Allen Long was gazing upon the largest marijuana field in the hemisphere, possibly the largest on the planet. And for just a fleeting instant, perhaps, in his own much smaller world, in a small pocket of civilization living on Jimmy Buffett time — a dazed population of freak-disciples whose gospel was spread by Cheech & Chong, a flock of wasted acolytes who were "waiting for Dave" — for just a fleeting instant, perhaps, Allen Long felt what Vasco Balboa must have felt when he ascended that final mountain peak and was met by the sight of the Pacific.

"More marijuana than you will ever need, sir."

Long was at a loss for words — as hard as that is to believe, as hard as that was for *him* to believe. For a full *moment* he could think of nothing to say. And finally it came to him.

He said, "I want it all."

Later that morning he entered the valley. As far as he knew, he was the first American to do so. This was impenetrable Colombia. The farmers of Sabana Rubia had never seen a gringo before. They were poor people, typically barefoot. Probably the most expensive, single material good a family owned here was an automatic weapon. They wanted to show Long their marijuana, and as he traversed the valley, they did.

Passing slowly through the fields, the party pressed on, four of them now, Augusto, Miguel, María, and Long, escorted by the Indian bodyguards. Del Río had turned back that morning, heading home on foot. They reached the Río Guasare at about four that afternoon. Long and María drifted off. As he was bathing in the river, Long heard Miguel call his name.

"Allen, Ricardo's man is here."

"Vaya con dios, lindo."

María turned back at the river, returning home with Miguel.

Long traveled for another two days, making the journey through Venezuela on a mule supplied by Ricardo's people. Augusto, in protection of Raúl Gaviria's interests, which were invested in the protection of Long, made the trip with him, seeing him all the way to Maracaibo. By the time he reached Caracas, it had been exactly seven days since Tony's boat had left the beach.

13   SMOKE ON THE WATER

Tony A., that capital letter being the surname by which everyone knew him best, was a rogue in the Golden-Age-of-Hollywood mode, "a throwback to another age," in the words of those who worked with him. A modern-day buccaneer, he gave new life to the term debonair. Tony was an authentic lady-killer with a perpetual, irresistible sparkle in his eye and a charm about him few could resist. He could just as effortlessly knock you off as sweep you off your feet — you and maybe six guys at the bar — and do it without losing the smile. Married to a highly regarded Miami lawyer, Tony, with eight children at home and as many girlfriends on the side, was as cavalier with his marriage vows as he was nonchalant in the conduct of business. Assuring his wife that he would never allow another woman to come between them, he promised her that when he fooled around, it would always be with several. Similarly, on every financial deal, he played both ends against the middle, unable really to help himself and unabashed in the face of discovery: "Hey this is the way we do business here. This is the Cuban way."

Like other Cuban-Americans in the upper echelon of the South Florida dope trade, Tony had honed his prodigious smuggling skills with the support of the Central Intelligence Agency, which had provided his covert operations training and continued to back his activities. The son of a lawyer, Tony had been a university student in Havana in the late 1950s when he, like many young, middle-class Cubans, took to the country's Escambray Mountains, later to be joined there by Fidel Castro's guerrilla forces, and fought to overthrow the dictatorship of Fulgencio Batista. Along with numerous other revolutionary officers, he was dispatched by Castro to a reeducation camp when the insurgency succeeded and the cigar-smoking dictator-in-waiting stepped out of the Communist closet. Escaping to the States upon his release, Tony was one of some 2,000 exiles recruited, trained, and outfitted by the CIA as part of the expeditionary force whose dream of retaking the island died an ignominious death at the Bay of Pigs in 1961.

With the failure of the invasion, this cadre of Cuban exiles continued to carry out covert operations for the agency, not only in Cuba but around the world (and not only internationally but domestically, as when they burglarized offices at Washington's Watergate complex in 1972), and they comprised the operational vanguard of the numerous anti-Castro groups that would control the political thermostat in Miami for the next forty years. Their unique brand of government service presupposed a lot of specialized, paramilitary training, and brought with it a significant layer of insulation against criminal investigation.

The drug business was a natural place for their talents.

Acting on behalf of the government and carrying no identification to prove it, they lived undercover in Florida, constantly training and hauling equipment. Discharging their duties would have been virtually impossible without official cooperation within the Miami police department. Tony's CIA liaison there was a politically powerful lieutenant named Jack, who, when he retired to practice law, continued to oversee and coordinate not only the exiles' government-sanctioned work but their criminal activities as well.

Of the Cuban-born drug traffickers who worked with Tony, many were CIA-trained; of the gringos who worked with him, most were former cops. (Some were still on the job.) Allen Long's arrival on the scene in Miami would result in a kind of weird, dope-dealing dialectic, a synthesis marked by the coming together of ex-cops and ex-hippies in a marriage of contradictions brokered by government-sponsored anti-Communists. It was a dialectic driven by a materialism free of all philosophical freight. What brought the counterculture, the cops, and anti-Communists to the same conjugal bed was nothing inherent in the mind-altering chemistry of the drugs. It was the money. Forget the antiwar movement, the war on crime, forget Castro. These boys had a business to run.

Long arrived at Kennedy Airport in New York on a direct flight from Caracas, and the first thing he did, from the first public phone he hit after clearing Customs, was call Tony at the Miami phone number that the Cuban a week earlier had written on the palm of his hand.

"Tony, this is Allen."

"Who?"

"Allen. You know, the guy you met on the beach."

"Hey, brother! How are you? I was kind of hoping you weren't coming back." Tony broke into a laugh, and said, "No, man, I'm just kidding. Good to hear from you. Where are you?"

Long said, "I'm in New York."

"Well, I was getting ready to sell this stuff. You better come down here."

Long flew to Michigan, arranged for transshipment of the pot to Ann Arbor, and flew from there to Miami with the cash necessary to secure it. He checked into a room at the Coconut Grove hotel, called Tony, who met him there, and before getting down to business, listened to Tony describe the adventure he and the pilots had missed on the boat trip back.

Tony had set sail for Colombia with two crewmen, one of whom, a kid named Nick, had never been to sea before; Nick, a relative of Tony's partner, had come along for the money and a taste of the outlaw life. The other crew member, Dwight, was a marine mechanic whose responsibility was to keep the boat running. The fun began after the boat, steaming home from the Guajira, had cleared the Mona Passage. (The Windward Passage offered the more direct route home, but would have put Tony too close to Cuban waters, where if the boat were stopped for any reason, his arrest would have led to almost certain execution.) Just below the Tropic of Cancer the boat hit a tropical depression. The wind was blowing maybe 55 knots, and the boat, pitching and heeling in thirty-foot seas, started taking on water. The engine quit. And so had Dwight — having overdosed on Quaaludes the day before, the mechanic lay unconscious. The boat, with no power, was unable to make headway, and fell victim to the storm that much more perilously. The storm was so furious and the turbulence it caused so disorienting that young Nick found himself doing what mariners throughout history have done when hit by inescapable seasickness sufficiently virulent to deprive them of reason. He jumped overboard. Or tried to. Tony caught him, grabbed him before he went over the rail, hit him hard enough to knock him out, and lashed him to the anchor winch on the bow.

Tony fought the storm alone.

With passage of the storm Tony finally got the engine running, but the bay shrimper by then had undergone irreparable damage, and was taking on water faster than the bilge pumps could empty it. With the boat slowly sinking beneath him, he finally established radio contact with the smaller vessels scheduled to meet him off the Florida coast. He managed to off-load all but a few of the bales before the boat went down. He had a bale in his arms when he stepped off the tip of the bow onto the deck of a Bertram, and the bay shrimper went under.

Long, straight from Sabana Rubia, had no trouble buying the story. Not that there was any reason to doubt it beyond the sheer hair-raising nature of it — years later, he would come to appreciate that his own tales sounded just as wild. Tony, as it happened, was a wellspring of fantastic stories. They always proved to be true, and always taxed the imagination, as did those of the other Cuban exiles Long eventually met through him. One, an underwater demolition expert named Hector, told Long of swimming alone one night from the hatch of a U.S. submarine into Havana Harbor, where, before swimming back, he blew up a Soviet PT boat. A curious collection of characters, Tony and his friends, at one time or another, all seemed obliged for some reason to volunteer alibis for the day of the Kennedy assassination in Dallas, and all appeared to know at least two other guys whose alibis did not stand up.

These were the people with whom Allen Long was about to do business.

"So what about the pot?" Long said, after listening to Tony's story.

"It's here."

"Then let's go get it."

"It's here," said Tony, "but I don't have it."

"Well, okay," Long said, "who's got it?"

"One of my partners has it," Tony said. "We have to make arrangements with him. That's how you're going to get it."

Long said he was prepared to pay for half the pot in front. Tony said it was up to his partners whether Long, in that case, got more than half the load. A meeting was set for noon the following day at a crab house in Fort Lauderdale. When Long arrived, two of Tony's partners were with him. One, a guy named Lonnie, was a former Miami police officer. The other was a character named Virgil.

"So, you're the guy with the airplane," Virgil said.

Virgil was a native of one of those small Bahamian islands where all the locals of English ancestry make do with the same last name. His family had immigrated to the Florida Keys, settling there, impoverished, with their rural roots intact. He had gone barefoot for most of his youth, and as a citizen now of the Conch Republic, he managed to get by without wearing shoes except on formal occasions. This, apparently, was not one of them. At the meeting in Fort Lauderdale, it was he who did the talking, and the temper of his remarks signaled a significant atmosphere shift — a forecast of the heavy weather that would overhang any business Long conducted in Miami.

Allen Long's appearance in Florida coincided with a cultural sea change, and in the swift and turbulent race of things its measure was hard to read. He arrived on the waters of a rising tide in the marijuana trade, and on its currents, beneath the surface of his ability to predict them, things like peace, love, and music were about to be washed away in the undertow.

In many ways, Long's arrival in Miami was like Mick Jagger's arrival at Altamont — Long had no way of knowing it yet, but Woodstock Nation was dead.

"We have your marijuana," Virgil said, "but you owe us a hundred dollars a pound for Tony bringing it in."

Tony had prevailed upon Virgil and Lonnie to free up the entire load on the promise of a second payment from Long after the pot was sold, informing his partners that the Colombians had given their personal assurance of Long's honesty.

"Okay," said Long. "Let's go pick it up."

"Well, where's the money?"

"I'll give you the money," said Long, "let's get the pot."

"No offense," said Virgil, "but we don't know you. Now, we have the pot, and we can keep it, nothing you can do about that, so if you want it back, give us the money first."

Three strangers — none of whom, Long was guessing, knew the words to "Purple Haze," all of whom, just by the look of them, were a good bet to be gun owners — insisting that he hand over a briefcaseful of cash. And no guarantee that he would get the pot.

Long had to think it over.

Hell . . .

"Here are the keys to my car," he said. "The money's in the trunk."

Virgil did not bother to check. Sliding an ignition key across the table, he said, "It's in the truck outside." He described a cab-over camper parked behind the crab house. "We want the truck back tomorrow."

Long did not bother to check either. He drove away with the load. When finally he opened the back of the truck, the marijuana was there. But the marijuana was not his. It was Tony's commercial Colombian.

Virgil just laughed in his face when Long confronted him on it.

"You didn't really think you were going to get the good stuff back, did you? That's gone," he said. "You're not going to see it again. This is what you get, that's it."

The news came as no surprise in Ann Arbor.

"Yeah, well, I guess that was to be expected," said Myerson. "Just go back and see if you can buy more. Tell them we want another two thousand pounds at the same price to make up for it. See what they say." This, of course, was where the discussion with Tony was headed anyway. "What's important is to see how many more pounds we can buy," Myerson told Long. "Here's the message . . ."

Tony, of course, played dumb when Long complained of the switch.

"Is that what happened?" he said, shaking his head. "Oh, that's too bad, I didn't know that."

Long said, "This is not right, Tony."

Tony laughed. "You think this is a game? You think I'm going to get sideways with my partners over this? Forget it."

Long, in fact, was prepared to forget it. "Let's go somewhere from here," he said. "Let's make this thing work better for both of us."

"If you want more, you'll have to talk to my partners," said Tony. "They'll want a certain price for it."

"We don't want more," said Long, and now it was his turn to laugh. "We don't want more, Tony, we want it all."

Long had spent no more than a few hours with these guys, and he knew exactly what they were doing. First, they were dealing with each other, so naturally they were getting ripped off, and getting ripped off on a regular basis. They were probably paying the Colombians $25 a pound and selling the pot for $150. And they were moving the product piecemeal, fronting out a few hundred pounds at a time and waiting for the money to come back. Every load was full of problems, real, imagined, often invented, and there were always disputes. Given the quality-control vacuum on both ends of the line, they were probably collecting about two thirds of the money due them, and they were likely to be paying the Colombians about three fifths of the money they owed. No matter what was said on the beach at Perico, the Colombians could be sure that they would never be paid in full: "Oh, it was full of seeds," they would be told, or something like that. They could be sure to end up with a minimum of 20 percent less than agreed on.

In Miami, with numerous people involved, none of whom trusted the others, every man was operating separately, each keeping his share of the load, searching for reliable customers, fronting to a brother, a cousin, sitting on the load forever, exposed on numerous fronts. Each of them was trying to develop a distribution network in South Florida, where the DEA and Customs had concentrated most of their resources. These guys were not going to last. Somebody was going to get busted and lead the government to everybody else.

"Here's what I can do for you," Long said, and laid it out for Tony.

"You can buy twenty thousand pounds?"

"Yes."

"At one time," Tony said, just to be sure he had heard Long correctly.

"I'll take the whole load. That's right. You bring me twenty thousand pounds, I'll take it all. And I'll pay for it all within a week."

Since the flights to Colombia had begun, Myerson's market had grown. With the quality he was getting, at the price at which he was getting it, he was in a position to sell not simply to his usual distributors, but to other wholesalers at his level. His reaction to the crash of the DC-3, the crew's escape, and the rescue of the load by Tony — his immediate response to hearing the story, lifted straight from the pages of a novel — had been: "How many pounds did you say he had on that boat?"

Long offered to pay Tony $200 a pound, $50 more than he was getting, for delivery in Miami of 20,000 pounds. He would pay $1 million on delivery, and another $3 million once the load was sold. Tony could rely on something like a seven-day turnover.

Tony, who had watched the DC-3 crash, said, "If you can do that, man, you'll never have to fly an airplane again. We will bring you more marijuana than you can sell."

"I dare you to do that," said Long, adding, however, that there was one very important condition. "The marijuana has to be good."

Long had reached this point in the pot business by treating it like any other marketing enterprise. It could be avocados or automobiles. What he knew was this: Quality drives the product. Jake Myerson could turn over 20,000 pounds of *good* pot in a week.

Myerson, when he met Long, was selling the best pot he could get his hands on, but as often as not it was the same pot that somebody else was selling. Taking a third of a load of grade-A dope, the balance of which might be going to two other Michigan wholesalers, he was typically competing for market share against the very same product. Pricing was a major concern. The further he was from the source, the more people between him and the merchandise, the less room he had to maneuver. The average wholesaler found himself several transactions removed from the Colombians — a guy in Miami, a guy in New York, maybe two guys in each of those places. Allen Long occupied an enviable threshold in being a direct link between Colombia and the market. Working in partnership with him, Myerson was in a position to dominate it, he and the one or two others in Ann Arbor who had similar connections, because few could beat his price for a product the quality of which was always assured.

When Long, on his first flight to Colombia, started rejecting bales on the runway, saying, "I'm not taking this," it was the first time the Colombians had heard someone say it. No pilot had ever said it, no boat captain had ever said it. "It has to be this color. This color or that. Gold or red. Nothing else." It was a psalm Long had sung from the shores of the Guajira to the hills of Aracataca. To the growers there, he had carried the word. "The reason you're getting only eight dollars a pound," he told them, "is because you're selling marijuana *this* color with marijuana *that* color in the same bag. Why not separate it. Sell that to everybody else, sell this to me, and I'll take it at fifteen dollars."

And now, after his trip through Sabana Rubia, he knew it was possible to get the quality he sought in volume. His first move was to put Tony together with Colombians who understood quality. Both he and Tony were working with the same loosely affiliated group of people in Colombia. Whoever was behind Tony's loads was hooked into Ernesto. Long reached out through Miguel.

"Go to Ernesto," he told Miguel, "and tell him from now on that Tony is to be loaded with the good marijuana only."

The Colombians were quick to oblige. Working with Long, they had been working with one of the very few smugglers who came back to Colombia and paid them exactly what he had said he would pay. He was paying them more per pound than anyone, and he was paying them in full. There was never a dispute.

The deal Long made with Tony and his crew was born of a simple reality. Tony's people, CIA operatives and cops, had the expertise, the connections, and the muscle to get marijuana into Miami. Maritime transport, landing the contraband, and securing it — they had these things locked up. They owned South Florida that way. Indeed, while they might have been exposed on the distribution side — and as hopelessly disorganized as they might have been there — the smuggling operation itself, as Long would later discover, was run with flawless proficiency. And more than that. They ran it with absolute impunity.

Organized and scrupulously supervised by Tony's handler, Jack, the entire operation was being run out of the Miami police department. With a mandate from Washington to see that CIA clandestine ops ran uninterrupted, Jack had access to the movements of the Coast Guard and other federal agencies; his access to criminal intelligence and his ability as a police lieutenant to misdirect the resources of those agencies immunized everyone involved.

Long was introduced to Jack on a visit to Tony's house. Stepping outside, carrying cognac and a Cuban coffee, he walked with Tony past the swimming pool and through the aviary to the back of his property, and passing through the rear gate, followed Tony across the neighboring yard to the police official's house.

Jack, tall, maybe five years older than Tony, greeted Long enthusiastically.

"Hey, there's somebody here you should meet," he said, and introduced Long to another guest, a county sheriff visiting from Georgia. Presenting Long to the man in uniform, he said, "This is the guy with the airplanes."

A nervous grin set up camp on the lower perimeter of Long's face. Suppressing a shudder, he shook hands with the sheriff, a kind of whimsical odium maneuvering within him as the lawman assured him that the airplanes in question would be welcome in his jurisdiction. Long, when it was polite to do so, took Tony aside for a talk.

"Tony," he said, "I can't do business with guys in black shoes."

"What are you talking about, man?"

"I just can't work with someone wearing a uniform and a gun." Not in the United States anyway. "I can't work with cops."

Tony said, "I got news for you."

Protected, thanks to Jack, not simply from arrest but from actual scrutiny, the Miami smugglers could move as many tons of marijuana as they could sell. Their problem was they had no market, certainly not one sufficiently large or secure to reward their potential. Long, with access to some of the larger and more reliable marijuana outlets in the country, was the solution to their problem. He could make them all rich overnight. And he stood to gain just as much as they.

He would pay them $200 a pound to deliver to Miami, $50 more than he was paying after factoring in the airplane costs and the pilots' share of the take. The plane was gone, the pilots had been eliminated, and gone as well was the crapshoot of putting together a ground crew, not to mention the constellation of risks that came with flying in and out of Colombia. On a 20,000-pound load, if he split fifty-fifty with Myerson, Long would make $2 million before expenses. And he did not have to go anywhere.

It did not take spreadsheets or time and motion studies to figure this one out. It did not even take an abacus to get a reading on the deal. He could do it on his fingers.

"Let's see if these guys can deliver," he said, laying it out for Lee Carlyle.

Long needed someone in Florida. You could not do this stuff alone. You had to have a partner. You had to have somebody just to watch your back. Lee Carlyle had been living in South Florida since 1972. He had been moving Jamaican pot, and though yet to turn his dime into a million bucks, he was doing pretty well. He was also pretty good at arithmetic. When Long called and told him he needed someone to cover his play, and was willing to cut him in for half, Carlyle said, "Cool," and he said it with no hesitation.

It was Carlyle who pulled all the local logistics together. He knew where to look for a safe house, knew a trucking company willing to do business. In Davie, a rural community featuring numerous cattle and truck farms about twelve miles southwest of Fort Lauderdale, Carlyle found a farm, 120 acres, with the house situated right in the middle of the property at the end of a half-mile driveway. From the house, the length of the driveway was visible all the way to the front gate, which cut off access from the highway.

In Davie, pickup trucks were ubiquitous, and it was not unusual to see tractor-trailers pulling in and out of farmsteads hauling hay, horses, cattle, feed, produce, and other agricultural freight. In a single semi-trailer rig, 20,000 pounds of pot could easily be concealed among crates of oranges, artichokes, or cucumbers, or whatever the current crop happened to be, coming out of somewhere like Homestead. Using a working farm that had been in operation for years — where such activity was not likely to draw scrutiny — and an established long-haul trucking company, Long avoided having to lease, buy, or sign his name to anything.

The owner of the farm was paid $5 a pound; the truckers received $10.

The price that Long paid Tony, $200 a pound, was for delivery of the pot to Davie. Up to that point all the expenses were Tony's; beyond that they were Long's. Tony would pick up the pot in Colombia and deliver it offshore in Florida. (Eventually the Miami smugglers would pick up the pot closer to home, turning maritime transport over to their suppliers, the Colombians, whose freighters delivered the pot off the Bahamas. At the time, Colombian captains and crews, unlike U.S. nationals, were deported rather than imprisoned when arrested by

American authorities.) Tony's people would land the pot in a small fleet of sport-fishing boats operating out of the Keys.

There would be at least four men involved in landing the typical haul. Tony's partner Lonnie would operate one boat. Virgil would operate a second. Long had yet to meet the other two men. One was a well-known Islamorada charter captain. The other was a guy named Frank, "Frank A.," as Tony A. referred to him. No relation. Frank A. was a former Miami police sergeant who sported the last name of a legendary (and violently late) New York crime family boss — which anyone could be expected to do if the (late) crime boss were his uncle.

These men were at the center of a smuggling enterprise that over the next two years would land over half a million pounds of marijuana in South Florida. The majority of the dope would be distributed by Jake Myerson in Ann Arbor. (As the numbers escalated, the Miami smugglers would develop additional outlets of their own.) In the middle, orchestrating the flow of traffic between Miami and Ann Arbor — between Miami and wherever it went, the traffic becoming so heavy that Myerson could not handle it all — in the middle, taking their dime, stood Allen Long and Lee Carlyle.

It was the beginning of a new era for Long, an era in which he just went to Miami every month or so and waited. All he had to do was be there when the phone call came in.

By 1977 boat builders in Florida had ascended to the cultural status of movie stars. This was the age of the "go-fast." Go-fast was the smuggler's term for those production power boats, first manufactured by Miami's legendary Don Aronow, famous for their deep-V hull design, and marketed under various brand names, including Formula, Donzi, Magnum Marine, and Cigarette. The last fell into generic use as a term for all similar offshore speedboats. Featuring twin inboard V-8 engines, or up to four high-performance outboards, the oceangoing racers were typically thirty to forty feet long and cost in the neighborhood of $100,000. They were capable of traveling over 75 knots through choppy seas (only slightly slower carrying a thousand pounds of marijuana or cocaine) and could outrun anything the Coast Guard had.

Bertram and Hatteras, the big sport-fishing boat manufacturers, were well established at the time. Bertram had dominated speedboat racing until Aronow came along. A fifty-foot Bertram or Hatteras sport fisherman, every weekend sailor's wet dream, could cost $450,000. And could carry a lot of pot: between 6,000 and 12,000 pounds of it. The advantage of a Cigarette or similar muscle-boat was speed. The disadvantages included not only the go-fast's limited capacity, but the fact that every one of them drew the scrutiny of the U.S. Coast Guard. A Bertram or Hatteras, or any other reliable sport fisherman, beyond its cargo capacity, benefited greatly from its ubiquity in the waters off South Florida. Late in the afternoon, on any given day, there were probably 350 charter boats out fishing the Gulf Stream between Fort Lauderdale and the Keys. There were so many of them, owned by so many legitimate people, that their very visibility made them invisible.

Steaming from the Guajira to, say, Orange Cay in the Bahamas, a Colombian coastal freighter could take anywhere from three and a half to seven days. To Orange Cay from the Keys was about five hours in a Hatteras. The typical off-loader would take his boat out fishing in the Straits all day, just waiting for the signal that his freighter was lying off Great Bahama Bank. On some nights, there might have been four freighters there unloading. Boats would be all over the place:

"Are you from Raúl?"

"No, I am from Rafael. Raúl is over there."

The setup invited the occasional rip-off: a guy with a death wish and a Cigarette, say, sneaking into the confusion, taking on some smuggler's dope, and speeding away. Or an off-loader who had business out there might simply succumb to greed. But such boat captains, while bold, rarely grew old. There was a price to pay. Various techniques — beyond retributive murder — were employed to prevent such losses. One was to provide the captain and off-loader with halves of the same hundred-dollar bill. If the serial numbers did not match up, the off-loader did not get the pot.

Tony's people would take on pot in the Bahamas at night, then fish the Gulf Stream, fully loaded, all the following day, coming in early that evening with all the other fishing boats returning to the Keys. Much of Tony's time was devoted to the purchase of real estate, to finding and buying up what the CIA called "holes" — safe houses situated on the various canals that snaked through the Keys at which the pot could be unloaded. The boat would tie up to the dock at the rear of the house, and sometime after dark, once activity died down, with no more boats coming up the canal, the unloading would begin.

Long was on hand one day when the two A.'s, Tony and Frank, were overseeing an off-load, and was struck by the proficiency with which they handled the job.

Frank A., until he became a cop, was completely legit, having moved to Florida with his father, a Miami businessman, whose brothers back in Brooklyn were pursuing more newsworthy careers ascending to stardom in the New York rackets. Frank owned a five-acre compound on the ocean in Key Largo. It had a high fence, a heavy gate, and a long pier, tied up to which he kept a fifty-foot sport fisherman. The day Long showed up at the compound there were eight guys sitting around. On a canal about four miles away, tied up at the dock of a pink stucco house — a "hole" procured by Tony — were three boats and 12,000 pounds of dope waiting to be unloaded.

At four in the afternoon, the county sheriff's office called the compound. Reports had been received of suspicious activity in the vicinity of the safe house.

"A heads-up from the locals," said Frank, hanging up the phone.

Tony said, "Call Angie."

Frank put in the call.

At the compound two hours later, a policeman came through the door. He came in by way of the kitchen wearing the uniform of a Miami sergeant. Beyond him, as he entered, Long could see a squad car idling in the driveway. Long, looking the cop over, figuring he could outrun him, was backing his way out of the kitchen when Frank started talking to the guy.

"Angie," Frank said to the sergeant, "we need to cool that neighborhood off. Go tell all the residents there to vacate their houses. Tell them there's an investigation, a drug operation going down at the pink house. Tell them vacate the premises or stay indoors, and stay away from the windows."

Angie left to take care of things, but at nine P.M., when it was time to move, all the off-loaders waiting at Frank's were nervous nonetheless.

"Come on, let's go, it's cool," said Frank, moving them toward the door. "Come on," he finally told them, "watch, I'll lead the way."

The off-loaders followed him out. A minute later Frank was back.

"They just needed somebody to open the door," he said, and everybody laughed.

The pot went into pickups fitted with cab-over campers, all equipped with air shocks, road-levelers like those installed in the limousines Long had used in Marin. At eight the next morning, with all the rush-hour traffic into Miami, the trucks headed for the parking lot of a strip mall near the farmhouse in Davie.

Letting the numerous truck drivers know where the stash house was located would have been a real security risk. That they might reveal its whereabouts to authorities, should they ever be arrested, was not the sole liability — a rip-off team coming in with guns, taking the load and leaving bodies behind, was another problem that came to mind. Long, to take delivery of a load, had set up a system of double cutouts. When he received a call that a boat was in, he would send people to sit on the house, people he knew he could trust, people from out of town. People like Little Eddie and his crew.

The driver of the pickup knew only that he was to drop the truck in the designated parking lot. He was to leave the keys in the ashtray, and disappear for an hour, maybe in the bar across the street from the strip mall. Seeing the truck arrive, Long would pick it up, drive it to the house, log it in — plate number, number of bales — and unload it. He would sweep it out, deodorize it, and have it back in the parking lot well within the hour. When the driver returned to the lot, the keys to the truck would be in the ashtray, and the pickup would be empty. And that was all the driver needed to know. Twenty thousand pounds of pot amounted to maybe ten pickup loads, and Long could count on seeing the same driver two or three times.

The quality of the pot Long was moving, all gold and red and stacked in abundance, made a stunning impression on the guys from New Jersey sitting on the safe house. There was no air conditioner in the house, and all the windows were kept closed. The smell of pot permeated the place, and Long did not want it escaping. He did not want the pungent aroma picked up by some serviceman reading a meter. Walking into the house, he was not surprised to find Little Eddie ripped on the fumes.

"Man this is . . ."

"Yeah."

". . . the best stuff . . ."

"Uh-huh."

". . . I've . . ."

"See . . . ?"

". . . ever seen."

". . . I told you."

Later that night a Peterbilt tractor pulling a forty-four-foot refrigeration van turned onto the property. It was filled with crates of avocados, sidewall to sidewall, from the reefer unit to the rear door, from the upper side-rail to the deck. When the smugglers set to work, all the cargo from the side door forward was removed from the truck. The marijuana bales were then loaded in and stacked against the front wall. A plywood bulkhead was erected behind it, the edges sealed with duct tape. A layer of plastic was taped over that. The produce was reloaded, as much as was needed to refill the space, and the truck was dispatched to Ann Arbor.

(It was only one of the methods used. No more than 14,000 pounds could be hauled that way — two trucks would be needed to move a 20,000-pound load — because the bales had to be kept one foot forward of the side door to avoid detection by police. Florida state troopers searched for dope by forcing a hollow pipe through the load, from the door to the opposite sidewall, extracting the pipe to check its contents for contraband.)

As soon as the pot arrived in Davie, Long paid Tony and his friends. A million in cash, sent down from Michigan. He flew to Ann Arbor to pick up the rest. In less than a week everyone had his money.

14 VIOLETS FOR YOUR FURS

"That stuff is bad for you," Constance said, cleaning up around the cocaine.

All the time he was operating in Florida, Long maintained residence in New York. His housekeeper, Constance, from Belize, came twice a week to clean the apartment, and if when she arrived there was no blow out on the living room coffee table, she could find it there within a few hours.

Long did not rise until one P.M., and by late afternoon, as often as not, the apartment was crawling with an assortment of coke-snorting troublemakers around whom Constance found herself navigating.

At just after four there would be several limousines parked on the street below, each having deposited on 68th Street a stockbroker who had punched out of his Wall Street office at precisely 3:48. Long's playmates treated the place as if it were theirs, and just like working stiffs everywhere they had fallen into a routine. There was no limit on the liquor and cocaine, but girls from the outcall service had to be paid and gone from the apartment by no later than six-thirty, when the boys got down to the business of colluding to churn stock. Selecting an issue to start pumping at, say, nine-thirty the following morning for a sell-off at two P.M., the crowd would then head home, leaving Long and the one unmarried broker among them to go running in Central Park.

There was no shortage of philosophies around the coffee table, and none better served to illuminate the world that Long and his friends were on top of than the following deconstruction of mankind's habits, which was ventured by one sage to the memorable music of rocks of cocaine being crushed:

"There are jewelry guys, and there are coat guys," he said.

"I'm a jewelry guy," responded one of the others.

"Most guys are jewelry guys. I'm a jewelry guy, you're a jewelry guy. Allen, he's a coat guy."

Long did not deny it, but he was justified in taking issue with the categorical nature of the assertion. Mink coats as sexual bribery were typically associated with older men. What made him stand out among his contemporaries, he insisted, was the fact that he was *also* a coat guy.

"I'd have to say I'm both," he admitted.

And he paid for his habits in ways that went beyond the expenditure of cash. One evening at Mary Lou's, a Ninth Street restaurant he favored, he was having a drink with a young record company employee he had romanced some months before, having surprised her back then with the black mink she was wearing at the moment. Now she had a surprise for him. The surprise arrived in the person of an ex-girlfriend of Long's who joined them at their table wearing a gray fox coat Long had bought her on the same day. ("You should wear your fur coat," he had told the latter, inviting her to lunch. "I don't have one," she had said. "Let's fix that," Long had replied.) She in turn was now followed into the restaurant by Cherie, wearing a diabolical smile and the white custom-made mink she had received from Long at the time he was fooling around with the other two. Long, contemplating the fix he was in, yearned for the Guajira and the chattering of submachine guns.

While Long and Cherie were clearly a couple, Long had readily seen to it, once they were settled in New York, that Cherie had her own apartment. While Long was smuggling pot, and investing his time and money in various legitimate projects as well — his own, chiefly in the music business, and those of various entrepreneurial friends in need of working capital — Cherie studied acting at the Neighborhood Playhouse. For a while she ran a small business of her own, designing children's knitted wear. In 1977 she put together a portfolio to seek out modeling work. Long hired the most expensive fashion photographer available, and Cherie eventually signed with the Wilhelmina agency.

Like women in the lives of most dope smugglers, Cherie had little impact on Long's business activities, and because those activities ate up so much of his life, very little call on his time. What made her different from the other people to whom he devoted attention was that it was she to whom he did the really significant lying and, in spreading himself around sexually, upon her that he was officially cheating. She would do her best to protect him, from his friends and from himself, and like others in similar circumstances she would inevitably fail.

As relationships went, theirs was dysfunctional even by the standards of the dope business, and probably would have been even in its absence. Both the children of absentee fathers (and, as it happened, schoolteacher mothers), neither was blessed with a stable frame of reference when it came to affairs of the heart. Long's father had left his wife and run off with an airline stewardess — at a time when the culture viewed flight attendants, stereotypically, as sexual trophies — and Cherie's dad, a high school coach, had managed to come up with an act that put that move in the shade. Cherie learned that her father, while living at home, before finally running out on her mother, was simultaneously raising another family across town.

Growing up in conjugal Disneyland, both would bring to their love affair an emotional history that was questionable at best. Nonetheless, for a good part of his career as a smuggler, Long's personal life, if you could call it that, would pretty much be seen by friends as the Allen and Cherie show. And for all the *Sturm und Drang*, his romance

255

with Cherie was the one against which all of his other infatuations were measured.

With Long, Cherie would travel to Aruba, Jamaica, St. Croix, and the Dominican Republic, and to numerous places around the country. And, of course, she would travel regularly to Studio 54.

The disco on West 54th Street was the hottest ticket in town, and its operators, Steve Rubell and Ian Schrager, had yet to be danced to jail by their felonies, when Long, with Cherie and some friends visiting from Virginia, first showed up at the door in 1977, only to be turned away. Made guys from Brooklyn, similarly snubbed, got right in the doorman's face, muttering, "You don't know who you're fucking with." Which was patently ridiculous — a joint like Studio 54, in order to stay in business, was dealing with wiseguys every day. Long, who did know who he was fucking with, knew better than to waste his time.

The following morning he was on the phone to the office of lawyer Roy Cohn, the notorious former counsel to the subcommittee of red-baiting Senator Joseph McCarthy in the 1950s. Now, some twenty years after nailing down his ignominious place in history, Cohn was celebrated by the New York media as the toughest lawyer in town. Among other things, he was a big-time mob lawyer. But Long was not looking for legal muscle. Long happened to know that Cohn was attorney for Studio 54. Getting a partner of Cohn's on the phone, Long explained that in trying to crack the door at the club he had been told he was "not on the list." Informed that "five thousand dollars will fix that," Long effectively "hired" the law firm, sending the money by messenger in cash. That night he showed up at the disco with Cherie and his friends, whispered to the doorman, "I'm on the list," and walked them in. There and at Xenon — same jive, different address — Long and Cherie remained regulars until both clubs ceased to be hip.

Studio 54 was neither the first nor the only public establishment in the country with a policy of ignoring the open use of illicit drugs on its premises. But the club, in the way it promoted itself, even in its decor, celebrated and effectively encouraged their use, and was by virtue of its visibility at the epicenter for their explosion out of the counterculture and into the mainstream. *High Times* magazine, whose Christmas card one year featured a photograph and the season's greetings of Andy Warhol and Truman Capote, threw private parties at the club at which one was likely to find himself standing with either or both of those celebrated Americans while waiting in line to avail himself of the large nitrous oxide tanks provided for the use of guests.

Studio 54, during the brief period in which it was the place to be seen, provided the backdrop for one of Long's more gratifying performances as a pot smuggler. It was a moment the likes of which came around rarely for Long: a chance to luxuriate publicly in his illegal accomplishments. He and Cherie were dining one night with one of his record business associates at the upmarket Maxwell's Plum, an East Side saloon of some social significance at the time. His associate had invited a friend, a wealthy investment banker, who, having acquired his wealth legitimately, was unafraid to brag, albeit discreetly, about his success.

"Real estate speculation and equity financing. That's my specialty," he told Long.

As it happened, he and Long would grow to be very close friends, but that night Long resented the supposition that there was a big shot at the table bigger than he. Long had a limousine waiting out front, and after dinner suggested that the two men and their wives hop in with him and Cherie, and head across town "to 54." There, to the throbbing music and the flashing of colored lights, God blessed the smuggler with the sublime opportunity to assert bragging rights of his own.

"This is really great pot," the banker volunteered, shouting to be heard over the deafening thud of the sound system, as he sucked on a joint that Long had passed around.

"You like that?" asked Long.

"I don't think I've ever smoked anything better."

Long nodded his head, gave it a second, and leaned in to speak into the banker's ear.

"That's *my* specialty," he said.

Smuggling pot was high-risk work and promoted bonds of sincere friendship between Long and the people he worked with. When Pablo

Cepeda paid him a visit in New York, there were two memories the high-strung *costeño* wanted to take home from the trip. He wanted to dance at Studio 54, and he wanted to meet Raquel Welch. The trip was El Demonio's first to the United States, and Long did everything he could to oblige. The first request he handled immediately upon Pablo's arrival. And Pablo cut quite a figure on the dance floor at the club. In blue blazer, gray slacks, and black lace-up shoes, it was almost as if he were in costume, but the weird impression he made on the disco's jaded patrons did not measure up to the impression they made on him.

"I cannot believe it!" he said, rushing up to Long at one point, his incredulity having rendered him breathless.

"What is it, buddy?" said Long.

"No one in my country will believe it!"

"What happened, Pablo?" asked Cherie.

He pointed through the crowd. And there, just off the dance floor, stood the source of his dismay. El Demonio had been pushed to the point of near insensibility by the sight of two cowboys kissing. Both were six feet tall, blond and cut like bodybuilders. Draped in Western roundup gear, right down to the rawhide riding chaps, shirtless, muscles rippling beneath matching leather vests, they were also draped around each other, swaying to the music, doing those kinds of things that Lawrence of Arabia left out of his official reports to the Crown.

"My people won't believe this," said Pablo. "John Wayne is *maricón?*"

"Pablo," Cherie was quick to assure him, "not all cowboys kiss."

And the same was true, Long wanted to say, of construction workers and cops, even if one could not prove it by the evidence of the dance floor. But Pablo, he figured, probably knew that already.

Pablo's rendezvous with Raquel Welch was equally memorable, but alas, it was memorable to everyone but Pablo. So drunk did he get at her show at Caesars Palace in Las Vegas that he would be unable to recall screaming "I love you, Raquel, I love you," just before passing out. Easy Matthews, who was along on the junket, caught him as he fell. The big redhead, laughing, hoisted the unconscious Colombian onto his shoulder and carried him out of the joint, transporting him in that fashion back to the Aladdin, where the smugglers were staying.

In Allen Long's New York, where the greatest sin, indeed, the only crime of any consequence, was being out of style, the money he made smuggling marijuana put him on everyone's A-list. But the acceptance he sought would never be complete, or at least be entirely trustworthy, until a year or so after he arrived.

Long was driving to Florida, making his way to Miami with a million in cash in his car. The money was in two Samsonite "two-suiters," a half a million dollars in each, in tens, twenties, and fifties. Passing through Virginia, he stopped in to see his grandfather. They were sitting in the den of his grandfather's house, and the elder Long, as always, was paying periodic visits to the bathroom, where he had his whiskey stashed in the toilet tank no more than an arm's length from the medicine cabinet, where he kept a bottle of mouthwash. His wife did not approve of his drinking, and like every alcoholic the old man had it worked out.

"This is what I made last month," Long said, unlocking the suitcases.

Long wanted nothing more than he wanted the approval of the man who had taught him to hunt and fish. He wanted his grandfather to be proud of him.

"How you makin' this money?"

"I'm a pot smuggler," said Long.

"What's that?"

"Marijuana."

"Marijuana?"

The old man laughed. He shook his head and laughed so hard that tears ran down his cheeks. They filled the furrows of his flesh. His hands were big, his wrists were thick, and his fingers, the size of sausages, all but obscured his face when he removed his glasses to dry his eyes.

"That's how I bought my first car," he confessed.

Using his handkerchief to dry his spectacles, he shook his head and reflected. He had run bootleg liquor, he said.

"Tennessee to Ohio."

He talked about moonshine and revenue agents. Long told him about the airplanes.

"Just one word of advice," the elder man said.

"What's that?

He gave his grandson three.

"Don't get caught."

It was shortly thereafter that Long was offered leadership of the family lock-manufacturing business. Long always saw it as his grandfather's acknowledgment of him as an achiever. And that was enough for the young scammer. Benefiting from the sad example set by his father, and seeing the offer for what it was — a promise of independence that would never be honored — Long declined the position, and not graciously. It was a negotiation whose low point came when his grandfather, in front of him, dismissed his father from the room. Long had challenged them to hand over control of the company to him in advance, telling them he was running a multimillion-dollar drug-smuggling enterprise — he had a Learjet waiting, he boasted — and was not about to give it up for $40,000 a year.

(Tom, his younger brother, ended up stepping into the job. And after almost twenty years with the firm, he still never received any stock. As general manager Tom returned the business to profitability, but was not allowed to reverse the company's long-term slide, which was precipitated by the profit-taking of his father and aunt, who together withheld the stock from him, their mistreatment of his brother being something for which Long would never forgive them. The corporation was eventually liquidated.)

In Florida, Long's business was rolling, propelled by its own momentum, the conspirators' appetite for money expanding with the nation's appetite for dope. Everything tasted like "more."

Moving 20,000 pounds on their first load, the smugglers moved 40,000 on their second. They went from twenty to forty right away. Doing a dozen boats over the next year and a half, they never did less than twenty, and sometimes they did eighty. They began moving so much pot that Myerson's people in Michigan could not sell it all. Long and Carlyle, in control of the flow, had to search out other buyers. In Washington, Easy Matthews started receiving significant weight. Carlyle opened a new market with wholesalers in Northern California.

Finding themselves at the center of a spreading network, outgrowing the stash house in Davie, Long and Carlyle moved their operation to Jupiter, Florida, to a bigger farm with a capacious barn on the property. They started moving so much pot, they hit a point of diminishing returns. A buyer, a distributor, with two months to sell 20,000 pounds, could move the weight through his own channels. But to sell 100,000 pounds in that time, if the smugglers wanted the money right away, he would have to sell it to other distributors, wholesalers with channels of their own, and he would have to sell it for a lot less.

Tony, after the initial deal had been struck, took Long aside for a chat.

"I don't want you to tell my partners," he said, "but you know, you wouldn't have made this deal without me."

Tony wanted an extra $5 a pound from Long's end on every load. Which amounted to a minimum of $100,000 on every boat that came in. Long subsequently discovered that Tony, God bless him, had gone to all of the others involved and made a similar pitch.

"Hey, I don't want you to think I'm greedy," he told them, "but I want an extra nickel from each of you for making you rich with this guy."

This was the "Cuban way" that Tony had been talking about. Everyone said okay, and everyone remembered not to say anything about Tony's nickel to anyone else. It was a measure of his charm. Everybody loved Tony.

Long figured Tony was making an extra $400,000 per trip. Or something in that vicinity. He was never quite sure how the Miami partnerships were set up. They seemed to be kind of fluid. Lonnie was definitely a partner — he was to Tony what Carlyle was to Long. Virgil and the others operated at a level of participation that probably changed after the first transaction.

With the operation up and running, Tony called Long in New York and asked him to attend a meeting.

"I want you to come down to Florida," he said. "Somebody wants to meet you."

Long flew to Miami and met Tony at Victoria Station, a restaurant not far from the airport. He found Tony and Lonnie there, seated with a Colombian gent. The man's name was Gilberto, he was somewhere in his fifties, and his outfit was a giveaway. The boots, the solid gold belt buckle, the ten-gallon hat — he was straight off the Guajira. Gilberto was the man behind the man Tony did business with in Colombia. And he had come to Miami to meet the American who was sending him all the money.

It was a social call more than anything: a General Motors executive in a show of courtesy to the sales manager of Chevrolet's highest-performing dealership. The meeting was conducted in that spirit, an exercise in camaraderie, but the two men did not part company without paying passing attention to business.

"How much merchandise can you sell?" Gilberto was curious to know.

Long let his ego answer.

"If the quality remains the same," he said, "I can handle one hundred thousand pounds at a time."

"Good," said Gilberto, all energy and corporate enthusiasm. "I will send it to Tony."

And he did. And Long moved it. He and Carlyle, it seemed, could move anything.

Carlyle was living north of Fort Lauderdale, renting a house with a swimming pool on a canal off the Intracoastal Waterway. Tied to the dock behind the house was his thirty-eight-foot Magnum sedan, midnight blue on black, with twin 400 horsepower inboard V-8s. In it he and Long would cruise the clubs along the Intracoastal, the hippest of which all had docks. At any one of them on a good night, Cigarettes were tied three deep.

In the way that Studio 54 presented the new look of drug consumption, Miami nightlife was the contemporary expression of drug dealing in the United States. Gone was the tie-dyed-good-vibrations-cop-a-lid standard of cool. There was nothing laid back about the scene. Guys like Long and Carlyle were no more a part of the counter-culture than the typical movie star.

There was nothing particularly political about marijuana anymore. And from the point of view of the dealer, there probably never had been. For him, even on campus, it had always been about business. For the dealer, even as a dedicated pot smoker, it had always been less about revolution than it was about conspicuous consumption. The latter was the real organizing principle, and Miami was the movement's Jerusalem.

None of the scammers in Miami could have found his way to a college campus. Had he done so, he would have been about as comfortable there as one of the bootleggers in *Guys and Dolls*. And thus it was not surprising that Lee Carlyle, in the forefront of the movement, had his problems with Jake Myerson. Not only was Myerson fairly well educated, but the Ann Arbor resident was active, by way of other interests, in the academic life of the university. As were many business-people in the city. What Carlyle saw in Myerson was a guy who preached the old pot-smoking principles and values, and promoted the political rectitude of the cause, but who was always very religious about the dough.

He saw Myerson as a guy with "a bad attitude." Myerson just rubbed him the wrong way. And the hostility was reciprocal. The two did not like each other at all, and their mutual aversion was manifest right from the outset of the deal.

"What do we need him for?" Myerson demanded, when Long brought Carlyle aboard.

"Hey, Lee's my friend," said Long. "I'm cutting him in."

When Long and Carlyle branched out to supply other distributors, Carlyle naturally asked the same question about Myerson, developing an understandable myopia as he and Long took in more money per pound from other buyers than Myerson was paying.

"What do we need him for?" Carlyle said "Why sell to him for two-twenty-five when we can sell it for two-seventy-five?"

Long grew weary of trying to impress upon his partner the advantages of the fast nickel over the slow dime. "No waiting, instant turn-around . . ."

"Allen, he's lying to you," Carlyle said. "He's not selling it for three hundred. It's going for three-fifty up there."

The beef intensified and took on more serious overtones when it became apparent to Myerson that Carlyle's prodigious intake of dope went far beyond the recreational. Carlyle was stoned, coked up, and drunk, it seemed, twenty-four hours a day. His tolerance for methaqualone was staggering. He was eating Quaaludes like they were candy, gobbling the pills by the handful. The popular hypnotic, marketed by more than one pharmaceutical house and bootlegged nationwide, had what Myerson saw as the distinct disadvantage of knocking Carlyle silly without knocking him out.

"This guy's trouble," said Myerson. "He's a liability."

Long was willing to concede that Carlyle lacked certain social graces.

"He's a complete fuck-up," Myerson said. "He's unreliable."

Carlyle *was* a fuck-up. Long knew that. But Carlyle was his friend. And Carlyle was his partner. And furthermore, in the end . . . well . . . Carlyle was no bigger a fuck-up than he, most of the time. Admittedly, Carlyle might have been slightly more dangerous. But Long was doing so much cocaine by now that he bore watching himself. As time passed and the money, flowing ashore with the predictability of the tide, began rising to the level at which it threatened to take up living space, Long, to put it in Myerson's words, was growing "more detached." (The characterization being a measure of Myerson's social graces.) He was throwing more and more parties at which he was the only guest.

It was a month after the meeting with Gilberto that Tony said he had a problem.

"The feds were at my house."

He informed Long that his old bay shrimper had come back up out of the water. The Coast Guard had found it drifting upside down off

Miami. There were still a few bales in the hull. The boat was in Tony's name. Tony had reported the boat stolen — legally he was in the clear — but there would be some heat on him for a while. Therefore, he would no longer be dealing hands-on.

"I'm sending someone else," he said.

Tony had, in fact, been visited by the feds, but that had happened sometime earlier. And it was not why he was stepping aside. If you could call it stepping aside. The truth was that Jack in Miami, sniffing the bureaucratic wind, had decided to sever the direct link between his operatives and the dope. Word had come down from Washington, where dope was beginning to draw a lot of political attention. The time had come for Tony and the others to distance themselves from the traffic, not to close down the operation, or even end their participation, but to insert a cutout that would put them beyond the reach of any criminal investigation.

Tony A. was a pioneer. On his own, like Long, he had traveled to Colombia and scared up a marijuana connection. One of the first smugglers to tap the Colombian pipeline, he transported the dope himself. As much as anything, it was an adventure for Tony, an outlet for his specialized talents, the kind of thing the government had trained him to do. Tony did not need the money. Doing contract work for the CIA, and simultaneously pursuing lucrative cover careers secured for them by the agency, he and others like him had already amassed legitimate wealth. They worked for agency front companies, and in some cases controlled them, establishing their own corporations with ever available CIA financing. Jack invested their money for them and over the years it grew. They owned real estate, held interests in local businesses, and they had substantial holdings of cash. Tony was rich before he ever sailed to the Guajira. He started smuggling marijuana pretty much because it was there. And he had done it for the collective good of his Cuban brothers-in-arms. It was lucrative, it was fun, and the government looked the other way.

Tony was a worker. He was downright cavalier about the money. Jack's job was to handle the money, Tony's job was to handle the job. One of the standing rules Tony observed was never to smuggle cocaine. So serious was he about it, and so nonchalant was he about the money, that once, rather than haul it, he threw a hundred kilos of coke overboard. Somebody else's coke. He just threw it into the drink. The coke had been secreted by Colombian traffickers within a load of pot Tony was transporting. It was destined for a dealer in Miami. Tony's habit, after hitting the Florida Straits, was to cruise the coast, off-loading the pot to numerous boats as he made his way to Key Largo. The coke dealer could have been associated with any of the guys on that end of the line. Tony suspected the guy was tied into Frank A.

(Tony eventually met the dealer himself. Heaving the cocaine over the side resulted in an ongoing relationship in which the dealer made repeated attempts to kill him. Finally Jack squared things away, bringing all the various forces of corruption in the Miami police department to bear on the solution.)

Now it was time for Tony to sever his connection to the dope. He would no longer be dealing with the Colombians. He was turning the operation over to someone else, a guy by the name of Jimmy, a Cuban exile who had worked for him, and who knew his way around boats. Tony was stepping aside, but he would still be making his money. He was going to retire "a little bit." Jimmy, who had trained with a different CIA cell, was the operation's cutout.

But Long would not learn this until much later. Long's assumption at the time was that Tony's wife was pressuring him to quit. Events would lead him to assume, also, that Jimmy — ruthless where Tony was charming, hungry where Tony was not — had effectively pushed Tony aside. Only later did Tony cop to the setup. All Long knew, or needed to know, was that he would be dealing with Jimmy from then on.

As he would later come to describe it: "This was a step in the wrong direction."

15   CEILING ZERO

Jimmy Alvarez was in his late thirties. He stood about five-feet-seven. His hair was black and wavy, and he wore it combed straight back, revealing the pale complexion and sharp patrician features that announced a highborn European ancestry. He had a broad face, a weightlifter's body, and a heart as cold as a New York bank lobby. He had been active at the Bay of Pigs, was protected by the CIA, was driven by ambition, paranoia, and greed, and had no wife or children. His family consisted entirely of a young girlfriend who was scared to death of him and 5,000 fighting roosters that he kept on a farm in Homestead.

In the fall of 1977 Long was in Miami, at the Coconut Grove with Cherie, when Tony showed up at the hotel unannounced, invited him outside, and, as a professional courtesy, explained that Long was about to be murdered.

"What are you talking about, Tony?"

"Jimmy says that someone stole two thousand pounds of his pot."

"And you believe it was me?"

"I told him that he must be mistaken," said Tony. "I said I would talk to you."

"So?"

"Before I go back," he said, "I just got to ask."

And look Long in the eye when he did.

"I just have to know," Tony said.

Long's blue eyes held fast, as though shot through with embalming fluid.

"Tony, I don't need to steal anything from anybody."

"Well, you know," said Tony, shrugging.

"No," said Long. "Don't give me that. You remember when you wanted me to steal that pot from Lonnie?"

"Hey . . ."

"And I said no? You remember that?"

"Man, that wasn't stealing."

Not according to Tony.

It had happened earlier that year. Lonnie, dispatching pickup trucks from Key Largo to the farm in Davie, had miscalculated the number of bales aboard. He had merely counted the trucks and multiplied. One truck was a bit bigger than the others, and Long had ended up with 2,000 pounds of pot he had not been charged for. Long had called Tony to straighten it out.

"Did you tell Lonnie yet?" Tony had asked.

"You're his partner. I'm telling you," said Long.

"But you didn't tell him?"

"No."

"Okay, let's keep it to ourselves," said Tony.

Long knew where he was going.

"I can't do that, Tony. Forget it."

Tony saw the screw-up as a free 2,000 pounds, a ton of pot that only he and Long knew anything about. Tony figured that rather than split whatever he and Lonnie were making, he would split $600,000 with Long.

"I can't do it, Tony," Long said.

Tony said he would take care of the Colombians, he would make something up. Lonnie would not have to make good.

"Forget it," said Long. "It's not gonna happen, Tony. It's not how I do things."

"Hey, don't you think he would do the same thing if he had the chance?" Tony said.

"Listen to what you're saying, man. Right now, you trust me completely. If I did this, how could you ever trust me again?"

"Hey, that's how it works."

Long said, "It's not how I work."

And now, on the street outside the Coconut Grove, he said it to Tony again.

"You know that's not how I operate. If Jimmy is missing some pot," he said, "I had nothing to do with it."

"Okay," said Tony, "we know who it was."

Long had no idea who it was. Numerous people had handled the shipment in question. One of them, whom Long had met, a young Miami restaurateur named Andreas — a hardworking Cuban family man just getting started in business — was later found tied to a chair in his restaurant with a bullet hole in his head. Long figured maybe it was him.

Jimmy adhered to a homicide schedule the way other business-men booked golf. Several months later, Long was in New York kicking back between shipments when Jimmy called from Miami.

"I want you to know that I am not going to kill you," he said.

Jimmy in a sentimental mood.

"Well, thanks, Jimmy," Long replied. "To what do I —"

"I am not mad at you," Jimmy said. "I know it is not your fault."

How nice, thought Long. "Okay," he said. He felt lucky.

"But I am going to kill Lee."

Shit.

"The money," said Jimmy, "is not important. It is the respect."

According to Jimmy, not only had Carlyle not paid him — to the tune of $420,000 — but Carlyle had insulted him. Long said he would fly to Miami and straighten it out. He asked Jimmy to hold off doing anything until he could get there.

"I'm sure it's just a misunderstanding," he said.

And then he called Carlyle.

"Fuck you . . . ! Fuck you and your Cuban friends . . . ! And fuck . . . !"

Right away Long had a feeling Carlyle was in trouble.

"Motherfucker . . . !" screamed Carlyle. "I'm not paying them shit . . . ! If they kill me, Allen, I guarantee I'm gonna fuckin' kill you!"

Yeah, he was in trouble.

Long flew to Miami, went directly to Jimmy's house, and explained the situation.

"Lee says he respects you tremendously, Jimmy. He told me he meant no insult. Lee would *never* insult you. It was just a mistake, a misunderstanding. I'm going to see him now."

"Excellent," said Jimmy.

He introduced Long to a Cuban gent, a recent arrival to the nation's shores, or so Long had to assume, for the young man spoke no English.

"This is the man who is going to kill him," said Jimmy. "He will go with you."

And kill Carlyle if he did not show the proper respect.

Long called Carlyle and arranged to meet him not far from his house in a parking lot off the Interstate. Long and Jimmy's hired assassin cruised to the meeting in a Cadillac Seville. Conversing in Spanish — on Long's part a very labored version thereof — they talked about the business at hand.

"Who is this man Lee?"

"He's my partner," Long explained. "He's a good guy. You'll like him. He just drinks a little too much."

It was about ten on a Saturday morning. Carlyle pulled into the lot in his black BMW coupé, stepped out of the car, and approached the yellow Seville in which Long and the Cuban were waiting. He wore cutoff jeans and a T-shirt, no more, and Long could see that he had been up all night. Carlyle stopped four feet from the driver's side window, folded at the waist, and rocked forward like a flamingo, craning his neck to eyeball the pair.

Long essayed a quick chemical analysis: cocaine, Quaaludes, alcohol . . .

As Carlyle extended his index finger to stick in the assassin's face, Long put his left hand over the assassin's right, which rested on the seat between them gripping a .38 caliber revolver.

"You Cuban motherfuckers . . ."

Oh, and he had had his coffee, too, it appeared.

"You Cuban motherfuckers . . ." he drawled, his eyelids holding at half-mast.

And that was just the beginning.

Carlyle from where he stood could not see the revolver, and Long from where he sat would not let go of the twitching hand that was holding it.

"What did he say?" asked the Cuban, turning to Long.

"He is telling you of the respect he has for the Cuban people."

"I don't think that is what he is saying."

Carlyle continued vomiting up verbiage, and Long continued to translate.

"He understands Jimmy's position, and he fully intends to pay . . ."

Carlyle growled out the last of his abuse, lowered his finger, and barked: "Did you tell him what I said?"

"Word for word," said Long.

Carlyle stalked off. Long smiled, nodded his head, and put his hand on the Cuban's shoulder.

"*Bueno!*" he said.

They returned to Coral Gables, where Long was pleased to report to Jimmy that everything was fine. He got Carlyle on the phone later that day.

"A gun?" said Carlyle.

"You are the biggest —"

Carlyle, suddenly sober, assured Long that he would phone Jimmy and make things right. He put in the call immediately. Apologizing to Jimmy, he was quick to affirm his abiding respect. He said that he had gotten the message and that he was grateful to Jimmy for giving him the opportunity to straighten things out.

He concluded by saying, "But, Jimmy, I don't owe you any money."

Carlyle was in Curaçao on an extracurricular sexual holiday, and his girlfriend was staying at his house, when two men wearing ski masks — professionals, good old-fashioned American gangsters — circumvented his $25,000 alarm system, killed his two Dobermans, and kidnapped his girlfriend at gunpoint, holding her for a week until Carlyle finally paid up.

So heavy was Carlyle into Quaaludes now, that one could hardly understand him when he spoke. Verbal congress with him was riddled with uncertainty, subject to immediate deterioration, vulnerable to the same critical vicissitudes that governed radioactive decay and things like collapse of the wave function. He was washing the quackers down with enough liquor to slur his speech in their absence. That he remained conscious at all was astounding, a tribute, no doubt, to the quality and vast quantity of cocaine he was doing. The first few hours of every morning Carlyle spent looking for his car. He could never remember where he had parked it before things went to black.

Things soon reached the point where Myerson insisted that Long introduce him to Jimmy that he might deal directly with the Cuban in the event of an emergency, like some complete, unexpected cocaine meltdown on Long's part. Long, Carlyle, and Myerson were returning from that meeting, heading to Fort Lauderdale, having just delivered $8 million to Jimmy, when Myerson and Carlyle got into it. All three men were high on coke. Carlyle had been dropping ludes and the pills were just kicking in. He was slurring his words so badly that they bordered on the inaudible. He was bellyaching about the price of pot in Ann Arbor, muttering at Myerson, going on to Long like Hamlet griping about his uncle. Myerson was giving it back to him. They started shouting each other down.

"Guys, guys . . ." said Long.

"Fuck you," responded Carlyle.

"Okay, fuck me," said Long. "Can you guys put an end to it?"

"Fuck you, fuck this guy, fuck you both, I'm leaving . . ."

Carlyle threw open the limousine door — at which point the driver deemed it prudent to pull over — staggered out of the car, and walked right into a boxwood hedge, screaming, "Fuck you both," as he tumbled, disappearing into the foliage, presumably to spend the night.

Myerson could not abide the guy.

The following day Long and Carlyle returned to Jimmy's house in Coral Gables to deliver another $4 million, the balance of what they owed. The cash was contained in sixteen cardboard boxes. Jimmy met them at the door with a submachine gun in his hands.

"You cannot bring that money in here," he said. "Take it away." Jimmy's paranoia was visible. His trigger finger was twitching. "If my friends find out I have all this money here, they will come and they will kill me. Take it away, turn around, go."

Backing Jimmy up were two other armed men. One was a guy named Dennis, an all-American type — never said much, always there, Jimmy's right hand. Long had never met the other guy. Both carried automatic weapons.

In the dope trade the day had arrived of the multimission sub-machine gun — the industry standard was the Ingram MAC-10 — and you could have removed the selective-fire switch from any of those used in Miami. It was like the movies now. The weapons in town were always on auto.

Beyond the doorway, on the living room couch, unarmed and out of range of any ejected cartridges that might start flying, sat a grim-visaged Jake Myerson — no doubt thinking twice right now about getting to know Jimmy. Long said he would hold the $4 million until Jimmy made arrangements, but before leaving with the money, they would have to count the $8 million they had delivered the day before.

"No way we are counting this fucking money," said Jimmy. "Forget that shit."

There was no way Long was leaving until Jimmy corroborated the amount.

There are certain conventions observed in the dope business. Some of them are intuitively obvious. Smugglers, for example, do not take checks. (Hell, they do not even take pesos. In the Western Hemisphere, and in much of the rest of the world, the dope business is conducted in United States currency.) Others make eminent sense after you think about them for a minute. For instance, standard procedure demands that the books always be balanced immediately. In the absence of canceled checks, counterfoils, and signed receipts — as in any cash business, especially one in which the ledgers are balanced by the barrel of a gun — money must be counted in the presence of both buyer and seller as soon as it changes hands. No phone calls the next day.

"No way we're counting it now," said Jimmy.

Doing so would take hours.

"Okay," conceded Long.

Jimmy's paranoia was positively radiant.

"We'll just weigh it," Long said.

Which was agreeable to everyone. The money was packaged and boxed by denomination for just such a purpose. One of the many gratifying aspects of doing business with Jake Myerson and professionals like Easy Matthews was their on-the-job courtesy. Both men made every effort to pay for at least half of their pot in hundreds. They even employed staff to help accomplish it — personnel whose job was to make the rounds of numerous banks converting to hundreds currency of smaller denominations.

Major distributors of pot, given the number of people with whom they were dealing, were already exposed on numerous fronts. Employing drivers and money handlers — large operations moved singles and fives by the truckload — put them that much closer to the heat. In the pot business, at the level at which Long and his associates were operating, the money, like the marijuana itself, had come to be viewed as cargo. (When the cocaine trade picked up a few years later, the money would represent the larger transportation problem for traffickers, the volume of cash exceeding the volume of the cocaine, every kilo of coke generating about three kilos of currency in singles, fives, tens, and twenties.) A quarter of a million dollars in hundreds, Allen Long discovered, fit nicely in fifty No. 10 envelopes containing $5,000 each. Five million dollars in hundreds, in a single stack, stood two stories high — just about twenty feet up — and weighed 110 pounds.

Like any respectable South Florida host, Jimmy had a precision scale in the house readily available to guests. The smugglers, emptying one of the cardboard boxes, placed it on the scale and came up with a tare weight. They reloaded the box, weighed it and all the other boxes, and then did the arithmetic, calculating a U.S. banknote at precisely a gram. They came up $100,000 short, which, out of $8 million-plus, fell well within the margin of error. Perhaps they overestimated the weight of the rubber bands. A hundred thousand was small change at the level at which everyone was operating. Long was spending around half that much every week in expenses. As Long was leaving the house that day, Jimmy, the way another man might hand him a cigar, gave him a Ferrari. A 308GTB.

"Looks new," Carlyle said, when Long stepped out in Fort Lauderdale.

"It's got about six hundred miles on the clock."

"Not a bad rig."

"You know, they're really pretty tight," said Long. "They're hard to move around in."

"They take some getting used to."

"I don't know. You want it?"

"It's not my kind of ride," said Carlyle.

Long gave it back a week later.

A hundred-thousand-dollar automobile Jimmy Alvarez would give away without breathing hard. Hide a nickel from him and he wanted to talk.

What Carlyle had pulled with Jimmy that had almost gotten him killed was what the Miami smugglers had been pulling on each other from day one. Jimmy himself was no exception. It explains why Allen Long was able to do so well in Miami — he was the first person with whom these crooks had ever done business they could actually trust to be honest. Virgil, Tony's pal, who had done the talking that day at the crab house, setting the tone for Long's initial South Florida transaction, was a good old boy in whom Long saw a sense of decency lacking in some of the others. Proving to be far more easygoing than had been apparent the day they met, Virgil, an honorable fellow, was quick to grow weary of doing business with Jimmy. And it was Virgil, working independently, who engineered the move that Lee Carlyle believed finally vindicated his position vis-à-vis Myerson.

"You won't believe this," Carlyle said, calling Long in New York and telling him to get down to Miami. "I made money for *you* for a change."

Carlyle, taking a load that Virgil had moved on his own, had sold 38,000 pounds of pot through his buyers in California.

"And instead of twelve dollars a pound, man, we made forty-seven."

They had made twice as much money as on the latest Ann Arbor load, and on half the amount of pot. Long cleared $780,000. One deal. That day.

"There's only one thing I ask," Carlyle said.

"Go ahead, ask."

"Now can we get rid of Jake?"

"Are you out of your mind?"

"Give me one good reason to do business with the guy."

"Turnover," said Long. "Just think for a minute."

"You think for a minute. Take a look at this deal."

"This deal took a month. With Jake it's a couple of days. And this deal was three different deals. Which is three times the exposure."

"It's four times the money. I'm telling you," Carlyle said, "we don't have to work with the guy."

One guy Carlyle was determined to work with, however, was Virgil. And Virgil was ready to go. Eager to strike out on his own, he saw Carlyle and Long as the guys who could help him do it.

"You can't tell Jimmy," he said. "And don't tell Tony."

The three of them, Virgil, Long, and Carlyle, were sitting in the "Florida room" of Virgil's prefabricated tract house. The room, about ten feet square, had known life as a screened-in porch before Virgil installed the jalousie windows that made the new designation official. In the concrete pad on which the room sat, Virgil had chipped out a hole in which he had laid down some 4 mil polyethylene. When the excavation failed as a fishpond, he had thrown into the hole a plastic fountain, which gurgled now as the three men spoke. The rest of the floor was covered in Astroturf. A year later, when Virgil was living in a custom-built place with water on three sides — a mansion complete with aviary and a sixty-foot power boat tied up to the dock on the bayside of Upper Matecumbe Key — the entire joint would be decorated in the style of the room in which Long was presently sitting.

"I won't stand in your way," Long said. "But I'm not going to jeopardize my relationship with these guys."

"Fair enough," Virgil said.

Virgil was moving on, and in doing so, moving up. The trip he was putting together was four times the size of his first, and he was not bringing the load into Miami.

Carlyle said, "I'm gonna *do* it."

Long said he would back Carlyle's play.

Long's own disenchantment with Jimmy and the Miami operation, in general, coagulated around a series of events in early 1978. Jimmy was taking a piece of a 25,000-pound load that belonged to a local businessman, a Calle Ocho retailer by the name of Enrique who insisted upon being called Don Enrique. Jimmy was taking $10 a pound for hooking the guy up with Long.

"I will get my share from Don Enrique," Long was informed by Jimmy. "You can pay *him* the money."

When Enrique flew to New York to pick up the cash, Long paid him for all but a thousand pounds of the load, holding back $200,000, explaining to him that the bales were no good. "They got wet. They're moldy," Long said. The last twenty bales were sitting in a warehouse in Virginia. "I went down to look at them. I can't sell them," he told Enrique.

"When are you going to pay me for them?"

"The pot's wet. It's no good, Enrique. It got wet in the hold of the ship."

"There was nothing wet in my load."

"Look, Enrique, you can ask anybody," said Long. "Ripping people off is not something I do." He was rich, and growing richer every day, he said. He did not need to steal anyone's money. But neither was he giving money away. "I'm not going to pay two hundred thousand for wet marijuana."

On a legal pad, over the dining room table in his apartment, Long laid out the numbers, providing Don Enrique with an itemized account of every dollar earned on the load.

"I understand the problem you have," he said, "but you can see the marijuana yourself. If you want, you can go pick it up. Or I will pick it up for you."

"Pick it up?" said Don Enrique, astonished.

"What I will do," said Long, "is I will pick it up myself, and bring it back to you in Miami."

"No. No. Don't bring it back to me. That won't be necessary. I believe you. I trust you," said Don Enrique.

They agreed to write off the twenty bales.

Two weeks later, Long received a call from Jimmy.

"Allen, you must come to Miami."

Jimmy picked him up at the airport.

In the back of the car when Long stepped in, sitting with Jimmy's man Dennis, was a guy introduced as Dwayne. Long had not met him before. He was pushing forty, he had dark hair and eyes, and was about the size of a mature Kodiak bear. You could probably bring him down, Long figured, if you loaded, say, .460 Weatherby Magnum. You definitely want to get him off his feet first, then you move in close, he told himself, using some decent power tools . . . Seeing Dennis was no surprise, Dennis was always there. But Long wondered why this guy was on hand. The .45 semiauto protruding from Jimmy's waistband added to Long's consternation.

Long thought of Jimmy as his friend, but he had to be careful, he realized, not to forget who he was actually dealing with. Take Tony A., for example. Tony was a man who owned plenty of guns, but never to Long's knowledge was Tony seen cruising the streets of Miami with one of them stuck in his belt. In Miami that made Tony a gentleman. Jimmy, on the other hand, Long was now quick to remind himself, was something else altogether. Jimmy, yes, was rich, he called himself Don Jimmy, he dressed in Brioni suits, he drove Ferraris, but he was still — What was the expression Long was looking for? Oh, yeah — he was still a fucking gangster.

Long stepped into the car.

"We have a problem, Allen."

"You know, Jimmy," Long mused aloud, "if I ever do a Greatest Hits album, that's gonna be the title."

Long turned to smile at the boys in the back. Jimmy explained the problem. The problem was that Don Enrique was not paying Don Jimmy.

"He says it is because you, Allen, owe him money."

Long said, "That's not true."

And he told Jimmy what had happened.

"Okay," Jimmy responded, after hearing the story, "that is all you have to remember. When I ask you to tell your side of things, when I say go ahead, speak, that is what you have to say."

"What do you mean, Jimmy? Where are we going?"

"We're going to meet Don Enrique."

They met him at an Eighth Street restaurant. It was about one in the afternoon. Don Enrique, clearly uptight, arrived with two associates, the three of them joining Jimmy and the others at a semicircular banquette in the rear.

The joint was packed.

"Hello, Enrique," said Long.

"Oh, it is you," Enrique said. "It is your fault."

"Wait a minute . . ." said Long.

Jimmy said, "Nobody talk."

It was going to be an interesting lunch.

At the table, getting a fix on the talent, Long was hard pressed to identify anyone in his immediate vicinity whose membership in the Farmington Country Club he would unequivocally sponsor. He was reminded of every gangster movie he had seen in a lifetime, and he envisioned himself, in CinemaScope, lying face-down in motor oil on a garage floor in Chicago, leaking vital fluids through the threads of a double-breasted suit, hemorrhaging in honor of Saint Valentine. You could have cut the tension with any of the knives with which the table was set. Or anybody at the table could have shot it. Jimmy was carrying a gun, Dennis was carrying a gun, Dwayne was carrying a gun, Enrique's two henchmen were carrying guns, Enrique was carrying a gun. At the table, Long alone was unarmed. Not that he wanted a gun. But right now, clearly, it was the wrong table to be at.

Waiter, excuse me, I'm at the wrong table.

Everybody ordered iced tea.

"Enrique, tell Allen what you told me," said Jimmy. "Enrique says you did not pay him, Allen."

"That is right," said Don Enrique. "He did not pay me for part of the shipment." Enrique turned to Long, and said, "That is Jimmy's part. You have to pay him."

"Listen," Long said. He turned to Jimmy. "I'm going to say this one more time, and that is going to be it. You, Enrique, came to my *house*. We went over the bookwork together. I told you the remainder of the shipment was no good. I said I'd bring it back to Miami. You said you didn't want it back, that you believed me, and that was it. And, Jimmy, that's the truth."

"No, that is not true," Enrique replied. "You owe me. *You* are going to pay Jimmy. I am not going to pay him."

At issue was 4 percent of the load, a thousand pounds of wet marijuana. Enrique still owed Jimmy his dime on the other 96 percent. He had not even paid Jimmy *that*. By Enrique's reckoning the $200,000

Long had held back was coming out of Jimmy's two-fifty. He was going to pay Jimmy fifty grand and call it a day.

Long said, "I'm not staying here."

As Long was getting to his feet, he felt Dwayne take hold of his arm, gripping him under the shoulder, like a Boy Scout about to usher him across an unusually busy street.

"Stay here," he groaned, pulling Long back into his chair.

Jimmy is the one who stood. He jumped up, reached under his *guayabera,* and pulled the .45 out of his waistband.

"I'm going to kill somebody at this table," he shouted, waving the pistol from one side of the table to the other.

It was Miami, it was Calle Ocho, no surprises here. The restaurant patrons kind of lowered their heads, but nobody in the crowd stopped eating.

"Somebody at this table is going to pay me," yelled Jimmy, "or somebody at this table is going to die."

It was not until he cocked the pistol that activity in the restaurant came to a halt. You could hear the silence fall. The only thing moving now was the barrel of the gun, swinging back and forth between Don Enrique and Long.

"I will pay," said Don Enrique. "But you," he said to Long, "you make a big mistake when you try to fuck me."

"You are going to pay, Enrique, correct?" said Jimmy.

"Yes."

"Very good. Now we will have lunch."

These were the kinds of people Long was dealing with as a matter of routine. Enrique, who had just threatened to kill him, had tried to rip Jimmy off, and had been prepared to let Long die for it if he could induce Jimmy to believe he had been shorted. This is what it had come to after a year and a half.

"It is nothing, my friend," said Jimmy.

If he and Jimmy were in fact friends, Long asked, why would Jimmy need to restrain him? Why the muscle? Why have Dwayne holding him down in the booth?

"Oh, I had to know the truth," Jimmy said.

"I *told* you the truth," said Long.

And he wondered if Andreas had died saying the same thing. He wondered if after the young restaurant owner had taken the bullet, one of the fifteen other guys involved in the load, some guy like Don Enrique, or even a "gentleman" like Tony, had shaken his head and said, "I didn't know they were going to kill him . . . That's too bad . . . Hey, don't you think he would have done the same thing if he had the chance?"

"You don't have to be a marijuana smuggler," Nat Weiss advised. "You'd be a terrific record promotions man."

In the record business Nat Weiss was more than a major presence, he was something of a legend. Developing and representing talent as the manager of numerous acts and one of the industry's more powerful lawyers, he had been instrumental in the success of some of the more famous names in music. Weiss had his own label at CBS, and he and Long had been friends since Long's days as an aspiring filmmaker in New York, when Long had approached him seeking to promote concerts. In 1976 Weiss had signed songwriter Robbin Thompson, whom Long was managing at the time. Remaining a source of advice and support to Long, Weiss never gave up on the younger man, whose energy and enthusiasm he admired. He was one of very few people Allen Long never thought he knew more than.

"Give record promotions a try," Weiss said, and offered Long a job doing it.

Long, fast on the heels of his lunch with the Dons Enrique and Jimmy, accepted Nat Weiss's job offer in the spring of 1978. He went to work in Special Projects and Promotions at Weiss's label, Nemperor Records. It had been years since Long had adhered to a work schedule, years since he had exercised the self-discipline required of a legitimate job, but he committed himself to trying, and he discovered that he actually enjoyed it. Not only did he like the job, but he found that he was good at it. For the first time in a long time he proved successful at something other than the dope business.

"I hear you did a great job in Dallas," he was told, when he returned from the Radio and Records Convention, at which he had represented the label. According to Weiss his success was reverberating through the corridors of CBS. He had "made a lot of noise," surprising many people with an outstanding performance in what was known to be an extremely tough business.

"Well, they weren't carrying submachine guns, Nat. You want to see a hard sell? Try negotiating with a guy named Ernesto."

"Yetnikoff and Lundvall want to meet you."

Walter Yetnikoff, president of CBS Records, and Bruce Lundvall, president of Epic, were among the more powerful executives in the entertainment business. They invited Long and Weiss to lunch at San Marco. It was the industry equivalent of an anointment.

Long did not show up.

When he walked into Weiss's office the next day, Weiss cut him off before he could speak. "Whatever you do, don't tell me the truth. Tell me anything," pleaded Weiss, "tell me your mother died. Tell me you were in an accident."

With the right story Weiss could probably smooth things out, he could probably salvage the job. But Weiss was not going to lie. If Long gave him the wrong story, if he gave him what Weiss supposed was the truth, Weiss would be hard pressed to save him.

But in the face of the problem before them, the slack that Weiss was prepared to cut him proved to be the problem itself. In the end, it was Weiss's faith in him that inevitably terrified Long. Fearing that one day he might fail to live up to it, Long left nothing to chance.

"Nat, I can't do this, I'll just let you down. Just like I did yesterday."

"Well, that's really sad," said Weiss.

Long had managed to go legit for a few months, and then, with the help of a quarter-ounce of cocaine, he chickened out of his future.

Long and Weiss remained friends. Weiss, who had never lied to him, never taken advantage of him, and had always responded when asked, continued as a source of encouragement and counsel, and like many who invested their belief in him, waited for his belief to be justified.

If you listened carefully, you could hear the sound of hearts breaking all over the place.

Cherie would have taken issue with the suggestion that her boyfriend was probably a drug addict. Cherie was not blind to reality, but even had she not been dragged so deeply into the strangeness of it all, enlightenment would have remained beyond reach. Cocaine, undergoing glorification at the time, was considered not only chic but relatively harmless. And upon many people its impact was mild. But these were people who were measuring their intake by the line, buying it by the gram, maybe doing it on the weekend. Few were the people of Cherie's acquaintance who were *not* doing coke, but the severe psychological free fall that was sweeping her up in its wake was not yet a common affliction. Long was measuring his intake not by the gram, but by multiples thereof, doing cocaine every day, and worse, laying it on every night. Cherie viewed it as simple overindulgence, much the way she viewed his random antics with other women.

But even as she remained naive to the ramifications of his drug use, Cherie had long since reached the point where she was no longer cavalier about the drug business. It had far outgrown the escapade, the small statement of personal freedom — the blow against the Empire — initially articulated by Long. He had left the counter-culture way behind him. If the man she loved was not already a gangster, he was fast approaching the point at which he would do until one came along.

Long's unwillingness to confide in her, his insistence upon leaving his troubles at the office, as it were, was a source of constant fighting between them. The rule, as he saw it, was clear, a proscription promoted, if not always observed, by professional outlaws of all kinds: You did not share information with the women in your life beyond what you were unable to hide. Silence was the strongest safeguard — for you, for them, and just as importantly, for your friends.

"They won't trust me," he told Cherie, "if you know what's going on."

Knowledge was culpability. Giving Cherie deniability went a long way toward protecting her, and in doing so protected him and any of those associates, those co-conspirators of his, against whom she might be forced to testify. You did not have to pass the bar exam to know that wives and girlfriends were a liability. Their innocence was not enough to prevent ambitious prosecutors from going after them, using them against you, threatening to lock them up if you refused to cooperate:

The drugs were in the trunk of your car when you picked her up for dinner. That makes her part of the conspiracy. She's facing forty years.

Which explained, in part, why drug smugglers were so generous in supporting the careers of prostitutes, not one of whom ever was known to ask, "How did things go today, honey?"

Long had used the drug business as leverage to get Cherie out of his apartment — he had rented her a place on Houston Street — but still, she spent much of her time there. Long was away a lot, and in his absence Cherie started using cocaine a lot to keep herself entertained. She found herself, now and then, picking the lock of his apartment to hit his stash when she ran out. Shortly before his failure at Nemperor Records, Long returned from a trip to Miami to find that, searching for cocaine, she had accidentally destroyed a treasured possession of his. An inlaid puzzle box, hand-carved of tropical woods, in which cocaine was occasionally hidden, the valuable piece of craftsmanship had been commissioned by Long from one of the many artists he supported. Cherie had splintered it beyond repair trying to get it open. The fight that followed the incident was as destructive as her assault on the artwork. Reckless, spiteful, and pointedly malicious, it ended with Long's leaving the bedroom to find JD Reed on the living room floor, kneeling on one of the Afghani prayer rugs he routinely gave away after using them to smuggle hash oil.

"What are you doing?" said Long.

"I'm praying for you, man."

Long and Cherie routinely rifled each other's stashes of cocaine, and it was nothing to get excited about. Long bought cocaine for both of them — he might be doing it in one room while she was doing it in another, it was like putting on a pot of coffee, an adjunct to other activities — and when his stash ran out, it was natural for him to hit hers.

Long bought blow in volume, but rarely did he do all that he bought. He always found someone to share it with, if only until whoever it was gave up and said good night.

While Cherie was breaking into the puzzle box, Myerson was flying to Miami carrying $2 million in cash, all hundreds, in a suitcase, the back end of a payment on a 20,000-pound load. He and Long were to meet and deliver the money to Jimmy together. Long was late by several hours — sell him enough cocaine, the way things were going, and he could be late by several days — and when finally he did show up, he had a young woman with him in the limousine. A stranger. Maybe she was a prostitute, maybe just a young coke freak he picked up in a bar. When Myerson pressed him on it, Long was unable to recall. And as if that in itself were not dangerous enough, Long had the limousine driver cruise the dark streets of downtown Miami, dragging Myerson and the forty-four pounds of money along, as he and his date looked for a connection.

A clinical fog had begun to roll in behind the squall line of cocaine, that brume of psychological uncertainty in which cause and effect are slowly obscured, where what at first appeared to be a symptom of spiritual chaos becomes the agent of the chaos itself.

Cherie, studying to be an actress, was "too stoned to do anything emotionally," she confided to a friend, having come to believe that the night before a scheduled class, Long always made sure to get her high, and in so doing insure her failure. She started spending more time at Houston Street. She started seeing other men casually. Long gave her a ring. He took it back.

Their days together were numbered.

"You know, man," Carlyle said, as though informing Long he had mail, "you need to come down here and pick up your money."

"Yeah, okay, I'll be there," said Long.

Virgil's load had come in, and Long and Carlyle, taking half of it, had moved 80,000 pounds of red through the system. Their share of the take was in cardboard boxes, stashed in the spare bedroom of

Carlyle's house in Fort Lauderdale. Long flew from New York on the company jet — they had one under lease now — to collect his cut of the cash.

"Half of that's yours, brother," Carlyle announced, leaning against the door frame, as Long entered the bedroom to confront the tableau.

"You're kidding."

The cash filled a stack of boxes that covered an entire wall.

"Whenever you're ready," Carlyle said.

Dividing it took the rest of the day.

". . . One stack for you, one stack for me . . . five thousand for you . . ."

By nightfall the two smugglers were effectively corraled, sitting on the wall-to-wall carpet with a narrow walkway between them and eight inches of money covering the floor. They had split over $3 million.

"You know," Long said, as they counted the last of it, "maybe it's time to quit."

"Oh, man," declared Carlyle, "don't say that. Not yet. Let's not quit yet."

"We have to walk away sometime."

"Buddy, I'm in it for the gold watch."

"We didn't get into this to do it forever. How much money do we need?"

Carlyle started laughing.

"Yeah," he said.

"What?"

"That's funny."

"What's funny?"

"Huh?" Carlyle gave him a look of bewilderment. "Are you serious?"

"What do you mean?"

"Man, we don't do it for the money."

And now Long found himself laughing. "Say that again, I don't think I heard you right."

"We do it. It's what we do. It's what we're good at," said Carlyle. "We're like everybody else. We do it because . . . It's what we fuckin' *do.*"

"What the hell are you smoking?"

Carlyle just smiled and shook his head.

"Smuggling pot," said Long, "is not something we're destined to spend our lives at. JD, maybe, but not us. JD's a guy who loves what he does. He would never think of doing anything else. Probably couldn't do anything else. He believes in pot. He's the next best thing to a missionary."

"Allen, being in it for the pot is no less ridiculous than being in it for the money. JD does it for the same reasons we do it."

"Wrong," said Long. "JD is a crusader. Pot, as far as he's concerned, is the one thing on earth that's legit. Pot's his job, it's what he does best. It's his destiny. You and I, we could do anything."

"Pot's the only thing you and I have been good at in our lives," said Carlyle. "We've never done anything but suck at everything else. And we probably never will do anything but suck."

"I don't buy that."

"Pot's the only thing you and I haven't been losers at since the day we were born, Allen. That's why we do it. That's why we're going to be doing it tomorrow, and the next day and the day after that. Face it. Pot's what we do. When the ship goes down, we're going to be on it."

They had come some distance from Guadalajara and that table at La Copa de Leche. Carlyle's dime had carried them far. A little bit too far, perhaps. To Long's way of thinking, the terrain in which they found themselves was beginning to look downright exotic. The lives of both had been threatened. Carlyle was driving around Miami with a gun in his car. There had been the matter-of-fact murder of Andreas, the kidnapping of Carlyle's girlfriend, the business with Don Enrique. And the money. There was just so much of it.

This was *real* criminal activity now.

In a year and a half, over the course of maybe a dozen boats, Long had made $8 million. In cash. No taxes. Granted, he was spending over $5,000 a day whether the boat came in or not. Fifteen hundred a day on hotel rooms. Limo on call twenty-four hours at something like $400 a day. An executive jet, a pilot and co-pilot ready to go, call it $3,000 a day. These were the necessities of life. With what he was spending on women and coke, he was looking at a total outgo of a quarter of a million a month — minimum — maybe $350,000 a month without buying anything of real value.

The airplane, of course, was a legitimate business expense. A six-seat Rockwell Jet Commander, with a little more headroom than a Lear, the plane, in addition to everything else, was essential to the transport of money. One could not fly commercial carrying $10 million in cash, nor on a scheduled airline could one hope to move that kind of money in the necessary three to four days. On call around the clock — plane, pilot, and co-pilot — the twin-engine jet offered speed, security, and efficiency. Long had leased the plane for a year at a cost of $150,00, paying another $75,000 to extend the lease for an extra six months. It cost additional money to take the plane up. Round-trip between Miami and San Francisco cost roughly $10,000.

The typical flight for Long started at Fort Lauderdale Executive Airport, and went from there to Washington, New York, and Ann Arbor, making stops as far west as San Francisco or Lake Tahoe, before heading back to South Florida, where limousines would be waiting for the money. The plane and the limos were leased in the name of a front company established by Carlyle, Real-to-Reel Productions, its ostensible mission being to pick up dailies and fly them to the company's film lab in Miami. Long generally tipped the pilots $10,000 in cash.

With cash representing the headache it did, the flight usually included a stop in Las Vegas, not to collect money but to exchange it, to convert the currency to the hundreds and fifties necessary for international payoff. At one of the city's larger hotels, through connections provided by Luther Reed, Long would launder the money through the casino, paying a one percent commission to the establishment. Depositing cash at the teller's cage in singles, fives, tens, and twenties, he would buy one hundred chips in thousand-dollar denominations, proceed to the roulette table, place a single thousand-dollar bet, lose it, then return to the cage and cash in the remaining ninety-nine chips for hundreds and fifties. Holding forth from a suite at the hotel, he would do this five or six times a day over a period of three or four days, before taking the jet back to Florida.

Occasionally Long and Carlyle used the jet simply for recreation.

"Let's fly to the Bahamas for breakfast," they decided, closing a disco one night, flying off with a couple of willing young women who had managed to stray into their orbit.

It was in that same spirit that Carlyle now, surrounded by $3 million, and sensing that his friend was glum, suggested flying out to the Coast.

"You know what? Miami sucks," he said. "Let's just take our entire scene and move it to San Francisco."

It was a $40,000 trip, with no reason behind it other than the fact that Long was in a grumpy mood, and Carlyle, who wanted to cheer him up, was nostalgic for the West Coast anyway.

Long said, "What the hell."

They stashed the money, grabbed a case of champagne, and flew to San Francisco. They checked into the Stanford Court for four days, putting the pilots up with a car and expenses for the duration of their stay.

And still Long could not shake the blues.

The guns, the Quaaludes, the coke. This was not the journey he had embarked upon six years earlier. This was not the same business he had drifted into back then. Once an illegal business is good to you, as you get better at it, as it gets bigger, other illegal things, Long discovered, become easier to do. Where do you draw the line? If it is okay to sell marijuana, is it not okay to sell cocaine? If it is okay to carry dope in your car, is it okay to carry a gun? Where do you say no? If people are out to rip you off, you probably *should* carry a gun. If they try, will you kill them? he asked himself. If they do rip you off, will you *find* them and kill them? Where, he wondered, do you stop?

This was not the marijuana business he knew. The coordinates of the enterprise had shifted observably. He was dealing with pot scammers who took people's lives, they had been shooting people for years. Before he showed up in Miami, all the smugglers he had known had been pot smokers. These characters did not smoke pot, they were in it for the money, nothing more. And now, as he looked at it, so was he.

He was not an outlaw, he was a racketeer.

He bought thousand-dollar suits and five-hundred-dollar shoes and traveled by limousine wherever he went. He traveled first-class when he was flying commercial and only when not traveling by executive jet. Crippled by a cocaine habit, he did not, as they say, get out much. All he saw were the insides of limos, the insides of airplanes, and the insides of luxury hotel suites. The only people he spent time with were drug dealers, or people who worked for drug dealers, or people who liked being with him because he was a drug dealer himself.

Allen Long's dreams of smuggler's glory, his quest for gold, his magnificent vision of El Dorado — all of his dreams had come true.

16 MUCH HAVE I TRAVELED IN THE REALMS OF GOLD

"Are you kidding?"

"If *you* want to," said Long, "go ahead. Do it. It's fine with me."

"We'll probably do five hundred thousand pounds with him," said Myerson, reminding Long that they had made $22 million working with Jimmy. "You'll make yours just being in the middle."

"No. But go ahead," said Long. "You guys do it without me."

When Long told Carlyle he was quitting, Carlyle told him he was insane.

"These are not my kind of people," Long said.

"It's crazy," mumbled Carlyle.

"You can say that again."

Carlyle would have said it again, but he could not remember it.

It would be natural to think that Allen Long had acquired a kind of dilatory wisdom, that he had seen the error of his ways and decided to go straight. But Long, for all his enlightenment, for all the retirement money at his disposal, was just not that kind of guy. Finding himself without spiritual coordinates, having somehow lost his position, Long decided that what he needed to do was — as they say in the music business — reinvent himself, he needed to get back to his roots.

He decided he needed to be a smuggler again.

Long was nothing more than a middleman now, a broker. He was just going through the motions. He was just another businessman, he might as well have been selling cars. It had been six years since he had smuggled his first load of pot and almost two since he had smuggled his last. Coming up on his thirtieth birthday, he was at an entrepreneurial standstill. In his journey along the contraband trail, he had stumbled into some bad terrain, a geography of the imagination in which the wilderness was closed. It was time to get back to the border. He missed the scamming, the adventure, he missed the creative thinking. He missed the thrill of going up against the prohibitive odds to deliver the goods. He missed the weirdness. He needed some action.

Allen Long had the soul of a smuggler. A smuggler, not a dealer. The two were not simply different, they were chromosomally distinct. Long was suffering the outlaw equivalent of classic gender dysphoria: He was a smuggler trapped in a dealer's body. It was time for reassignment surgery.

Carlyle would continue working with Virgil, selling to his people out west. He and Myerson, happy to be rid of each other, would do no business together. Long would strike out on his own. But trying to move large loads of marijuana without a guy like Jimmy Alvarez posed a challenge that was growing more difficult. Jimmy's operation offered more than financial security, it offered safety, a comforting layer of insulation against arrest. Long wanted to get free of Jimmy, but he did not want to get caught.

The government, concentrating its resources in Miami, had turned up the temperature in South Florida. Jimmy was one of few smugglers there who could move weight with any success. Since 1974 marijuana consumption had quadrupled. By 1978, according to the DEA, more than a third of the nation's adults, and one in five of its teenagers, were frequent drug users. And they consumed about twice as much pot every day as they consumed in cocaine all year. Some 42 million Americans smoked pot. Dope, by far the biggest business in Colombia, generating greater revenue than coffee, had by now surpassed the tourist industry as the largest employer in South Florida. It was the largest retail business in the state.

More than 70 percent of the marijuana coming into the country was now coming from Colombia. In late December 1977, a few months before Long made his decision, the government had initiated a six-week-long enforcement effort called Operation Stopgap. The DEA conducted an average of two flights a day over the Guajira and offshore waters, monitoring mother ship traffic, identifying clandestine airstrips, picking up aircraft tail numbers, and forwarding the information by radio to Miami. The U.S. Coast Guard had blockaded the Yucatan Channel and the Windward and Mona Passages. Happy with their numbers, federal agencies had followed up the initiative with a similar effort in April.

Within two years the feds would virtually shut down the Caribbean. With Customs, the Coast Guard, and the DEA augmented by U.S. armed forces, government interdiction efforts would grow so intense that large shipments of pot from Colombia would pretty much come to an end. It was due in great part to the government's success that Colombian marijuana traffickers switched to moving cocaine, a product far easier to conceal, expanding a market in the United States that had been relatively small up to then. The government campaign against importation of pot would eventually give rise to a domestic marijuana industry of great agricultural significance. But more than that, it would be instrumental in creation of the market for cocaine, a market that would change the cultural landscape of the country, inevitably darkening its domestic politics and the geopolitics of the hemisphere. Bureaucracies would grow up around it. Preoccupation with cocaine would drive careers, in and out of government. Soon the prospect of a drug-free society would become economically unthinkable; in the absence of a war on dope, at $30 billion a year, a large chunk of the nation's gainfully employed population would be out looking for work.

Long saw what he perceived to be the future of Colombian pot in the 160,000-pound load of *punta roja* that Virgil had moved. The feds, growing fat on interdiction in the Caribbean and the Gulf, were not looking for loads farther north. Virgil, bringing it into Chesapeake Bay, had landed his load in Baltimore. And the pot had come right into the harbor. No mother ships, no go-fasts — it came right into town on a barge towed by an oceangoing tug from Colombia.

What, in the eyes of the government, could be as unlikely as that, Long wondered. How about moving Colombian pot, specifically Santa Marta Gold — all of which grew on the country's northeastern coast — a thousand miles west before shipping it north? How about moving the pot off the Guajira to, say, the port of Buenaventura on the country's Pacific coast, avoiding the Caribbean altogether, and shipping the pot north from there, smuggling it into California?

For the next year and a half, Long worked on a single move. It would come to be known as "the Pacific trip," and in many ways the Pacific trip would come to define him as a smuggler. For sheer ambition and logistical complexity, it showed off all his talents. If the trip did not sound the overture to the future of Colombian pot, it did play as something of a crescendo, and in it were echoed all the sentiments that had driven Long's pursuit of his dream.

As a statement of artistic purpose, the move found its parallel in the annals of rock and roll, in a remark attributed to the late Jim Morrison, legendary lead singer of the Doors. Early in the band's career, playing a small club before a near-empty house, Morrison had closed the act with a physical, characteristically theatrical, signature assault on the microphone stand. Falling to the floor with it, writhing and screaming the set to a conclusion, he took the show over the top, as histrionic and dangerously energetic as if playing before a sold-out stadium. Or so the story goes. Asked what inspired him to do so in the face of such obvious indifference — there was no audience present to speak of — Morrison replied: "You never know when it's going to be your last performance."

The midtown Holiday Inn, situated on the outer reaches of civilization in Manhattan, within loud-hailing distance of the Hudson, within shotgun range of the New York headquarters of the Drug Enforcement Administration, served always to highlight Allen Long's deficiencies as a tour guide. Its position in the hierarchy of New York hoteldom was best illustrated by the confusion it suffered, in his and the minds of many, with the Howard Johnson Motor Lodge six blocks south, where the FBI in 1970 had arrested fugitive Angela Davis, the gifted social philosopher and theoretical Communist who after her acquittal on murder and kidnapping charges sought spiritual refuge, it was rumored, on an ample parcel of improved real estate in Northern California, there to distribute her wealth, America liked to believe, among various dealers in imported automobiles, each according to his needs, and miscellaneous day help with nothing to lose but their chains.

Long's choosing the Holiday Inn in which to contravene the federal conspiracy statutes had nothing to do with the hotel's proximity to DEA headquarters and little to do with the FBI. It suggested not that Long possessed a refined sense of that which was fitting and just. There were a couple of conventions in town. Everything else was booked. It was Miguel's first visit to New York, and agreeing that "it would not be a good idea" for the Colombian to stay at the apartment — why supply potential prosecutors with that kind of ammunition — Long, who had intended to put his friend up at the Plaza, had reserved the only room in the city he could find.

"Isn't this where they popped Angela Davis?" he said, looking around the lobby, as the assistant manager working the desk was putting him through to the room.

"Howard Johnson's," the young woman said, handing him the phone. "They control the means of production on the Connecticut Turnpike."

At five P.M. Long was standing at the window of Miguel's room, looking down on West 57th Street. The sidewalks were acrawl with pedestrians. The vehicular traffic in both directions was choked by the afternoon rush. On the far side of the street, a uniformed cop with his hat pushed back was asking a bearded man in a business suit if he could possibly cool the reefer. Gesturing patiently with his nightstick, pointing north by northeast, in the general direction of Newfoundland, the patrolman appeared to be telling the young exec, "Pal, the park's just over there."

"Ernesto can do only half," Miguel said. "The other half we will get from the people in Valledupar."

"It has to be good," said Long, turning away from the window.

"Only the gold and the red," Miguel replied. "We will pay them now. For next year's harvest. They will grow the marijuana just for you."

Miguel poured Scotch for both of them. He handed a glass to Long.

"And," said Long, "you are looking for a ship."

"There is a man in Cali. You will meet him when you come."

"Okay," said Long, raising his glass. "Now we will talk about the important things."

"Sir?" asked Miguel, raising his own.

Long downed the Scotch in one hit, set the glass down, and clapped his hands.

"Where would you like to eat tonight, and how many women do you want?"

The trip, in order to pay for itself, had to be worth at least $15 million. It had to be a 60,000-pound move. An investor asked to put up $500,000 had to receive ten to one on his money. At a meeting at the Trident hotel in Port Antonio, Jamaica, to which Miguel, Myerson, and Easy Matthews traveled with their wives, and Long traveled with Cherie — lunch every day was the same, lobster salad and Dom Pérignon — Myerson and Matthews agreed to invest a half a million each in the load. At a minimum sale price of $300, they and Long stood to make $5 million apiece.

The logistics of the move were head-spinning. The plan was to move the pot to Buenaventura by air, and from there by Colombian freighter to the Northern California coast. The move required the purchase of a cargo plane, a freighter, and the lease of a helicopter. Necessary personnel included three pilots, a ship's captain and crew, and several off-loaders both in Colombia and in the United States.

It was like a pot-smuggling WPA project.

Long would be bringing some old friends together. And they needed a good place to talk. He set up a meeting in Las Vegas.

A city engorged with gamblers, hustlers of every stripe, and citizens from all over the country with nothing but time on their hands, Las Vegas, Nevada, was a short-odds favorite on any day to be playing host to a complement of wiseguys in collusion to violate the criminal statutes. The town was a national boardroom, of sorts, in which the underworld was free to convene, a dead end not only to the American Dream, but to the federal conspiracy investigation as well. As circumstantial evidence presented before a grand jury, a trip to the desert metropolis was about as persuasive as a trip to the lavatory. It was Vegas. A man never had to explain what he had been doing there.

Long arrived on the FBI breakfast flight, and when he exited the terminal at McCarran, JD Reed was waiting outside, leaning on the fender of his car, the brim of his Stetson cocked forward about 40 degrees off the horizontal. He grabbed Long's luggage, threw it in the car, handed him a twenty-eight-ounce Mason jar filled with bootleg 300 mg Quaaludes — "a gift from my dad" — and drove him to the Aladdin.

Reed was on probation. In the years leading up to the Colombian loads, while flying pot out of Sonora and selling it to Long in Richmond, Reed had also been moving boats out of Jalisco. In 1976, just before the first flight to Perico, he was arrested off-loading some 800 pounds of Mexican weed at a dock in Newport Beach, California. He made bail, and continued to postpone his court date, succeeding with the help of a lawyer paid for by Jake Myerson. Not until two years after his arrest did he go before a judge.

Three *days* after his arrest Reed was aboard the maiden flight of the DC-3 to Colombia. When the plane hit the trees on takeoff, and he jumped out with his survival gear, he naturally figured "I'm livin' here." As it was, he missed a date with his parole officer. He told him he "went fishin'." When the DC-3 was abandoned, and Long started middling pot in Miami, Reed returned to moving his own loads. In 1978 he finally appeared in court to answer the charges out of Newport Beach. Facing a maximum of five years in prison, he was sentenced to ninety days in jail and put on three years' probation, for the duration of which he was determined to behave himself. He would not be part of the Pacific trip. He had just been released from custody when Long arrived in Las Vegas.

When Long flew into town, followed in short order by Will McBride, his own arrival immediately followed by that of Frank Hatfield, Reed was on hand to welcome the boys to Las Vegas like a member of the Chamber of Commerce. He was there just to say hi. And just maybe to get high. And party a little. With Long in town, he knew there would be plenty of that. After ninety days in jail, he allowed, "I could use me some of that under yonder." Within an hour of their getting together, what *none* of the four men could use was a driver's license.

"So the guy tells me," Hatfield was saying, "'I like to look to my left and see nothing but engines. I like to look to my right and see nothing but co-pilots. Now that's a safe airplane. You take off in a jet, you're already in an emergency. Look behind you. You're on fire . . . !'"

"Allen," said McBride, holding up a joint.

Long was standing at the window with his head against the pane, talking to a pigeon roosting on the ledge outside the hotel room.

"Hey, buddy, how's it look up there?" Long whispered, tapping the glass. "You catch that breeze out of Barbados?"

". . . He tells me, 'If God wanted us to fly jets, son, he wouldn't have given us the sound barrier.'"

"Allen."

Long walked over to where the others were sitting, took the joint from McBride, and threw a thumb back in the direction of the window.

"Pilot talk," he said.

It had been almost two years since Long had worked with Hatfield and McBride. During that time, the pilots, doing business with Miguel, had made four flights to the Guajira in Hatfield's twin-engine Titan, but had met with little success. For what it was worth, McBride informed Long, they had found a 4,000-foot runway of hard-packed dirt about ten miles west of Perico.

"Which," he pointed out, "would have been kind of nice to know about when we were flying the 3."

Hatfield, smiling, turned to Reed.

"Let's not set sail on *that* sea of heartbreak," he said.

Reed raised a beer bottle to salute the notion.

Long, in Las Vegas, hired the pilots to find, purchase, and outfit a cargo plane at least as large as the DC-3 to handle cross-country transport of the marijuana within Colombia. Because buying such an airplane in the States would draw the immediate scrutiny of several agencies, bureaucracies extending from the FAA to the Department of Defense, it was agreed that McBride and Hatfield would do their shopping elsewhere. They left Las Vegas with expense money and an eye on Central America.

"Action, action, action. That's the answer to your question. We do it for the action."

Long and Reed were taking the sun on the stern of Reed's thirty-two-foot Sea Ray, anchored off the Valley of Fire on the edge of Lake Meade.

"Yeah, you and me and Belle Starr," said Long, "before she lost her looks. The money never sucked either."

"She sucked for the money, as I remember."

"The old girl was never much of a tournament player."

"Strictly C.O.D."

"Hooking for the James gang, she never made as much as we did."

"She should have sold them weed."

"Sorry you can't help me on this one," said Long.

"Tell Ernesto I said *hola.*"

A few months later, in Costa Rica, the pilots picked up a DC-4. With new avionics, the plane came in at about $250,000. In February 1979, six months after the Vegas meeting, Long set out for Colombia.

"You must be careful," Miguel told him.

"What's the problem?"

"Raúl Gaviria is looking for you."

Oh, yeah. María.

On the trip through Sabana Rubia, Long and María had shared their dreams, mostly María's dreams, for Long's dreams changed dramatically once he had entertained hers. María wanted to see the world. She hoped one day to fly her own plane. She wanted to see New York, Hong Kong, London, Paris, and Rome. She was *different* from traditional Colombian girls, she wanted Long to know. "I am not going to be like that," she insisted, of the timeworn values embraced by her friends and other Latin American women. The very feminine values, as luck would have it, that made her attractive to the Neanderthal in Long. No, she was a modern girl, she said. She wanted — and Long did not need to hear it to run from it — to be just like *American* girls.

"How bad is it, Miguel?" he asked.

"I believe it is serious, sir."

"As bad as a bullet with my name on it?"

"Worse, I am afraid. A tuxedo."

Just like American girls.

"I will be careful," said the fugitive bridegroom.

Long flew to Colombia, avoided María and her uncle, and spent several days traveling the country, setting out from the Guajira with Miguel and Pablo, visiting Buenaventura, Cali, Bogotá, and Valledupar. Looking at pot, laying out bribes, securing working relationships with numerous strangers, he stayed two weeks in South America.

Through Chase Manhattan, N.A., in Panama, Long bought a 170-foot Colombian freighter, the *Pituro Uno*, docked in Buenaventura. The ship, making regular runs between Peru and Colombia carrying ceramic tiles, was simultaneously being used by Colombian smugglers to bring coca leaves into the country for processing in the labs around Cali. The $480,000 Long paid for the freighter bought with it the compliance of the Colombian authorities who had been cooperating with the Cali traffickers.

Through Matthews, Long found a smuggler in California who would help orchestrate the off-load. The plan was to have the *Pituro Uno* lie seventy-five miles offshore, and to remove the pot by air. Long secured a lease on a helicopter, a Sikorsky S-64 Skycrane, available from Georgia-Pacific for $60,000 a month in the summer. Capable of lifting over 20,000 pounds of cargo slung from its long fuselage boom, the helicopter had an operational range of 230 miles. Long bought a 5,000-gallon fuel truck to support the five trips necessary to off-load the freighter in 12,000-pound increments.

The pot would be brought ashore in the King Mountain Range on the north coast of Mendocino County, lowered from the Sikorsky into open-top tractor-trailer rigs running on logging roads.

The marijuana, purchased from two sources in Colombia, would be moved from separate locations. Ernesto would provide 30,000 pounds on the Guajira, and a second trafficker engaged by Miguel would provide another 30,000 in Valledupar, capital of César department, on the southern slope of the Sierra Nevada. The bales, triple-wrapped in 12 mil heat-sealed plastic and wound with heavy-gauge web netting, were to be transported in a total of four trips, air-dropped from the cargo bay of the DC-4 into a lagoon about a hundred miles north of Buenaventura. From there local villagers would move them by motor launch to the *Pituro Uno*. Successful test drops were conducted from 800 feet over the lagoon near Perico. The necessary Colombian coast guard commander cost $20,000.

Everything came together in the summer of 1979. The marijuana was cured and baled, all the money had been spent, and Long had a two-month window of opportunity in which the helicopter would be available, when Miguel called him in New York.

"Sir, we have a problem."

Without one, it would not be smuggling.

Ernesto's pot was ready to go, but in Valledupar, according to Miguel, police had received information that a shipment was about to be moved. Of the 30,000 destined for the airstrip there, the first 10,000 pounds were loaded aboard a tank truck that had been converted to carry dope, but with the heat coming down, the traffickers were afraid to move it. Long flew to Colombia, where he and Miguel, as time slipped away and their options rapidly diminished, made the decision to send the load, having little choice but to rely on the effectiveness of the scam, the bogus tank truck, itself. To thwart suspicion that the tanker was carrying anything other than bulk fuel, the truck had been rigged to pump gasoline from fuel drums hidden inside, one installed beneath the overhead tank hatch and the other behind the rear outlet.

With Long and Miguel preceding it through, the truck was detained at the first roadblock it hit. The police were obviously ready. They climbed all over the tanker, they pumped out gallons of fuel, they were certain there was dope aboard. Inevitably left scratching their heads, they reluctantly let the truck pass, but they were so sure that the truck was dirty, and so indignant in the face of defeat, that they radioed ahead, alerting officers at the next checkpoint. There the truck underwent the same scrutiny. The inspection yielded a similar result, but the truck was nevertheless refused passage. The smugglers were told they could not proceed, and their protestations of innocence were ignored. "We know you have marijuana," they were told. The truck was staying put.

Citing their rights got them absolutely nowhere. A smuggling arrest was never at issue. It was bribe money the cops were after. After the truck had been held for an hour, Long gave Miguel the last of his cash and instructed him to make the payoff. It took another hour for Miguel to convince the officer in charge that the $8,000 he had given him was all the money he had. The officer let the truck pass, but he clearly was not happy with the story. He radioed his cousin, an army colonel, who met the smugglers at yet a third roadblock fifteen miles down the road.

Negotiations with the colonel began at the roadblock and ended an hour later over beers in a nearby café. Long explained that he had no more money. The colonel explained that more money, and nothing short of more money, would activate the barrier gate behind which the truck was stalled. The conversation ended in a standoff, the deal was hopelessly deadlocked, and it seemed the marijuana would never make the airstrip when Miguel made an inquiry of the colonel.

"Would you accept a check?"

The colonel said he would do so gladly.

Miguel wrote the colonel a postdated check in the amount of $10,000. The colonel, after thanking the smugglers, urged them to alert

303

him in advance next time. In doing so, he advised them, they would avoid such inconvenience as they had experienced today and reduce their expenses to a single payoff.

Which is precisely what Ernesto on the Guajira had done in preparing to move his share of the load. And Ernesto did not rely on transactional bribery — he did not buy the service per se, he had bought and long since owned its provider. The payoff, covering a wide range of conditions and requirements, secured him the working equivalent of a blanket policy, the kind made available by insurance companies and promoted in much the same spirit.

With the colonel's help, moving the pot to the airstrip in Valledupar was accomplished in a matter of three days. But by then enough time had slipped away to queer things on the Guajira. There, thanks to a U.S.-sponsored drug-interdiction offensive, the bribery so assiduously applied by Ernesto was destined to go unrewarded. He would not be allowed to ship his pot, he was informed, until a respectable amount of time had passed. Long did not have time. There was only a month left in the operational window within which he was required to move.

He had 30,000 pounds ready to go, and 30,000 pounds would not do it. Moving half the load would pay for the trip, and he and his partners would walk away with a million dollars each, but Long, who was obsessed by now with the trip's being a serious crowd pleaser, wanted to move it all. Rather than move the 30,000, he gave up on the Sikorsky, and hustled to make other arrangements in California. Myerson led him to some Bay Area smugglers with a lease on an old Navy dry dock, who were preparing to bring loads of their own up from Colombia using a small fleet of fifty-foot trawlers, sailing them through the Golden Gate and right into San Francisco Bay. For a usurious 30 percent of the load, they agreed to meet the *Pituro Uno* and bring Long's pot ashore.

He would wish he had taken the million.

By the time he made it back to Colombia, Ernesto's marijuana had been busted, sacrificed to appease the DEA, and the smugglers in Valledupar, to secure their investment, had sold off the 30,000 pounds they were holding. "Not until next year," Miguel said, would he and Pablo be able to amass another 60,000 pounds of quality pot.

Six months later the *Pituro Uno* was busted. Eventually, by way of the DC-4 and a single San Francisco trawler — traveling directly to Buenaventura to make pickups in the lagoon — three loads of pot belonging to Miguel, a total of 45,000 pounds, ended up in Ann Arbor. But Long did not learn that until later. By then he had been cut out of the deal.

The failure of the Pacific trip had cost him the trust of his partners, more than a year of his time, and about $3.5 million in cash. What he had seen as an opening to the future closed with the unmistakable sound of a door slamming on the past. Out of work and without a plan, Long called Tony A. in Miami. And it was Tony who showed him the future. It was Tony who helped him see where the dope business was *really* going.

He said: "Jimmy wants to talk to you."

Since Long had last done business with him, Jimmy had taken up residence in a three-million-dollar house he had built on a vast expanse of ranch land in the shadow of a Costa Rican volcano. He had been spending as much time there as in Miami, and it was there that Long reached him by phone.

"This man Santiago is killing me," said Jimmy.

Santiago was the Colombian middleman from whom Jimmy was now buying his pot. And Santiago, Jimmy alleged, was overcharging him for the product.

"He has grown too greedy," Jimmy complained.

Long understood this to mean that cheating him had grown too difficult.

Jimmy wanted Long to supply him with a new connection in Colombia. Long did not even bother to ask, "Whither Gilberto?" the original Colombian connection, with whom he had lunched at Victoria Station. That setup had been doomed to go south the instant Long stepped out of the deal. He had been the glue that held it together. In his absence, there would have been a host of "problems" — discrepancies, alleged "contingencies," a "misunderstanding" here and there. Simply put, Gilberto would not be getting his money. No doubt, he had cut Jimmy off, refusing to do business with him. If "this man Santiago" were in fact guilty of overcharging Jimmy — and on that, the jury was still out — he was, as they say in California traffic court, "guilty with an explanation, Your Honor."

Long's professed misgivings about doing business with Jimmy had diminished in the course of a year and a half, and what remained of them he was able to set aside in the face of his failure to land a load on his own. Jimmy was a worker, you had to give him that. There would always be money in doing business with him. Long, seeking a new connection for him, reached out to Miguel in Barranquilla, who came back with the name of Samuel Calderón Sanchez. This was the man, Miguel said, to whom he would introduce Jimmy.

"That is his name!" shouted Jimmy when Long conveyed the news. "Calderón, that is the one!"

And Long just had to laugh. Thanks to Miguel, Jimmy had just accomplished the otherwise impossible. Jimmy had, without trying to, succeeded in jumping Santiago, in going around him to his supplier. Had Jimmy intended to do so, it never would have happened. Neither Jimmy nor Calderón could have made themselves known to each other. Santiago, who brokered their business, would always remain between them, he would always be entitled to a piece of their deal.

Positively blissful at the prospect of dealing directly with Calderón, Jimmy instructed Long to meet him in Miami. In the Everglades just west of Miami, Jimmy owned a ranch, the centerpiece of which was neither the lavish house nor small hotel situated on the property. Its focal point was the cockfighting ring to which breeders and high rollers from all over the Caribbean were drawn to bet on fighting roosters like the thousands Jimmy owned.

"Let's go dig up some money," he said.

He and Long headed for the ranch. There Jimmy unearthed a trunk containing $850,000 in cash. Returning to Coral Gables, he transferred the money to briefcases, and the following morning set off to Bertram, where he bought two fifty-eight-foot power boats. Long shook hands with Jimmy on a fifty-fifty split. With an 80,000-pound load in the offing, he was looking at a $4 million payday.

The partners flew to Costa Rica.

La Finca de Don Jaime— or as others called it, Jimmy's place — as an ode to conspicuous consumption was state-of-the-poetic-art. The money he had spent to build the house, with indoor pool and a gymnasium, was a third of what he had spent on the barn. With ceramic tile floors, its numerous stalls were appointed each in the manner of a first-class hotel room, and accommodated what some considered the finest Andalusian horses in the Western Hemisphere. Jimmy had flown in the breeding stock from Austria and Spain. The stable was monitored by video camera twenty-four hours a day, except on those occasions when Jimmy threw a party, when he turned the horses out and equipped the stalls to house his guests. The ranch was also home to a congregation of fighting cocks, which were put up in individual cages. The sun did not rise quietly over the Finca de Don Jaime. The day after Long's arrival, and every day thereafter, he was awakened at dawn by the crowing of some 2,000 roosters, not blind (or deaf) to the piercing reality that he had helped generate the money that Jimmy had spent to accumulate them.

In residence at the ranch, anticipating the arrival of the vaunted Calderón, in addition to Long and Jimmy — and the ever-present Dennis — was a Miami Cuban named Hector, the same CIA contract employee who had blown up that PT boat in Havana Harbor. Hector, employed by Jimmy, was related to Tony A. by marriage. Tony, let it be sufficient to say, had a nickel on everything that went down — from everybody.

When Calderón arrived at the airport, traveling with Miguel, Long and Jimmy were there to meet him. When Miguel introduced Calderón and Long, a look of recognition passed between them, but neither could place the other. It was on the ride back to the ranch that Long remembered where he had met the dark, heavyset Colombian who was seated with him in the car. It had been on the Guajira one night, the night Miguel told him about the burros.

Long remembered the night very well, a quiet night in Riohacha in 1976. He had been in Colombia selecting pot between flights of the

DC-3. Returning from the fields with Miguel, walking through the jungle, he had seen two young boys jumping quickly through the brush, chasing a small donkey. Miguel, catching sight of them, provoked laughter in his fellow Colombians with an observation in Spanish that Long did not manage to catch.

Long asked about it that evening.

Because it would be unwise for a gringo to be seen spending the night in town, Long was camped with the Colombians in a compound near Riohacha, an outdoor encampment used by the local *contrabandistas* as a staging area, and for the storage and repair of equipment: trucks, guns, and other tools of the trade.

Sitting around the campfire that night, drinking *aguardiente*, Long asked Miguel what everyone had found so funny earlier in the day.

"Oh," said Miguel, "the little boys, they were trying to fuck the burro."

"Come on."

"You have never fucked a burro?"

"Are you serious?" said Long.

Miguel seemed genuinely surprised.

"Oh, yes, sir, it is done all the time."

Long laughed, certain that his friend was putting him on, convinced that this was some sort of time-honored gag the Colombians enjoyed at the expense of every visiting gringo.

"Oh, yes, sir," Miguel insisted, "they were trying to fuck the burro. You have never done this?"

"No."

"Oh, it is very good. Very sweet," Miguel said, kissing his fingertips, spreading them open like a bouquet. "Good pussy."

Long was incredulous now.

"Miguel, you fucked a donkey?"

"Not only me, sir," answered Miguel. "I bet you that every man here, around this fire, when he was a little boy, fucked a burro."

And with that he began polling his countrymen . . .

"*Sí* . . ."

"Oh, yes . . ."

"Very good . . ."

"*Muy buena* . . ."

. . . each man, in turn, answering in the affirmative.

"In my country, Allen," Miguel explained, "you learn when you are a boy that there are two kinds of women, the *señoritas* and the *putas*. The *señoritas*, they do not fuck. The *putas*, the whores, these are the ones who fuck. But we are only boys, we don't have any money to pay them. And so, when you reach the age where the desire to fuck is so great, it is a tradition, you fuck the burros. The burros have no disease like the dogs. My father, when I was a little boy, he told me: 'Don't fuck the dog!' And you cannot fuck the chickens, because later they will die. It is only the burros you can fuck. Every man, when he is a child in Colombia, fucks a burro. And it can be very good."

As Miguel explained this to Long, the smugglers around the campfire nodded their agreement, ventured amplification, and injected words of wisdom. One man among them did not speak. He was larger than the others, darker, his skin tone a deep mahogany, mulatto where they were mestizo. His hair was black and thick, his features almost simian. Standing outside the conversation, he was working at a makeshift table over which he had thrown a dropcloth, cleaning automatic weapons by the light of the fire. He had pulled them out of a sack . . . Uzis, Ingrams . . . a half-dozen submachine guns, and his attention to them was proprietary. All were loaded and ready to go, and all of them were his. Snapping in their magazines as he finished oiling the weapons, he added audible punctuation to the conversation taking place, the intermittent click of steel on steel mimicking the crackling of the fire. Other than that he was silent.

"This is a very dangerous man," Miguel had said, pointing him out to Long, "very famous here in the Guajira."

This was Samuel Calderón Sanchez.

A rising power in the marijuana business, Calderón, according to Miguel, had already killed twelve men. His most recent murder was of a witness to another murder he had committed. As the witness was about to give evidence, Calderón had run up and shot him dead right on the steps of the courthouse.

Calderón's reputation for ruthlessness and the fear he inspired among his countrymen had not yet been matched by wealth. Only recently had the killer turned his prodigious criminal talents to smuggling. Calderón, that night on the Guajira, did not make himself known to Long. He merely said hello. To attempt to effect a connection with the American was forbidden by the rules of the trade. Any business they did would be conducted by way of Miguel.

The night on which he had met Calderón was a memorable one for Long, if for nothing else than for being so instructive. There he sat before the campfire, the flames casting shadows across the brown, weathered faces of the armed *contrabandistas* of Colombia. All had 5,000 to 10,000 pounds of pot stashed somewhere in the jungle. Sitting there on boxes and rickety chairs in their cowboy hats and boots, on the dirt floor of a lean-to under a shed roof of corrugated tin, they were drinking *aguardiente* and discussing sexual congress with animals to the sound of submachine guns being cleaned. And Long would never forget being reminded of how far he was from home.

The events of the evening came back to him now, traveling to Jimmy's ranch from the airport in San Jose.

In the two years since that night in Riohacha, Samuel Calderón had ascended to a position of preeminent wealth and power as a smuggler. He now owned a significant interest in Colombia's Aerocondor Airlines, a commercial carrier recently subverted by traffickers, and turned to the purpose of smuggling large shipments of cocaine. His reputation for mercilessness, which put that of Jimmy Alvarez in the shade, foreshadowed the emergence later of the cocaine cartels in Colombia and the tide of violence upon which they rose.

"There is a time in Colombia," Long understood, unburdening himself of the understanding in a conversation he had with Carlyle after the Pacific trip went bad, "a time when if you don't kill someone, you don't get the job done. That's how things are handled. You pull the trigger. And everything gets taken care of."

The time was rapidly approaching when no one who did business in Colombia did so without blood on his hands.

Jimmy turned the horses out and put his guests up in the stable, checking each man into a stall. He made reservations at his favorite restaurant, a local dining establishment that he owned.

"Down by the river," he said.

By the river on his ranch.

Jimmy's wealth and the distance it placed between him and the indigenous population had engendered in the drug kingpin severe paranoia. He believed that the locals were trying to poison his roosters and slaughter his horses, and were just waiting to murder him. It had driven him to desperate measures. That he might dine out whenever the fancy struck him, without fear of assassination, Jimmy had built his own restaurant. It sat on a verdant spit of land at a bend in the river traversing his property. Supporting a roof of thatch, featuring an indoor-outdoor barbecue pit and handmade tables and chairs, it was open to the air and not open to the public. The restaurant served Jimmy exclusively. When Jimmy felt like dining out, he picked up the phone, called his cook, and instructed him to slaughter a pig and break out a couple of bottles of Château Lafite. He then called the maintenance man and told him to turn on the lights, the brightest of which was the neon sign installed on the roof that read: "Jimmy's."

At the door of the restaurant, Long and the others were greeted by a pair of white-jacketed waiters. A pig was roasting, rice and beans were cooking, and the table was set with several bottles of seventy-year-old Bordeaux. It was there, that night, in front of his other guests and putative business partners, that Jimmy, with a "by the way," informed Long that his cut of the load had been reduced from a half to a third. He had taken on another partner, he said, the man who would be handling the Florida off-load, using Jimmy's Bertrams to meet Calderón's freighter offshore.

There was little Long could do but accede to the new terms, however incensed he might be by their unilateral adoption. At a third of $8 million, he was still looking at a nice piece of change. He was in for $2.6 million, and all he had to do was go to Colombia and pick out the best pot he could find.

Conversation over dinner proceeded from that particular slap in the face to an orgy of whining and self-justification, with Jimmy and Calderón, two of the wealthier men in the dope industry, complaining about the exorbitant amount each of them had been losing to Santiago. The undisguised rapacity with which they cut out the middleman who had helped to make each of them so rich failed to make more than a passing impression upon Long, whose achievement, after all, had been to bring together these two creatures of God.

Calderón's digs in Barranquilla were the city-mouse equivalent of country-mouse Jimmy's Costa Rica crib. The extravagance of its forty-grand shower stalls, outfitted in marble and gold, was cast into vivid relief by the city's intermittent provision of municipal services. The morning after his arrival, Long, at Calderón's insistence, availed himself of the use of one, spending as much time therein as he deemed gracious under the circumstances — under no running water, hot or cold — to be greeted upon his exit by an ain't-I-livin'-good smile from his host.

"The next thing I do," Calderón announced, "I will build a power plant."

From Barranquilla, with Hector in tow, Long set out for the Guajira, stopping in Santa Marta to check into the Irotama. Prized for its location, amenities, and service — for a long time it had been the city's only first-class hotel — the Irotama, quite innocently, had become a way station for every smuggler in the Western Hemisphere. Checking in was like genuflecting at Mass.

Out near Maicao, beyond Riohacha, in the dust of the high Guajira, Long got down to business, looking at truckload after truckload of marijuana, none of which was any good. He rejected about 400,000 pounds, finally amassing a shipment of some 80,000, maybe half of which was acceptable. The pot was not great, but four weeks had already passed — Long had picked up a terrible sunburn — and the time had come to move.

"What do you say?" asked Hector.

"It makes me high," said Long.

Period. End of evaluation. It was garden-variety, low-octane loco weed. It was not something the Rastas would ever want to write songs about.

"But there's no pot in the U.S.," said Long. "I guess we ought to send it."

"Good."

Using Ernesto's people, they loaded the pot aboard Calderón's freighter, a thousand pounds at a time, five trips each in sixteen *cayucas*. From the beach, in the dark, on a moonless night, Long watched the ship's mast light bobbing above the swells. Looking at a take of some $2.6 million, he hopped aboard the last *cayuca*, motored out, boarded the freighter, and saw that the pot was stashed securely below. From the bow of the dugout, as he stepped back aboard to return to the beach, he kissed the stern of the freighter, sending it on its way.

They celebrated that night on the Guajira.

Calderón moved boats through the Caribbean where other smugglers could not, busting right through a U.S. task force that looked like the flotilla deployed at the Battle of Midway. Long was unsure how Calderón did it, but the pot arrived off the Marquesas Keys eight days after leaving the beach.

When Long arrived in Florida, Jimmy told him, "I need more Bertrams." They drove to the Everglades to dig up cash, and on the way Jimmy explained that to recoup his added expenses, he would be cutting Long's share down to 20 percent.

"Jimmy, we're partners, remember? It's getting ridiculous, it's gone far enough. I don't want to hear any more of it."

The pot came ashore, and Jimmy was too busy to meet.

"You cannot come here now," he told Long.

"Jimmy, I have a truck here in Florida, I'm ready to pick up my share."

"If you come here now, Allen, I will kill you."

Long let a couple of days go by, called Jimmy and said, "I'm coming over."

"Okay, my friend, it is not a good time, but okay," Jimmy said.

Evening had fallen. The house was in darkness but for the light of a few lamps. Jimmy sat alone at the dining room table. He motioned Long to a chair. Weapons covered the table, from end to end, from side to side, like a lawn. The weapons were new, many still packed in shipping grease. There were submachine guns, automatic rifles, and shoulder-fired grenade and rocket launchers.

"They got go-fasts now," Jimmy said.

Jimmy was talking about the U.S. Coast Guard. It was no secret that Jimmy now, in addition to pot, was moving large shipments of cocaine. And he did not intend to be stopped. His Bertrams, fully loaded, did maybe 27 knots. Unable to outrun the Coast Guard crews, he would blow their Cigarettes out of the water.

M-72s and M-79s. Rockets and grenades. This is where Long's adventure had brought him. This is where he had been led by the escapade he had decided to undertake almost ten years before, sitting there over a couple of joints in El Coyote's penthouse apartment.

"I'm ready to pick up my share of the load," he said.

"Yes, I know, I understand," said Jimmy, making room on the table in front of him. "But there are some things we need to talk about."

Jimmy flipped the page on a legal pad, and started playing with numbers. First of all, the load had been sold, he said. Long would not receive a share of the product to sell, he would be paid a share of the profit. Jimmy multiplied the weight of the load by a dollar figure significantly lower than reasonable, and started subtracting from there.

". . . Two new Bertrams, that is nine hundred thousand, and then, you see, I have a partner who does the off-load, he gets thirty-three percent, so we have to subtract that, and then I had to pay for the marijuana, we subtract that, then all the expenses . . ." Take this off, take this off and this off . . . "and your share is one hundred and fifty thousand dollars."

Long's payday, last seen at 20 percent, went from an already unacceptable $1.6 million to $150,000 in maybe a minute and a half.

He said, "You know what, Jimmy, this is no good, and I'll tell you what I'm gonna do. I'm gonna have someone else come down and collect my money for me."

Jimmy drew a pistol, and placed the muzzle against Long's head.

"I like you, Allen," he said, "but I will kill you right now unless you take the money and agree to walk out the door."

Long's sunburned face surrendered its color. Something awful happened inside of him, something in Long of cellular origin. It seemed to rise in the germ plasm, a kind of genetic dread that had survived evolution, inflecting man's history as he ascended the food chain.

"Jimmy," he said, "I can't do it."

"Take the money."

Long stood up and turned around. Standing behind him was Dennis — inches away, in suspension, it seemed, like a barracuda at feeding time — holding an AR-15 aimed at his chest.

"Allen," said Dennis, extending a briefcase, "take the money."

The room was strung with invisible tension. Opposing vectors of excitement traversed it like the lines of force on a chessboard. The room, in low light, lugubrious at best, had assumed all the charm of a meat locker.

"Jimmy," said Long, "this wallpaper is new."

The wallpaper was silk. A pale silver silk moire. Jimmy's girlfriend had spent $3,700 for the job.

"Came out nice," Long said.

Jimmy narrowed his eyes. He shook his head.

"What the fuck, man, are you talking about?"

"It would be a shame to mess it up with my blood."

Jimmy smiled, said, "Allen, I like you. You are a good man, and you make me laugh. So, please, take the money. I do not want to, but I will kill you if I have to."

There was a very subtle point at issue. If Long took the money, he was accepting the deal. It was saying that Jimmy owed him nothing. He would not come back at Jimmy, or send someone else to do so.

While Jimmy knew that Long was no gunman, he could not let him leave empty-handed and be sure that Long would not someday send someone to collect his money, or in some fashion close the books. And why, reasoned Jimmy, wait for a showdown? If Long did not take the money, better to kill him now.

Not so subtle was the coldness that came over Long in the echo of his own words, hearing himself advise Jimmy that he would send someone else to collect, a coldness that told him he was now one of them, in that instant, with that threat, a gangster himself. As he stood there, with weapons targeting him from opposite sides, it was his own behavior that startled him most.

"Allen, take this money, and we will talk about a percentage for you on the loads I do from now on."

"Jimmy, I don't think you're going to be doing any more loads. If you treat me like this, you're treating everybody like this. Nobody's going to work with you."

"Allen, please take the money."

"I don't want to die, so I'll take the money, but I'll never do business with you again."

"As you choose," Jimmy said.

He took the money, walked out of the house, and when the door closed behind him, it was over. In every real way it was finished.

Walking into the game a pioneer, Allen Long was now an anachronism.

The adventure was complete. He had seen it to a conclusion.

"Something funny?" said Jimmy, as he was showing him out.

"Me," said Long, unable to shake the absurd smile from his face. "It's me. It's what I was thinking. You wouldn't understand."

But he told Jimmy anyway, and he left the house laughing.

"I was just thinking," he said, "this would make a great movie."

EPILOGUE

There are three ways out of the dope business, the most dramatic of which will always be dying on the job. Of the other two, quitting while you are ahead or going to jail, the second is by far the more common. Those who have chosen the former — you have eaten in their restaurants, worn their sportswear, listened to music on their record labels, or maybe you have rented their real estate — are admittedly difficult to count. Those who have suffered the latter, they, and their customers, have provided 50 percent of the population of the nation's prisons over the last decade. Walking alive out of Jimmy's house that night, and faced with a choice between the two, Allen Long inevitably did both.

A little more than a year later, to use the words of JD Reed, "the dominoes started to fall." Of the North Americans involved in what the government would ultimately claim to be one of the larger marijuana-smuggling conspiracies of its time, virtually all wound up in prison.

Jake Myerson went down first. In 1982 his Ann Arbor operation was busted, and Myerson started cooperating. He was required to name names. Released from prison after serving three and a half years, he is the owner of a legitimate business and is a pillar of his community today.

Will McBride was doing business with Myerson when the feds closed Myerson down. Working with Canadian smugglers, he was landing boats in North Carolina and shipping the pot to Ann Arbor. Busted, McBride cooperated, and was required to name others. He served four years of a twelve-year sentence. McBride, who had "never wanted to be a farmer," said, "I always thought I'd be a rock and roll star, an astronaut, a movie star, a lawyer, or politician. I never expected to be an international criminal." Upon release from federal prison, accepting the opportunity presented by a friend, he went to work in advertising. He owns his own company today.

Frank Hatfield's participation in their enterprise was a few years behind him when he was arrested in 1984 on information provided by Myerson and McBride. He served three years of a five-year sentence. He fought to retain his pilot's license, but the license has done him no good, the necessary medical certificate being impossible to come by because his conviction is drug-related. "It was more beautiful than any woman I'd ever met," he recalled of the DC-3. "It was such a scammer's airplane. It saved our lives," he said. Acknowledged to be an extraordinary flyer by professionals who have heard of his exploits, today he drives a truck for a living.

Buddy Blanchard, in exchange for his cooperation, was allowed to plead guilty in U.S. Court to two counts of tax fraud, on which he served reduced jail time, and was required to surrender his license to practice law in Virginia.

JD Reed was arrested in 1984 on marijuana charges unrelated to his work with Long and the others. Busted on a Virginia indictment, convicted on the testimony of co-conspirators, he was sentenced to thirty years in prison, all but eleven of which were suspended. Unlike most with whom he had worked over the years, Reed refused to cooperate. While serving his state time, he was picked up and tried on federal charges, and sentenced under the government's racketeering statutes for engaging in a continuing criminal enterprise. After doing three years on his state conviction, he did nine years' federal time. Asked what he could have offered authorities in exchange for a lighter sentence, he answered with a look of bemusement. "I never got that far with them. I don't think that way," he said. Noting that he was never arrested for anything he did by himself, he hastened to add that nobody else was ever arrested because of him: "If it was a cop, I wouldn't give him up." He saw his capture as inevitable. The business got so big, he said, and there were so many amateurs working, that it was only a matter of time. Reed, who served hard time because he stood up, never held it against those who did not. Today he is self-employed, earning his living as a cabinetmaker. Reed's father, Luther, died of heart complications in 1985 after completing a five-year sentence on his federal conviction for manufacturing bootleg Quaaludes. He was fifty-nine years old.

Abe succumbed to cancer in 2000 at the age of sixty-five.

Miguel and his friend Dr. Pablo Cepeda today earn their money legitimately. Neither was ever arrested.

Gilberto, the Colombian behind all the marijuana Long distributed out of Miami, was murdered on the Guajira sometime in the 1980s. His prominence and his estimated $100 million in cash, according to what Long was told, made him the target of leftist guerrillas, and refusing to pay their protection money, he was killed in a shoot-out with their forces during an assault they made on his farm.

Samuel Calderón Sanchez was gunned down outside his house in Barranquilla.

Raúl Gaviria escaped prosecution when the Black Tuna Gang was busted in Miami. He lives in Colombia, a prominent member of a politically influential family with lucrative commercial interests.

María, escaping marriage to an American dope smuggler, went on to marry the Colombian version. Today she is the mother of five children. To Long's knowledge she has never seen Paris.

Tony A., who had retired from the dope business, was arrested in 1982 on charges arising out of his reluctant response to a call for aid from his relative Hector, who had not. Tony served seven years of a twelve-year sentence. Hector escaped to Spain, where he lives today. Tony remains the only man Allen Long knows ever arrested for cattle rustling. Deer hunting on Florida panhandle property owned by his partner Lonnie's family, Tony and his pals shot a cow that had found its way into the woods, or an "Italian deer!" as Frank A. exclaimed, being the first to draw a bead on the creature. Testing new ordnance for the CIA — they were hunting with automatic weapons — they managed only to wound the cow. By the time they caught up with the animal, it had walked as far as a local church, outside of which it finally collapsed dead. The local sheriff, who had always had it in for these troublemakers, one of whom, according to Tony, had been sleeping with the lawman's wife, threw them all in jail. It was a nuisance arrest more than anything. Nobody was surprised when the government showed up and squared things away. Today Tony is a successful real estate developer in Miami.

Lonnie, a former Miami police officer, was arrested on unrelated drug trafficking charges while Tony was in prison. He drew a sixty-year sentence, and is still incarcerated.

Frank A., arrested in 1982 on tax-evasion charges, is believed to have turned state's evidence. He disappeared from the minimum security lockup at Eglin Air Force Base in Florida, presumably entering the federal Witness Security Program under an identity provided by the government. Only the U.S. marshals know where he is.

Jack, Tony's CIA handler, suffered a heart attack at his law office in 1989, just as the DEA was moving in on him, and died a few months thereafter, never having regained consciousness. He was fifty-five.

Virgil was never arrested. Having quit while he was ahead, he is a wealthy man today, with substantial holdings in South Florida.

Jimmy Alvarez is still in business.

El Coyote was never seen by Long after their trip to Guadalajara.

Ives, erstwhile saloon owner and documentary film producer, whom Long had not seen in more than twenty years, was, in Long's words, "still clipping coupons" — living on the proceeds of his stock portfolio — when Long in 1998 ran into him walking on West 57th Street in Manhattan.

Pomeroy was last seen by Long at the helm of a sailboat off Sausalito in 1988. He had just launched a business bottling and distributing a new brand of spring water.

Easy Matthews was convicted in 1990 on tax and drug charges unrelated to his work with Long, and served two years of a four-year federal sentence. A successful family man, and the owner of an equally successful, legitimate business today, he still drives the same car he was driving when Long first met him in Richmond in 1974, a four-door sedan that was eight years old even then.

Myles, Matthews's partner, sentenced in 1990 on charges of pot distribution and tax evasion, served 27 months at Eglin, where he enjoyed himself immensely. "If I had kids, any one of these guys, I'd let them baby-sit," he said of the people he did time with. This he said to his mother in a phone call from the facility. "On the outside," he told the parole board, just prior to his release, "I was working eighty hours a week. In here I'm working thirty." Today he distributes T-shirts to the tune of $30 million a year.

Lee Carlyle in 1983 took up alligator farming in Sebring, Florida. In 1999 he was arrested, having found his way back into the marijuana business, and is currently serving a federal sentence.

Cherie Harris, after she and Long split up, enjoyed a brief career as a model, discovering that she could "be successful without being a star." As a client of Wilhelmina and subsequently Ford, she did well on the commercial side of the business. "I put braces on my sister, a fence around my momma's house." In 1990 she returned to Richmond. Today she is married and the mother of a ten-year-old son.

The trajectory of Long's career was a predictable one. It followed pretty faithfully the breaking curve of pot smuggling's passage through the culture as an indulgence of the aficionado. Long was one of numerous gringos who all walked away at about the same time to leave dope trafficking to the professional felonry. No less predictable was the retirement package with which Long departed the business.

Jimmy's 80,000 pounds had arrived in Miami a week before Christmas 1980. Earlier that year Long and Cherie had finally put an end to things, and Long had since taken up with a young Fort Lauderdale businesswoman, a former girlfriend of Carlyle's. She and Long had been sharing a house for about a month when Long walked out of Jimmy's. Of the $150,000 that Jimmy gave him that night, Long owed half to Miguel, who was waiting for him in Aruba. With Miguel's $75,000 in a briefcase, Long left home the following day, flew to Aruba, delivered the money, stayed a couple of nights on the island, and when he returned to Fort Lauderdale the house was empty, the safe was empty, and the young businesswoman had stolen his half of the one-fifty.

With that, Long returned to New York, knowing little more at the time than what he did *not* want to do with the rest his life, but before he departed South Florida, he took a shot at earning some necessary seed money.

He had been approached by a guy named Vargas, a Miami Cuban who had been directed to him through Gilberto's people on the Guajira. Vargas had a load in. He had 15,000 pounds that he needed to off. Long, in need of cash, and agreeing now to move the load, reached out to Carlyle, who arranged for delivery of the marijuana to a warehouse in Pompano Beach. The warehouse was one of a series of storage bays and other businesses, auto repair places and the like, set back from the road surrounding a parking area on the edge of a palmetto swamp. Long and Carlyle took delivery at night, and the following morning, Long, with JD Reed in the car — it was the day Reed's probation ended on his Newport Beach conviction — drove into the facility surprised to find that none of the businesses was open. The parking area was empty but for the presence of a refreshment cart at which two men in sunglasses were drinking coffee.

"There's definitely something wrong here."

"It don't look right," muttered Reed.

Long, circling the car, left the place without stopping.

The police report told the story:

The night before, unknown to Long and Carlyle as they were inside weighing the pot, a pair of homeless, yet nonetheless civic-minded, alcoholics were camped out with a bottle up against the rear wall of the storage bay. Like most of the nation's citizens, especially those registered voters within the municipal orbit of Miami, these two American taxpayers appreciated the meaning of expressions like "really good shit," and overhearing the smugglers' conversation, they reported it to the police, who that morning set up a command center in the diner across the street.

Once it became clear that no one was going to claim the marijuana, the cops moved in and seized it.

Long called Vargas.

Vargas said, "Somebody has to come to Miami and explain this."

When Long showed up for the meeting, he was thrown into a car by Vargas's men, driven to a house on the edge of the Everglades, and dumped on the floor.

Vargas put a revolver on him.

"Where is my money, you motherfucker?"

"Kill him!" urged the others present, brandishing weapons of their own.

"Motherfucker, you stole my money!"

"Hey!" shouted Long. "I didn't steal anything."

"I am going to blow your fucking brains out!"

Vargas put a foot on Long's face, placed the barrel of the revolver behind Long's ear and cocked the hammer.

"Go ahead, blow my brains out. Kiss my ass. If you're gonna kill me, kill me. I didn't steal anything."

He handed Vargas the police report. He had hired a lawyer to obtain the report when a warrant was issued for the owner of the storage bay.

"You see it?" he asked Vargas.

Vargas saw it. He threw it aside.

"Fuck that," he said, "we are going to kill you."

But the twitch in Vargas's trigger finger lost some of its urgency as he pondered murdering for no reason now the only buyer he knew for any future shipments of pot.

Long said, "Why don't you get the Colombians over here. They own the pot. You guys haven't lost anything. It's the Colombians who lost the load. It's their say whether somebody gets killed."

Vargas said okay.

Long had no idea who they were, but two Colombians eventually showed up, and the pair of them were straight off the Guajira: cowboy hats, no English, and neither of them capable of reading the police report Long was offering in support of his innocence. But Long walked them through the numbers, explained that it was an official document, and more than that, after that, he said, "Do you know Gilberto?"

Oh, yes. They knew Gilberto. Everybody knew Gilberto.

"Well, my name is Allen. Call Gilberto, and ask him about me."

No, Gilberto's name was enough. Calling him would not be necessary. The pot was not stolen, it was seized by the police. No problem, Long owed nothing. And the Colombians said so to Vargas.

Vargas and his associates apologized.

"Sorry, man . . ."

"Yeah . . . "

"Hey . . ."

"You know . . ."

Long was free to go.

The Colombians departed immediately, followed by Vargas's henchmen, one of whom, before leaving the house, tossed Long the keys to his car. The anthracite gray BMW sedan had been driven there by his kidnappers and was parked on the street out front. Long, left sitting there with Vargas after everyone else had gone, stood up and walked to the door. So quickly had everyone vanished that Vargas still had the gun in his hand. Vargas got to his feet, stuck the revolver back in his waistband, and then slowly he sat back down, staring into the middle distance, his hands draped over the arms of an easy chair.

"Allen," he said, when Long opened the door.

"Yeah," said Long, before stepping outside.

"Allen, I don't have a ride home."

Long had the only car.

"Can you give me a ride?" Vargas asked.

Long drove Vargas home.

And Long was now out of the game.

But what happened that night in the Everglades, serving or not to enlighten him, was loaded with the freight of a parable. Examined even casually, it illustrates all you need to know about the dope business.

At the time, in Colombia, Pablo Escobar was in meteoric ascendancy. Escobar, the legendary architect of the Medellín cartel, was shot to death some twelve years later, and in the five years leading up to his eradication the streets of Colombia ran with the blood of the cocaine-financed murder of more than 60,000 people. The dead included more than a thousand police officers, sixty judges, seventy journalists, a governor, an attorney general, two cabinet ministers, and four of the six presidential candidates running in the campaign leading up to the 1990 national election. How many civil servants and public officials chose the *plata* (silver) over the *plomo* (lead) one could only speculate. Add to those naked statistics the fact that Allen Long on the floor of an Everglades house, with a foot on his face and a gun to his head, was waiting for salvation in the form of two strangers who, when they arrived, brought with them the comforting air of the Guajira. And all you need to know about the dope business is that the Colombians were the good guys.

With the arrest of Myerson and McBride, Allen Long became a federal fugitive, indicted on charges stemming from the original conspiracy and all the subsequent business he did with Myerson moving loads out of Miami. Long had moved back to New York by then, having made the decision to go straight.

In 1984 Long ceased to exist. For the next seven years he remained at large, a fugitive from justice, living under false identification. He supported himself by way of various legitimate jobs and the occasional small-time pot deal. A botched attempt to secure a passport — the papers held up, but Long did not; he bolted from the passport office in fear that he had drawn suspicion — led to a second identity change, and an outstanding arrest warrant on a charge of passport fraud. In 1987 he married a twenty-six-year-old German national he had met in the Caribbean. In December of that year his first son was born. In 1991, a year after his second son was born, the government finally caught up with him. He was arrested in Tampa, Florida.

The crimes that Long was wanted for were so far in the bureaucratic past that the prosecutors who inherited him saw very little political sunshine in the prospect of building a major case against him. There was no one for him to give up. Long was the last man standing. A plea agreement was in everyone's interest. In exchange for his pleading guilty to a federal marijuana trafficking conspiracy in the Middle District of Florida and passport fraud in the Virgin Islands, all other charges were dropped, and he was sentenced to five years in prison.

Officially considered a flight risk on the basis of his fugitive status, Long commenced his sentence in the maximum-security facility in

Atlanta, one of the nation's tougher joints. Transferred eventually to medium-, then minimum-security facilities, he was released from federal custody in 1995 after spending a year in pretrial detention and serving thirty months in prison. Having worked his way back into the music business, he lives today behind what he describes as "that white picket fence I always dreamed of," and attributes the current success he enjoys to the encouragement and support of his wife, to the second chance she gave him. "If it hadn't been for Simone, I would never have gotten where I am now." She and their children, Matthew and Sean, are "the real reward of my life," he says. The family lives in Virginia.

ACKNOWLEDGMENTS

The author first ran across this story as it was happening. The project, as proposed to him then, was a book very much of its time. Had it been written then, as a report from the front, it would have been in some ways ahead of its time, its journalistic value amplified by a wealth of inside information. The story would have been newsworthy, possessed inherently of an instructive edge, enlightening as a result of its immediacy. Now, any shock value the material holds, if any at all, derives from simple historical throw weight. That a loaded, top-of-the-line BMW could once be had brand-new for $17,000 is a good bet, one supposes, to liven up, however briefly, the national conversation.

Allen Long, over the course of his career, in addition to the Mexican pot, the Jamaican ganja, and the Thai weed he managed to smuggle, moved 972,000 pounds of pot out of Colombia. That is a lot of dope by any standard. The $8 million he made doing it, to be fully appreciated, must be measured against a standard that existed when you could put yourself in the leather and walnut interior of a high-performance German sedan for a fifth of what it costs today.

The book presents a story from out of a time and place fogged in not only by the passage of years, but by an atmospheric shift in the political and cultural spirit of a generation. The effort to illuminate that time and place absorbed most of the research muscle applied to the book, and was made more challenging by circumstances inherent in the material. First, the people whose story it is, when not trying to reinterpret it, have spent the ensuing years trying to forget that time in their lives, and second, even at their most willing, have had to admit to being completely stoned while much of it was going down.

Unlike other, more famous American fortunes, Allen Long's was made illegally. Certain participants in the crimes reported cooperated in the writing of the book on the condition that their real names not be used. Those who sought such cover did so not to avoid incriminating themselves — they have been prosecuted for their crimes, and their convictions are a matter of record — but to spare themselves and their families the negative personal and professional consequences of what they consider to be ancient history. Accordingly, some names have been changed. Allen Long's is not one of them.

Because the need to protect their identities makes it impossible to thank them individually, the author wishes to thank collectively all those people who shared their stories. In the absence of their trust and generosity the story could not have been told. The author is particularly grateful to Cherie Harris, whose faith in the project was exceeded by no one's, and who, as the first to believe, was responsible in large part for originally bringing the author and the material together.

For their help in the preparation of the manuscript, for the research material they provided, or for other personal and professional efforts in support of the project, the author wishes to thank: Vincent Amicosante; Marjorie Braman; Arlene Burchell; Rosalba Butler; Patrick Cavanaugh; Bruce Fishelman; Michael Gochenour; Ryan Harbage; Myra Hicks; Joe Lewis; Russ Maguire; Jay Mandel; Marianne McCaffery; Ross McDonald; David Riley; Dianne Ripley; Richard Rosenthal; Jamie Saul; Andy Valvur; and Amy Weinberg. Specific acknowledgment is due Mary Ryan, particularly for her guidance; no one lived with this project through more changes than she.

Were it not for Jennifer Rudolph Walsh, this book would have remained nothing more than a notion, an idea for a book, forever. She made it real by decree. The force of her magic is absolute. It is hard to imagine anything she cannot do, and one of the more terrifying manifestations of her sorcery is that once you surrender to her power, it is hard to imagine anything *you* cannot do. Were it not for Michael Pietsch, who invigorated and constantly dignified the process that led to its completion, the enterprise would have been unworthy of the effort. His contribution to this book is immeasurable; in the absence of his participation its vision would never have been realized.

The story itself should demonstrate that whatever Allen Long has to prove in this life, it is not his courage. But nothing he has done up to now proves it better than his agreement to do this book. Given the opportunity to hide behind a pseudonym, he declined. He is not naive to any of the implications of his decision, or to the consequences it holds for his family. The author wishes to thank him for his faith, his patience, and for the hours he sacrificed in the struggle to get the story right, and to thank his wife, Simone, and his sons, Matthew and Sean, for so graciously indulging the chronic interruption of their lives that writing the book forced upon them.

Special thanks is owed the following people, in default of whose assistance the author would still be sending up flares. On a different field of combat they would be awarded medals for valor; in action on another planet — call it Hollywood — they would be suing for production credits: Walter Bastian, whose lighting the way into Latin America was merely the most visible of his contributions. His encouragement and enthusiasm, mobilized here as behind every enterprise, no matter how slight, make showing up for work worthwhile even on the worst of days; because he is paying attention, you want to look good *all* the time. Thomas Butler, whose place in the scheme of things is inexpressible in all but the dead languages. *Semper honos nomenque tuum laudesque manebunt.* Sara Nelson, whose untiring friendship has occupied the horizon like a hospital ship, unqualified year after year.

No man has ever had a greater ally, a surer source of aid and comfort, or more reliable source of intelligent counsel. Her generosity and that of her husband, Akira Yoshimura, can never be amply rewarded. Philip Richardson, who managed to insinuate himself into the project in so many different ways that his contribution to its success, difficult enough to quantify, is that much more difficult to qualify. His talents are kaleidoscopic. Watching his mind at work is like walking through the Renaissance with a fever. The first phone call was always to him. Stephen Sullivan, that rare friend who can articulate the first-person pleasures of flying at twice the speed of sound; rarer still, a friend whose idea of fun, when flying that fast, is to do it upside down. The author and a grateful nation wish to thank him for not doing it stoned. To him and his wife, Rebecca, for their confidence in him and their encouragement of him not to give up and seek honest work, the author is deeply in debt; without them, this book would not have been written. And finally, preeminently, for that which defies the power of all alphabets to specify, Patricia Riley. She is the music you hear in the background.

INDEX

Abe, 77–78, 94–95, 319, and Reed, 98–99

abrazo, 35, 169

Aerocondor Airlines, 310

Aeschylus, 212

airstrip, in Colombia. *See* Perico

Alejandro, 44–47

ALL Air, Inc., 107, 109

almuerzo, 197–98

Altamont, 240

Alvarez, Jimmy, 266, 269–75, 293, 305–307, 311, 312, 313–16, 321; disenchantment with, 277–82

Andreas, 269, 288

Andrés Pérez, Carlos, 137

Angie (Miami police sergeant), 249–50

Ann Arbor, Michigan, 78, 92; marijuana market in, 95, 192–93, 243

Ann Arbor Sun, 93, 96

Aracataca, Colombia, 198, 200–201, 243

Aristotle, 212

Armando, 198–200, 218, 224, 225

Aronow, Don, 247

Aruba, 140, 141, 322

Aspen, Colorado, 73, 90–91

Atlantic Records, 89

Augusto, 226–31, 233–34

Bahía Profundo, 130, 202

Baranquilla, Colombia, 113–14, 197, 312

Bassett, Leslie, 19

Bassett, Steve, 89
Bay of Pigs, 236, 267
Benito (cabdriver), 114, 115
Bertram boats, 248, 306, 311, 313, 314
Big Jim, 60, 70–71
Billboard, 89
Billy (off-loader), 185, 187
Black Tuna Gang, 130, 320
Blanchard, Buddy, 108–109, 190, 318
Blonde on Blonde (Dylan), 19
Bogotá, Colombia, 224
Braniff Airways, 164
brotherhood, birth of, 173, 174
Byrds, The, 20

C-47 Skytrain, 17, 107. *See also* DC-3
cachaca, 224
Cactus Jack, 85
Caesars Palace, 258
Calderón Sanchez, Samuel, 306, 307, 309–10, 312, 319
caleta, 123, 152
California: logistics of load to, 297; off-loading in, 301–302, 304; opening market in, 261
Camarones, Colombia, 122
Capone, Al, 14
Capote, Truman, 257
Carlyle, Lee, 245–47, 261, 262, 276–77, 293, 322; and coke, 195, 196; drug habit of, 264, 272; in Mexican pot trade, 38–40, 43–44, 52–54; and Myerson, 263–64, 276; start as smuggler, 37; threat on life of, 169–72
cash: problems with, 273, 274–75, 286–87, 289; as cargo, 274–75
Castro, Fidel, 236

CBS Records, 87, 88, 282, 283
Central Intelligence Agency (CIA), 142, 249, 265, 267, 307; clandestine operations of, 244; and Cuban exiles, 236; role of in dope trade, 236
Cepeda, Pablo (El Demonio), 117–19, 121, 125, 130, 223–24, 319; in U.S., 257–59
Chase Manhattan Bank, Panama, 301
Chateau Lafite-Rothschild, 37, 311
checkpoints, security, 117. *See also* roadblocks
Chicago distributors, 38–39, 53
cigarette boat, 247–48
coastal freighters, Colombian, 246, 248
cocaine, 220, 265–66, 314; cartels, mercilessness of, 310–11; cultivation in Colombia, 141; development of Colombian trade in, 294; money in, 274–75; negative karma of, 71, 195; at Perico, 175; and pot, incompatibility of, 195–96; price of, 194; small market for in Seventies, 196. *See also* Allen Long
cockfighting, 306
code of silence, 74–75
coffee, Colombian, as contraband, 140
Cohn, Roy, 256
Colombia: cocaine trade in, 141, 294, 325–26; drug interdiction in, 211, 219, 304; drug use in, 154–55; internal customs system in, 117; marital fidelity in, 199; narcoeconomy of, 127–28, 140–41, 143, 294; quality of

marijuana from, 93–94, 198, 243;
value of marijuana from, 96
Colombian Coffee Federation, 140
Columbia Records, 89
Concorde, 223
connections, protection of, 74,
137–38
conspicuous consumption,
significance of, 263
conspiracy laws, 133–34, 298
Constance (housekeeper), 253
contraband, branding of, 171
costeños, 140–41, 224
Counts Four, 20
course of smuggling flight, 5–6,
164–67, 177–85
courtesy, among smugglers, 274
covering losses, conventions for, 168
crooks, culture of, 35, 137, 191, 274,
275–76
Crosby, 25–26, 29–36
Cuban Americans, in South Florida
dope trade, 93, 236
Cuban exiles, and CIA, 236
"Cuban way," 235, 261
Culiacán, Mexico, 38

Dante Alighieri, 217
Darlington International Raceway,
South Carolina, 176, 184–85
Davie, Florida, 246, 250, 261, 268
Davis, Angela, 296
Davis-Monthan Air Force Base, 107,
150–51
DC-3, 17, 106, 107, 130–31, 145;
auxiliary fuel tanks of, 150;
durability of, 163; fuel
requirements for, 118;
identification marks of, 206;
Long's purchase of, 106–109;

operation of, 165; use of parts of
in Colombia, 142–43
DC-4, 300
Del Prado Hotel, Baranquilla, 114
Del Río, 225, 226, 229–30, 232–33
deniability, function of, 284–85
Dennis, 273, 278–79, 315
Department of Defense, 300
deus ex machina, defined, 212
Don Enrique, 277–78, 279–82
Don Julio, 125–27, 222
Donzi boat, 247–48
Doors, The, 295
dope business: conventions in, 168,
274; U.S. currency in, 274
double cutouts, system of, 250
Douglas Aircraft Company, 17, 150,
163
Drug Enforcement Administration
(DEA), 106, 293, 294; and
Colombian drug interdiction, 219;
in Florida, 242; New York
headquarters of, 296
drug interdiction, 7, 117, 248, 294,
314; Colombian, 211, 219, 304;
costs of, 294
drug trade: attractions of, 174,
175–76, 287–88; as business,
84–87, 237; logistics of in South
Florida, 246–47; and music
industry, 88–89; risks of, 145, 216,
288–89; turnover in, 85; volume
in, 84
Dwayne, 278–79
Dylan, Bob, 19, 20

Eclair camera, 42, 43, 50
Eglin Air Force Base, 320, 321
El Coyote, 24–29, 30–33, 35–36, 39,
321

El Tigre (Del Río's man), 232
emeralds, 140
Epic Records, 283
Ernesto, 9, 122, 125, 127, 145, 152, 154, 155, 170–73, 283, 304; and cocaine, 195
Escobar, Pablo, 325
Euripides, 212
Eurotrash, 90
executive jet, Long's use of, 288–90

F-4 Phantom jets, 182–83
FAA investigators, 206–208, 300
Falstaff, 190–91
FBO operator, 203–204, 206
Federal Bureau of Investigation (FBI), 296
federal drug profile, 73
Felipe (cousin of Benito), 114
finca: of Jimmy Alvarez, 307, 311; of Pablo Cepeda, 218
firearms, absence of in pot culture, 14
five-dollar herb law, Ann Arbor, 92
Fleurette, 60, 69
flight operation: logistics of, 131–32; briefing for, 144–45
Forcade, Tom, 196
Ford Agency, 322
Formula boat, 247–48
Fort Lauderdale Executive Airport, 289
Francisco (uncle of Tomás), 47–49, 61
Frank A., 247, 249, 266, 320
Fuchs, Howie, 75–76, 77, 79
fuel gaskets, 150–51

gangster tactics, 279, 281
ganja, 98

García Márquez, Gabriel, 200
Gaviria, Raúl, 130, 202–203, 225, 234, 300–301, 320
gifts, to Colombians, 142, 205, 217
Gilberto, 262, 264, 319, 324–25
go-fast boats, 247–48, 314
Godfather, The, 69
greed and self-preservation, primacy of, 191
gringos, doing business with, 116
ground operations manual, 132, 143
ground-to-air radio, 146–47
Guadalajara, Mexico, 27, 29
Guajira, 4, 139; gun culture of, 8–9, 14, 145, 153, 231; drug interdiction on, 7, 211, 304

Hammond, John, 89
Harris, Cherie, 80–81, 105–106, 192, 193, 205, 254, 255–56, 257, 322; and Long's cocaine addiction, 284, 286; relationship with Long, 255–56, 284–86, 322
hash oil, 98–99, 192
Hatfield, Frank, 5, 6–11, 15–17, 102–105, 109, 203–204, 299–300, 318; escape from Colombia of, 212–23
Hathaway, 132, 143–44, 161
Hatteras boat, 248
Hawthorne School, 19–20
Hector (relative of Tony A.), 238–39, 307, 312, 320
helicopter, lease of, 301–302
Hell's Angels Motorcycle Club, 56, 57
High Times magazine, 196, 219, 256–57
"holes," 249

Holiday Inn, midtown Manhattan, 295–96

honor, among crooks, 74–75, 190–91, 268–69, 275–76

hot list, FAA, 206–208

Howard Johnson Motor Lodge, New York, 296

hypoxia and night vision, 164

Indian Springs, nuclear test site at, 89

Inferno, 217

Ingram MAC-10 submachine gun, 273

International System of Units, 38

Irotama Hotel, Santa Marta, 117, 202, 312

Ives, 26–27, 51–52, 55, 72, 321

Jack, 236, 244–45, 265, 266, 321

Jagger, Mick, 240

jail, attitude about, 106, 194

Jeff, 76–79, 86–87, 91, 95. *See also* Myerson, Jake

Jeppesen Airport and Information Directory (J-AID), 131

Jesús, 39, 40

Johnson, Hillary, 90

Jupiter, Florida, 261

Kennedy, John F., assassination of, 239

Key Largo, 249, 266, 268

kidnapping, 272

Knoxville Metropolitan Airport, 207

La Finca de Don Jaime (Jimmy's Place), 307, 311

Lake of Wells, Nevada, 89

Las Vegas, Nevada, 298; money laundering in, 289

Little Eddie, 74–75, 79, 114, 250

Long, Allen: career in filmmaking, 24, 40, 42, 43–44, 52, 53–54, 58; childhood of, 22–24; cocaine addiction of, 50–51, 180, 181, 194, 253–54, 272, 283–86; as deal-maker, 174, 214, 242; death threat to, 268–69, 315–16; disillusionment of, 277–82, 289–90, 291; earnings of, 204–205; enters marijuana trade, 61–68, 293; escape from Colombia, 223–34; as fugitive, 326; grandfather of, 23, 259–60; legitimate career of, 87–88, 89, 282–83; lifestyle of, 288–89, 291, 327; personality of, 181–82, 259–60; plea bargain, 326–27; relationship with Cherie Harris, 255–56, 284–86, 322; in Richmond, 79–80; as Spanish speaker, 114–15, 220; youth of, 19–22

Long, John, 23–24, 255

Long, Tom, 193–94, 260

Long Manufacturing Company, 23, 260

Long T46, 23

Lonnie, 261, 268–69, 320

Lundvall, Bruce, 283

McBride, Will, 5, 83, 90, 102, 103, 105–106, 130, 203–204, 299–300, 318; arrest of, 326; escape from Colombia of, 212–23

McCarthy, Joseph, 256

MacDill Air Force Base, 181

McGuinn, Jim, 20

machismo: in drug trade, 68; on the Guajira, 12, 153–54

Magdalena River, Colombia, 113
Magnum Marine boat, 247–48
Maracaibo, Venezuela, 135, 167,
   225, 234; Long and Myerson in,
   136–37
María, 122, 129–30, 198, 202,
   223–34, 301, 320
mariachis, 30–31
marijuana: Colombian economic
   dependence on, 143; cultivation
   of, 48–49, 141; distribution of,
   78–79, 83, 251–52; forest of in
   Sabana Rubia, 232; harvest of, 44;
   increase in trade of, 239–40,
   293–94; off-loading of, 61–68;
   packaging of, 188, 198; price of,
   242, 243, 246; processing of,
   123–24; profits from, 261; quality
   of Colombian, 93–94, 198, 243;
   subculture of, 14, 43; symbolic
   nature of, 21; from Thailand, 93;
   types of Colombian, 93–94
"marimba," 126
marimberos, 126
Marin County, California, 59, 69–70
marital fidelity, in Colombia, 199
Martinez, Joey, 44–47, 49, 51
Mary Lou's, 254
Matthews, Easy, 83–84, 85, 95–96,
   258–59, 261, 274, 297, 321
Maxwell's Plum, 257
Medellín cartel, 325
metric system. See International
   System of Units
Miami: gun culture in, 14, 273, 279,
   280; nightlife in, 262–63; police
   department, 236, 244–45
Miguel, 117–19, 121, 125, 138–40,
   170–73, 197, 220–22, 296–97, 319
Miguel, Sr., 139–41

military, Venezuelan, 136–37
military patrols, Colombian, 215,
   217–18, 229, 230–31
mink coats, as sexual bribes, 254
mochila, 231
Moisés, 116–17, 121, 139
mona, 94, 120
Mona Passage, 238
Morrison, Jim, 295
Motion Associates, 24, 55, 87
music industry and drugs, 88–89
Myerson, Jake, 162, 188, 189, 190,
   192–93, 241, 243, 247, 293, 297,
   318; arrest of, 326; and Carlyle,
   263–64, 272–73, 276; courtesy of,
   274; as financier of Colombian
   trip, 99–102, 109; and Jimmy, 272,
   273; to Maracaibo meeting,
   136–37. See also Jeff
Myles (partner of Easy Matthews),
   83, 321

N-number, 206
Narco Avionics, 146
Neighborhood Playhouse, 255
Nemperor Records, 282, 285
Newton, Wayne, 192
night, flying at, 164, 166–67
North Carolina, spring climate of, 164
Northern California, pot market in,
   261

off-loading: basic rule of, 143–44,
   160; in California, 302, 304;
   failure of, 157–59, 167–69;
   logistics of, 131–32, 143–44,
   176–77; of Mexican marijuana,
   61–68; payoff for, 188–89, 190;
   after second trip, 185, 188; in
   South Florida, 248–51

One Hundred Years of Solitude
   (*Cien Años de Soledad*) (García
   Márquez), 200
Operation Stopgap, 294
oxygen, use of in flight, 164

"Pacific trip, the," 295–305
Pan Am conversion, 150
passport fraud, 219, 326
Patton, George S., 174
pay phones, 77, 130, 135; security
   protocol for, 133–34, 134–35
Perico, 124, 145, 155, 175
perico, 155
pilots: brotherhood among, 204,
   207–208; dress of, 164
Piper Navajo Chieftain airplane, 85
Pituro Uno, bust of, 305; purchase
   of, 301
Plazuela de los Mariachis,
   Guadalajara, 29–30, 37
police: department, Miami, 236,
   244–45, 249–50; former officers of
   in dope trade, 237, 239
Pomeroy, 56–57, 59–68, 70, 195, 321
Port Antonio, Jamaica, 297
Portete Bay, 211
pot and cocaine, incompatibility of,
   195–96
pot smokers, number of in
   seventies, 5, 70
power boats, production, 247–48,
   306, 311
Puerto Galeón Hotel, Santa Marta,
   128
punta roja, 93, 128, 295

Quaaludes, 54, 187, 264, 271, 272,
   290, 298
Quicksilver Messenger Service, 60

Radio and Records Convention,
   Dallas, 283
Real-to-Reel Productions, 289
Reed, JD, 81–83, 89–90, 91, 93,
   97–98, 151–58, 285, 298–99, 317,
   318–19; and Abe, 98–99; and coke,
   194, 195; in Colombia, 113–21; as
   off-loading expert, 176, 218
Reed, Luther, 177, 185, 186–87,
   319
Ricardo (cousin of Pablo Cepeda),
   225, 234
Richmond Times-Dispatch, 171
Río Guasare, 227, 234
Río Palomino, 4, 122, 211, 218
Riohacha, Colombia, 117, 135, 211,
   307, 312
rip-offs, in marijuana trade, 240,
   241–42, 250, 290
Rita, 41, 42–43, 52
roadblocks, 218, 226, 303–304
rock concerts, filming, 87
Rockwell Jet Commander airplane,
   288–90
ruana (poncho), 226, 231
Rubell, Steve, 256
rubia, 94, 120
rubia de la costa, 120

Sabana Rubia, 225, 231–34, 243
Santa Marta, Colombia, 113, 117
Santa Marta Gold, 5, 94, 96, 120,
   127; price of, 127–28
Santiago (Colombian middleman),
   305, 312
Schrager, Ian, 256
Sierra de Perija, 226
Sierra Nevada de Santa Marta,
   Colombia, 4, 93, 94, 127, 167,
   200, 227

Sikorsky S-64 Skycrane, 301
sixties, marijuana culture of, 14, 21,
    95, 263
smuggling: brotherhood in, 257–59;
    channels of affiliation in, 74;
    increased volume of, 260, 262;
    risks of, 145, 216, 288–89;
    situation ethics in, 191; thrill of,
    174, 175–76, 287–88; volume of
    in 1976, 211; and waiting, 63
smuggling trip, first to Colombia,
    145–59; mistakes of, 160–61
Sony Trinitron, 142
Sophocles, 212
South Florida: dope trade, 236;
    logistics of drug trade in, 246–47;
    off-loading in, 248–50; volume of
    traffic in, 247
South Hill, Virginia, 22–23
souvenir T-shirts, 220
sport-fishing boats, ubiquity of, 248
stash house, 246, 250
state troopers, Florida, 252
Studio 54, 256–57, 262
Summer of Love, 21, 59
"Sweet Virginia Breeze," 89

T-6 trainer, 61, 64, 66
telephone records, prosecutors' use
    of, 133–34
Tepic, Mexico, 47–48, 61
Teterboro Airport, New Jersey, 77
Tex, 61, 64, 66
Thailand, marijuana from, 93
"the man," 114–15
Thompson, Robbin, 89, 282
Tomás (street hustler, Mazatlán), 47
Tony A., 213–14, 235, 241, 264–66,
    320; boat trip from Colombia,
    237–38

Tourneau, 205
Trade-A-Plane, 104, 106–107
transmigration, of souls, 97–98
Trident, Sausalito, 60, 69
Truman, Harry S., 19

Upper Matecumbe key, 277
U.S. Coast Guard, 248, 294, 314
U.S. currency: in Colombia, 114; in
    dope business, 274; as wallpaper,
    201
U.S. Customary System of
    measurement, 38
U.S. Customs, 294

Valledupar, Colombia, 297, 301, 302,
    304
Vargas, 323–25
Variations for Orchestra (Bassett),
    19
Victoria Station restaurant, 262
Villa, Pancho, 48
Villanueva, Colombia, 225–26, 227
Virgil, 239, 240, 247, 261, 276–77,
    286, 293, 321
Virginia Commonwealth University,
    80
Virginia Youth for Goldwater, 23
Volvo engines, 169

Wadleigh, Michael, 42
Warhol, Andy, 257
Watergate burglary, 236
Wayne, John, 258
weather interference, 180–81
Weiss, Nat, 282–83
Welch, Raquel, 258
Wexler, Jerry, 89
Wilhelmina Agency, 255, 322
Winterland, 60, 69

Witness Security Program, 320
Woodstock (film), 42
Woodstock, 21

Xenon, 256

Yetnikoff, Walter, 283
youth vote, in Ann Arbor, 92
Ypsilanti, Michigan, marijuana law,
    92–93